X

Inter/vention

Inter/vention

Free Play in the Age of Electracy

Jan Rune Holmevik

foreword by Gregory Ulmer
afterword by Ian Bogost

The MIT Press
Cambridge, Massachusetts
London, England

© 2012 Massachusetts Institute of Technology

For information about special quantity discounts, please email special_sales@ mitpress.mit.edu

This book was set in Stone Sans and Stone Serif by Graphic Composition, Inc. Printed and bound in the United States of America.

Library of Congress Cataloging-in-Publication Data

Holmevik, Jan Rune.
Inter/vention : free play in the age of electracy / Jan Rune Holmevik ; foreword by Gregory Ulmer ; afterword by Ian Bogost.
    p.   cm.
Includes bibliographical references (p.   ) and index.
ISBN 978-0-262-01705-3 (hardcover : alk. paper)
1. Mass media—Philosophy. 2. Digital media—Philosophy. 3. Mass media—Technological innovations. 4. Mass media and technology. I. Title. II. Title: Intervention.
P90.H655   2012
302.23'101—dc23
                                                                    2011026379

10 9 8 7 6 5 4 3 2 1

For Cynthia

In memory of all the innocent victims of the July 22, 2011, terror attacks on my homeland of Norway. Your ultimate sacrifice for our democracy will never be forgotten.

Contents

Foreword by Gregory Ulmer   ix
Preface: MyStory   xvii
Acknowledgments   xxiii

1   Widescope   1

2   Hacker Noir   23

3   Choral Code   55

4   Venture   91

5   Intervention   115

6   Ludic Ethics   137

7   Burning Chrome   153

Afterword by Ian Bogost   161
Notes   165
References   169
Index   183

Foreword: Becoming Electrate

Gregory Ulmer

Inter/vention emanates from a moment of insight. Jan Holmevik became who he was already through a realization, like the Buddhist monk in the riddle who meets himself coming down the mountain. The terminology used in *Inter/vention* to discuss identity experience (mystory, widescope, punctum, avatar) derives from pedagogical experiments developed for learning within the digital apparatus (electracy). Specific to electrate identity is first-person undergoing of group awareness, for the new dimension of identity added to spirit and self (orality and literacy) is that of collective subject. A context for the event was Holmevik's perplexity about his career in games, as hacker, player, and teacher. The Blood Elf paladin Raik, Holmevik's avatar in *World of Warcraft*, has "killed" more than thirty thousand alliance characters. In his twenty years of virtual killing play, Holmevik is an exterminator. He reflects on this play in the context of the virtual consultancy, the EmerAgency, bringing to bear on public policy formation the new resources made accessible to reason through electracy. The enigma is Columbine, the team Harris and Klebold, and their love for the first-person-shooter genre popularized by DOOM. The enigma resists cause-and-effect logic, as it resists almost every category of understanding available through the existing institutions inherited from the oral and literate traditions (i.e., religion and science). We live now in a condition of permanent exception, the philosophers report, a state of emergency, "man overboard." But the alarm is not one of those fire bells or smoke sirens that make it physically impossible to go about your business. It is a silent alarm routed elsewhere while we persevere in our own striving.

Holmevik's intuition of an answer to the riddle, the inception of epiphany, was triggered by the sting or punctum experienced while reading Gibson's (1986a) story *Burning Chrome*. The scene of encounter with the matrix in the story triggered the memory of an occasion during Holmevik's role as guild master for the *Equinox* community in *World of Warcraft*, "a ludic collective that would help players achieve goals that sometimes required upward of forty people to work together in unison." On one evening in 2006, *Equinox* defeated the Lord of Fire. "I experienced real community that night," Holmevik reports, and yet (citing Virilio), "there remains an irreducible gap." *Inter/vention* connects this experience of community with a certain candidate for heroic type of the new apparatus: the hacker, who may be to the Internet what Charles Baudelaire's ([1863] 1986) *flaneur* dandy was to the modernist city. Much of the book consists of the history of "hacker noir," expressive of an attitude of play that is to electracy what materialism is to literacy. The anecdote of the six chopsticks illuminates the state of mind, calling attention to the first-person capacity for "fun" that becomes metaphysical in electracy. Electracy contributed to Holmevik's epiphany by providing a frame within which retrospectively he grasped the culture he was helping to create. He understood that the gambit of civilization is underway today in the mode of entertainment.

During this learning process, I received the invitation to collaborate with Holmevik, Ian Bogost, and the Game Studies group at Clemson University in the RCID program directed by Victor Vitanza. It was a case of a theory intersecting with a practice, to their mutual benefit. Holmevik frames his history of hacking and the Open Source or Free Software movement with the concepts and vocabulary of apparatus theory, so the purpose of this foreword is to offer some background on the provenance of this theory. A shorthand version is that programming is to electracy what alphabetic writing is to literacy. Holmevik's theoretical insight connects the metaphysical principle of "chora" with the universal machine of computing. Chora is *genos*, a third kind (neither intelligible nor perceivable), constituting the mediating interface hosting the integration of Being and Becoming in Plato's *Timaeus*. Jacques Derrida refunctioned chora in grammatology as trace (referenced in the term "electracy," combining "electricity" and "trace")—proposing not a new metaphysics but the principle that any metaphysics is relative to its apparatus. The terms "Western metaphysics" and "literacy" are synonymous. The caveat is that programming and writing, respectively, are only one dimension of a three-part matrix that also includes institutional practices and identity experience (individual and collective).

Early in his career, Derrida invoked grammatology, defined as the history and theory of writing, to develop his insight into this interdependence of metaphysics and technology. Grammatology as a method conceives the possibilities of creating electracy through an analogy with the emergence of literacy out of orality. I first became aware of grammatology by reading Marshall McLuhan and his sources, such as Eric Havelock, Walter Ong, and

Jack Goody, all of whom address the role of technology in the emergence of literate civilization. The source for the concept of "apparatus" was French media studies, specifically the book edited by Theresa Hak Kyung Cha, *Cinematographic Apparatus: Selected Writings* (1980), which includes influential and widely anthologized essays by Jean-Louis Baudry. The purpose of this argument was to counter the technological determinism associated with some readings of McLuhan, to insist instead that communications equipment (alphabets, cameras) are social machines—as much ideology as technology, with the invention of photography, for example, involving several different invention streams or genealogies. Derrida himself borrowed the term "grammatology" from the French archeologist André Leroi-Gourhan.

The most recent version of grammatology is found in the multivolume study *Technics and Time* by Bernard Stiegler (1998, 2008, 2010), who draws substantially on André Leroi-Gourhan and also Gilbert Simondon, along with the whole movement of poststructuralism with which Derrida is associated. The new feature of the argument introduced by Stiegler goes beyond the previous view of the apparatus as having three registers (technology, institutions, and identity) to propose that technics and nature (including human nature) have separate and autonomous ontologies that are rhizomatic, intertwined, and interdependent. Part of the point is that technics precedes "humanity," that a certain animal became human, fulfilled its potentiality, through the prosthesis of tools. With the Industrial Revolution (which is to say, since the inception of electracy), the dominant power in this relationship is on the side of machines. It has been said, in fact, that humans are the sex organs of machines. Machine becoming is immanent, happening entirely through historical evolution, full of contingencies and accidents whose vicissitudes are documented by James Burke in his television series *Connections*. The remaining role for humanity in this process, Stiegler argues, is as governor, functioning as an *operant* (collective) subject for the materialized object (the term is from Jean-Joseph Goux). Electrate metaphysics must take into account the interdependence of these two ontologies, constituting a new understanding of reality as an emergent construction (we are making it up as we go along).

How does the operant subject function as governor? Stiegler understands this project within the terms provided by philosophy (literacy). The becoming of technics is guided by human becoming, and the classical definition of human becoming is represented by a phrase that Friedrich Nietzsche took from Pindar as his motto, mandating that the human project is "to become what one already is." Plato needed Chora to mediate his dualistic ontology, with Being and Becoming as separate orders, different realities.

Aristotle collapsed this dualism into an immanent order, with Being as essence, as the principle of order within material entities. In Aristotle's metaphysics, immanence has two dimensions—the potential (dunamis) and the actual (energeia). The prototype of change was that of a plant, whose growth through time is guided by its essence (its nature). An acorn becomes what it already is (an oak tree). Aristotle invented a concept to name this becoming: entelechy ("being-at-work-staying-itself"). The aporia of Aristotle's account concerns precisely human entelechy. Aristotle took up the problem of human becoming in his Ethics, to say that the telos or end of humanity is happiness, well-being. The impasse in this line of thought is due to the fact that, unlike plants, humans exercise choice, through practical reason, making decisions requiring good judgment that shifts the grounds of acts from necessity to contingency. There can be no science of judgment. It is a virtue (a disposition) and cannot be taught. Therefore, Aristotle subordinated practical reason to pure reason, committing the literate tradition to the path leading to technoscience (as Martin Heidegger explained).

Stiegler is not committing the operant subject to entelechy, a term that today only serves as a metaphor, since there is no telos for the posthuman (a term that perhaps names this human-technics rhizome). It is understood that human decision is ontological, in a condition better described by complexity theory, with identity as an emergent effect, thus inverting Aristotle's priority, now favoring potentiality (the virtual) over actuality. Even so, readers of Stiegler are left with the aporia intact, since everything we have learned about human judgment since Aristotle (everything produced by the institutions of the two apparati, religion and science) leaves us as perplexed as ever about well-being, with ever more decisions consigned to machines. The insight of apparatus theory is most relevant at this point—that the apparatus is as much cultural as it is technical, with the invention process drawing on separate and diverse genealogies. This framing allows us to see that Stiegler's grammatology is incomplete. There is another factor at work in history, one that like technics also is prior to and constitutive of animals becoming human. This factor is *play*, a point familiar to readers of *Homo Ludens* ([1938] 1955). Becoming human means playing with tools. Here is the pivot of Holmevik's realization.

Heidegger was concerned about the fact that Western metaphysics forgot about being itself to deal only with beings. This forgetting produced a one-dimensional technoscientific civilization whose good intentions lead to disaster, whose consultants are ever more frequently astounded by events "that no one could have foreseen," and whose insistence on awarding Nobel Prizes in Economics to academics who notice that humans tend not to behave "rationally" will have been one of the great embarrassments of our era (like theologians perplexed by the ineffectuality of miracles). Another classic, *Man, Play, and Games* (Caillois [1961] 2001), helps place this second genealogical factor of play into the frame of grammatology. Roger Caillois identified four categories of game: Agon (competition), Alea (chance), Mimicry (simulation), and Ilynx (vertigo). Vertigo and simulation tend to dominate in oral civilizations, organizing the periodic festivals associated with agricultural cycles, structured by the symbolic exchange of gift economies. The effects of possession and mask are fascinating, powerful, and a check on progress according to Caillois. When civilization was able to break the dominance of these institutions and shift to organization structured by competition and chance, as happened in Classical Greece, it was a major advance. The vehicle of this break was the presence of clowns within the ceremonies, whose parodies opened a dimension of reflexivity against trance. Hacker noir reanimates gift economy against the commodity form.

Vertigo and simulation are still with us, just as is the sacred, but subordinated, degraded—surviving in carnival rides and contaminating society in the form of drug abuse. A task of the institution formation of electracy, emerging within entertainment organized in our historical circumstances in the mode of capitalist corporations, is to ontologize and make accessible as an intelligent dimension the ludic drive and its game categories. Holmevik's recognition of entertainment as the site of apparatus emergence is a guiding idea of *Inter/vention*. Entertainment is not something superficial, not a matter of spare time in the apparatus, but a fundamental counterpart to work and productivity, with equal claim on the human project. Literacy produced science over the course of two and a half millennia, and religion evolved within orality over a much longer period. Entertainment as an institution of electracy is in its infancy. Holmevik's trajectory opens a chora, an opportunity for invention, whose purpose is to take up the practical implications of a technics-play rhizome. Gilles Deleuze and Félix Guattari's ([1972] 1983) notion of "desiring machine" is another version of "apparatus." The difference between a tool and a machine, they say, is that the former is an agent of contact and the latter a factor of communication. A reason for refunctioning chora today, relative to its original purpose to mediate a dualistic metaphysics, addresses our situation of technics-play. Holmevik's insight is that programming is choral and makes possible communication between humans and equipment.

What is at stake in this vision of choragraphy may be seen in the work of Jean Baudrillard, as an estranged spokesperson for the French theory that Stiegler invokes as the best hope for understanding what humans want.

Baudrillard is exemplary for his melodramatic and hyperbolic presentations of positions tested more cautiously by his peers. Nonetheless, the entire poststructuralist project is condensed in Baudrillard's attempt to identify manifestations of symbolic exchange, the gift economy, Georges Bataille's General Economy, merged with commodity form in postmodern society. Holmevik understands that hacker noir and the Open Source movement occupy this dimension, with an optimistic view of what this hero may accomplish. In our coming collaboration, it is my role to emphasize what the theory proposes. Baudrillard's *Fatal Strategies* ([1983] 2008) is a convenient point of reference to help appreciate what it means when play and game become metaphysical in electracy. A shorthand version of the proposal is just that play is no more inherently benign than is technics and similarly holds as much promise for disaster as for thriving.

We are formulating now an agenda for the EmerAgency, inviting consultations with hacker noir. The issue is what Holmevik calls "pervasive life" (what I call "N Life") to name our condition of information sprawl, in which (to use old-fashioned terms) base and superstructure are merged. Technoscience is ontological, meaning that we are making up reality as we go along. All previous standards of measure have been dismissed, leaving only money and the commodity form as a structure of universal equivalence. The capitalist model of infinite growth broke with entelechy without finding a replacement and disavows any General Economy (death, the sacred). The real replies in the discourse of catastrophe, to assert *death*. What the corpse was to the Baroque, Walter Benjamin ([1972] 1999) noted, the commodity is today (an allegory), and this is one framing for Holmevik's body count. The reply is not subtle. The Accident (as in Paul Virilio's [2007] Museum of the Accident) is our version of Nemesis (the Greek term that Freud found in a lexicon, translated as "Unheimlich," the uncanny). Individuals (selves) act, and the real replies to the operant (collective) subject, and this is the return of the repressed (that is, this is how the General Economy appears). Technoscientific consultants are stumped, and their problem-solving capacity is blocked because they lack appreciation for one major dimension of events. They forgot about play.

Here is where Baudrillard is useful, in a way that illuminates also Holmevik's recognition of electracy. Baudrillard attempted to think the contemporary scene from within the terms of entertainment as the institutionalization of the new apparatus. His move beyond right and wrong, or true and false, seemed perverse to many, who did not recognize that he was taking up the project of the third axis institutionalized in electracy—pleasure-pain—first formulated by Immanuel Kant ([1790] 2000) as a capacity in its own right, equal to pure and practical reason. The axis of aesthetic judgment concerns neither salvation nor utility but rather ecstasy. *Ecstacy.* Against the scientific calculations of Game Theory, working out all the rational (logical) options of competitive decision, Baudrillard proposed that we are engaged in a different category of game altogether, identified by Caillois as Ilynx. You could say desiring machines, but Baudrillard's analogy was seduction (as against John von Neumann's poker), and an old song lyric described the state of mind (*Yes I'm in a spin, love is the spin I'm in*). We enjoy spinning, spinning. Spinning does not answer "Why?" Consultants fascinated by calculation are oblivious to ecstacy, spinning, and enjoyment (and their opposites) as primordial, irreducible motives driving human behavior. Caillois warned that when possession and mask (vertigo and simulation) are combined, they are dangerous, and Baudrillard's point is that this is exactly what happens in the spectacle. The Greeks created tragedy to help focus attention of emerging literate citizens on the consequences for the group of individual acts of blindness. *Ate* refers to blindness for the individual and calamity for the collective. Antigone's choice is the prototype.

A candidate for an equivalent focusing form in electracy, which does for Ilynx what tragedy did for *Ate*, is slapstick comedy. Karl Marx ([1867] 1906) observed that if a commodity could speak, it would be the most empathetic creature imaginable, since it would regard every person it met as a buyer. We may picture a product coming to life as *Rameau's Nephew* (Diderot [1772] 1987), the consummate flatterer. Comedy, especially silent cinema, shows a related angle when the object is a machine. Albert Bermel noted how in cinema machines replaced servants in the old Commedia dell'Arte roles adapted by the silent comedians. The servants in these farces (for that is our mode) took every opportunity to thrash their masters with a slapstick. When the doctor starts expounding on Latin roots, a beating will soon follow. In the updated version, antagonistic machines defy the intentions of their human operators in every possible way. The first zanni that come to mind when thinking of Commedia are Pantalone, the Captain, Pierrot. Perhaps we don't even recall Columbine, a lady's maid, often the only rational figure in the story, whose stage business concerns the Innamorata. Those who named the Colorado High School probably were not alluding to Commedia, but this is how the real communicates.

Attempting to express his epiphany, his realization of the absurdity of existence, the protagonist of Jean-Paul Sartre's *Nausea* explains his feeling: "Funny—no; not quite that, nothing that exists can be funny; it was like a floating, almost entirely elusive analogy, to certain situations in vaudeville" (Sartre 1965, 61). Call it the absurd, or vertigo. There is in events a fatal dimension, which is not everything but must be taken into account. It cannot be saved. It cannot be fixed. It may only be played. The real in its reply to the operant subject communicates in the manner of oracles, as Baudrillard noted when identifying not all possible options but the fatal (predestined) one. *The real neither conceals nor reveals, but intimates.* Fortunately, we do not have to rely on the measure of last resort (catastrophe) to chart the edge of pervasive life. There is another channel open between players and technics, besides Accident, and that is programming. We are in love, seduced, and ask for Columbine's *intervention.* A machine, Deleuze and Guattari stated, is constituted from the moment there is communication between two portions of the outside world that are really distinct in a system that is possible although less probable. They were citing one Pierre Auger (conductive inference hears "augur"). We are hoping hacker noir helps us avoid yet another thrashing. Let the collaboration continue.

Preface: MyStory

> I do not know of any other way of associating with great tasks than play: as a sign of greatness, this is an essential presupposition.
> —Friedrich Nietzsche

I have been a gamer for as long as I can remember. When I was growing up, my family always played games, and every Christmas there would be a new board game under the tree. I can fondly remember such titles as *Othello*, *Mastermind*, *Cluedo*, *Scotland Yard*, *Ludo*, and many others. Games created a social atmosphere and provided us with activities that we could do together as a family. In some ways, games and the traditional family dinner were the only activities that brought us all together. Games also provided an opportunity for me and my friends to have fun together on those cold Norwegian winter days when we couldn't play outside. Games were not just something of a pastime for me, however, they always held a special fascination. Inside the game there was a world of endless adventure and opportunities, and no matter how many times I played them, they never lost their allure. In short, games were integrally part of my family, community, education, and adventure. Writing this book is also the culmination of that history. It is first and foremost about playing and the role that play has in our lifelong learning processes.

When I was about eleven or twelve, I designed my first game. It was a board game that I called *World Trader*. The game was loosely based on *Monopoly* and a couple of my other favorite games. The playing board was a big 5'-by-3' beautiful and highly detailed map of the world mounted on a thick piece of cardboard. The objective of the game was to sail around the world and buy and sell cargo to the highest bidder. Once you had earned enough money, you could upgrade your vessel, or buy bigger and faster ships, and eventually amass an entire merchant fleet. The rules were simple because the purpose of the game was not to win. In fact there was no discrete winning condition. Instead players were encouraged to build their shipping empires and have fun seeing them grow while exploring trade routes and profitable cargoes while avoiding the many hazards of the high seas such as storms, pirates, and the dreaded hundred-year wave. *World Trader* was a game of adventure and exploration, but it also had educational aspirations as it turned out, although that was certainly not a conscious design decision on my part at the time.

That winter I also spent a lot of time in my family's woodworking workshop creating a *Chess* set from scratch. The little town Geiranger, in which I grew up, did not have any stores where you could buy games back then, so when I wanted to learn how to play *Chess*, I built the game myself. You have a lot of time to learn and contemplate the rules of the game and the abilities of each particular piece when you literally spend days painstakingly carving each one. What fascinated me about *Chess* wasn't necessarily the competitive aspects of the game or the multitude of strategies of the game play as such. Rather, what I found interesting was the *drama* that unfolded on the *Chess* board. Pawns lining up to defend their King, marching into battle only to be struck down by vastly more powerful Bishops, Rooks, or Queens. Yet in spite of their lowly rank and limited capabilities, the Pawns' presence and role on the battlefield could easily change the tides of war. When the powerful and awe-inspiring Knights came charging from behind to threaten the enemy King, it was the spectacle of it all, the rustling of plate armor and the neighing of horses, that had me captivated.

Until the 1980s and the advent of the affordable personal computer, my experience with digital games was mainly limited to a few arcade titles such as *Pac-Man* and *Space Invaders*. These games had become increasingly popular in the 1970s as pay-for-play systems, and in larger cities around the world, gaming arcades became immensely popular gathering spots for people of my generation. In the small town where I lived, however, we only had four or five different arcade machines that everyone played, and while I certainly spent my share of coins playing, I have to say that I grew tired of them pretty quickly. Saving the world from hordes of invading aliens in increasingly faster and more complex attack waves never did appeal to my sense of adventure and accomplishment. Once you had mastered the basic hand–eye coordination skills, it became a matter of figuring out the appropriate strategies for each new level and executing those with as much dexterity and lightning reflexes as you could muster. Most of these games that I played had no real winning condition; you kept playing (and paying) until you could no longer keep up with the speed or complexity of the game. Achieving the elusive high score was an important motivator for many players, but it never held any real appeal for me. There is a famous *Seinfeld* episode from 1998 where George discovers that the old pizza parlor *Frogger* machine they all used to play in high school still has his high score on it. Apparently for George, whose accomplishments in life are not perhaps the most outstanding, this high score still represents a major point of pride. Thus, in typical Seinfeld fashion, he and his friends proceed to buy the machine only to realize that if they unplug it to move it, the high score will be lost. The episode ends with a hilarious top-down scene where George tries to move the machine, which by then had been hooked up to a battery courtesy of Kramer's friend "Slippery Pete," across three lanes of busy traffic—just like the frog in the original game. Interestingly enough, this is also an intriguing commentary on how our lives and very existence today seem to depend more and more on fragile electricity-powered digital representations of who we project to be.

With the advent of the home computer in the 1980s, new and exciting opportunities for engaging gaming experiences emerged. When I first went to college in 1985, I bought a Commodore 64, which was one of the most popular home computers at the time. To me, that machine changed everything that I had been taught to believe was a separation between work and play. Not only did I write my first college term paper on it, which was a huge convenience in its own right, I could easily switch between work and play within the same digital environment. In this way, the computer came to represent a world in which work and play could and should coexist. In a very real way, this book and the ideas within started for me back in 1985 with that brilliant blue Commodore 64 screen that just said READY. There were no menus to choose from or windows to type in. That blue screen was the window to what has become a pervasive and perpetual learning/creative lifestyle in a highly mixed-reality environment.

Although there was no shortage of games to play for the Commodore 64, my fascination with them soon turned to how they worked and how to make them. At the time, computer magazines such as *Byte* and many others would publish listings of code that you could type in to program simple games and other applications. The first game that I programmed on the Commodore 64 was *Lunar Lander*. It was a very simple game, consisting of only about 100 lines of BASIC code, and the goal was to maneuver a little spaceship across a rough lunar surface and find a safe place to land, all the while meteors kept falling from the sky. This game taught me how to manipulate objects in a game and make them move across the screen. More important, however, building games from listings of code that others had written allowed me to learn computer programming in a new way that was intuitive, fun, and interactive. I had become a hacker. Not in the sense that most people think of hackers today, which is a criminal who uses his or her skills to break into computer systems and steal information or wreak havoc. No, the kind of hacking I mean is the practice in which people share code and learn from each other by improving on and republishing each others' programs. I will talk a lot more about hacking and hackers later in this book, but I need to reclaim the original meaning of that term here at the outset so there is no misunderstanding as to its meaning later.

I never bought any books or took any classes on computer programming, which is typically the form of learning that we are taught to adopt. All that came later. The way I learned how to program computers was simply through reading listings of code and figuring out what the program did and how it worked. Then, once I had a firm understanding of it, I could make changes and modifications to it so that it eventually did what I wanted it to do. In this way, to me, the art of computer programming became a fascinating "game" in its own right where you would "play around" with the code until something brilliant and fun emerged. Some of my computer science professors later told me this was not the "right" and literate way to learn programming. They were wrong. Not only was it a lot more fun to learn programming by hacking together a game than, say, programming a member database for your local nonprofit or some basic sorting algorithm, it was also a lot more satisfying to be able to play that game, share it with others, and get their feedback and input on it.

After my first year of college, I took a break to do my military service and work as a K–12 schoolteacher. Being the "new hire," I was charged with teaching religion to a class of eighth graders who had no interest in the subject. As a gamer, I turned to games as a way of engaging with them, and we made a deal. If they would commit to the class and do well, I would create a text-based adventure game for them. The premise of the game was to escape from school at the end of the year. I modeled the game "dungeon" for The Escape from Eidsdal School after the actual floor plan and released one section of the game to the students each quarter. In order to finish that section, they had to find a certain teacher, who was represented by a nonplayer character (NPC), somewhere in the building and answer his or her quiz correctly. Once they completed the quiz, they would get a key that allowed them to progress to the next section of the game. The game took all year to complete, and the students became deeply involved in the design of quests and other activities that were put in so they could go back at any time and pick up more knowledge by exploring books and other game artifacts. There were no high scores or timers. Instead the game encouraged students to explore the concept of learning as an adventure that should and could be both fun and engaging. Much to my surprise and satisfaction, I later learned that the game was being played by students at that school for many years after I left.

Back in college, I went on to study history and computer science, and it was there that I first discovered the Internet and the online multiplayer games known as MUDs (Multi-User Dungeons); I have devoted a whole chapter to them later in this book because not only did they shape the future of my career, they also gave rise to all subsequent multiuser games and virtual worlds that exist today. What attracted me to MUDs was primarily their multiplayer functionality. Previously, digital games had for the most part offered up single-player experiences, but with MUDs, adventure gaming with other people in a shared online world added a whole new ludic layer that very closely approximated the shared experience of traditional play. By the early 1990s, MUDs had attracted a sizable following among college students, and some players had even begun to think about how they might be used for educational purposes. At that time, one place more than any other helped to put educational and professional uses of multiplayer games on the agenda for new media scholars: Amy Bruckman's MediaMOO at MIT. I first read about MediaMOO in a science and technology studies newsletter in 1994 and soon found my way to purple-crayon. edu, which was the domain of MediaMOO at the time. What I found was a completely new and intriguing digital space that combined the playful and exploratory nature of the dungeon-based adventure game with the kinds of networking and conferencing activities so typical of professional academic life. Best of all was that the underlying source code for the MOO system was available free to anyone. Within a year, I had embarked on a whole new research-and-development trajectory that led to the creation of the online multiplayer educational system LinguaMOO (1995) and enCore Xpress (1997), an early web application that became quite popular within several academic fields. The book you are about to read is a result of that ad/venture that began so many years ago.

Acknowledgments

This book represents a long and exciting ad/venture in electrate learning for me, and it is appropriate here at the outset to acknowledge those who have most inspired and influenced my work. My friend, colleague, and dissertation advisor, Espen Aarseth, was the first person to show me that there could be an academic career working with digital games and virtual worlds, and I am thoroughly grateful for his support and encouragement. Victor Vitanza is one of those people whose presence in my life goes far beyond what I can possibly describe here. He has always believed in me and given me opportunities to teach and publish that I can never hope to repay. Steven Katz and I came to Clemson the same year, and since then he has been an ardent supporter of me and my work. I place tremendous value on his friendship, scholarship, and poetry. Thanks are also due to my other colleagues in the English Department at Clemson University, who welcomed me in and allowed me to continue my research and teaching on the threshold between game studies and rhetoric.

I also extend my gratitude to Gregory Ulmer, whose theoretical work on electracy most directly inspired me to write this book and who generously agreed to write the foreword. Ian Bogost's work on procedural rhetoric continues to inspire me as well as many others who are interested in bridging the gap between ludology and rhetoric. I am very thankful to him for doing me the honor of writing the afterword. In addition to these major influences, I want to thank Stuart Moulthrop, whose work at the intersection of new media and games gave an invaluable voice to the work I had been doing for years—inter/vention. The students in the Rhetoric, Communication, and Information Design doctoral program at Clemson University gave me the opportunity to share both Ulmer's and Bogost's work with them, and I will always treasure the many inspiring class discussions and Serious Games colloquia we've shared these past few years. In the same vein, I want to thank current and former members of my *World of Warcraft* guilds,

Equinox at Argent Dawn, EU (2005–2008), and Venture at Argent Dawn, US (2009–present). I also want to extend my sincere thanks to all those who have been involved with the enCore Consortium and carried forward the work that I began. I owe you all a debt of gratitude.

My editor, Doug Sery, and the staff at the MIT Press deserve a big thank-you as well for helping me make this book a reality; even more important, they deserve to be recognized for the very important work they continue to do as the premier publisher of game studies titles. I am also grateful to Terry Harpold and the other reviewers of the manuscript for their positive and productive feedback on my work.

I want to thank above all my wife, Cynthia Haynes, who has been my collaborator and soul mate for all these years. She has been at my side, always supportive and always with encouraging words at those times when frustrations ran high and I doubted my ability to see this project through. This book is for her.

1 Widescope

Always and ever differently the bridge escorts the lingering and hastening ways of men to and fro, so that they may get to other banks and in the end, as mortals, to the other side. . . . But only something *that is itself a location* can make space for a site. . . . Thus the bridge does not first come to a location to stand in it; rather a location comes into existence only by virtue of the bridge.
—Martin Heidegger, "Building Dwelling Thinking"

I am somewhat like an amphibian—one foot on land, one in the water—regarding my stance in relation to the rhetorical landscape on either side of the stream of game studies, itself flowing only by virtue of language, code, and embodied play—only by virtue of the bridge. This is a classical dilemma and one that has haunted our thinking since Plato. Steven Katz likens the split to a dream/nightmare in that "Plato's dream of disembodied thought, the Pure Forms to which the Philosopher-King's mind trends, tends ascends, apprehends, has been the un-over-stated project of the West, has been and is being realized, but in and through the very media—poetry, rhetoric, and its descendants—he distrusted if not despised" (Katz forthcoming). But I am quite comfortable moving from dream to nightmare, river to rocky bank. It is the nature of being human, of playing the game of life. In my work I have consistently sought opportunities to integrate work and play in both industry and academia. Research has, however, always formed the foundation on which work and play coexisted for me. But play has also always been the *mode* with which I conducted research in this foundation. This means that foundationalism is countered by a playful antifoundationalism. But I do not mean to cast foundationalism as some basis for absolute truth. I think of the base on which work and play interact as more of a surface (and a porous one at that) than as some ground zero of truth. As Jacques Derrida explained in his classic essay "Structure, Sign, and Play in the Discourse of the Human Sciences," there is no center that functions as the absolute point of origin or reference. Structure, in other words, is destructured by the free play of language, which is nothing more than "a field of infinite substititions" (Derrida [1966] 1978, 289). *Free play* will denote both a metaphor and a practice of the inter/vention at work in this book.

Although antifoundationalism might seem the obvious counteracting notion to foundationalism, as Patricia Bizzell defines it, "anti-foundationalism is the belief that an absolute standard for the judgment of truth can never be found" (Bizzell 1986, 39). Yet the most essential part of her definition follows: such a standard can never be found "precisely because the individual mind can never transcend personal emotion, social circumstances, and historical conditions" (Bizzell 1986, 40). And this is why I begin this book with these three elements of the problem of academic treatments of the work/play dichotomy. My personal emotions, social circumstances, and historical conditions will have been my foundation, and my antifoundation, on the way to what I believe is a new and different contribution to humanities and technology studies in general and to digital game studies in specific. It is also an approach supported and exemplified by both Derrida's theory of *free play* and Gregory Ulmer's work on *electracy*, from which this book's title takes its primary cue.

To cross these various terrains, it is necessary to construct a series of bridges. This is a device we regularly expect from architecture and engineering, but bridges are also useful as conceptual strategies for moving thought from here to there. In this book, I am building a bridge that both connects and disconnects thought. Stuart Moulthrop rightly questions whether we "should be satisfied with a regime where play and reflection remain separate" (Moulthrop 2005, 211). It is my aim to reconnect play and reflection by means of electracy but also (as Ulmer aims to do) to invent electracy by means of play. Ironically, a lot of ink has been spilled on pages such as these, and quite a few heated debates have occurred at conferences featuring game studies scholars and literary scholars. The debates over ludology versus narratology have dominated and shaped the field of game studies in the past decade. Yet as Terry Harpold wisely argues, "[understanding] the qualities of a moving field, and not only being swept along by its currents, requires conscientious investigations of its precursors, and, equally as significant, of the inertias and atavisms that persist within it" (Harpold 2009, 2). Espen Aarseth, Janet Murray, Markku Eskelinen, Harpold, Moulthrop, and many others have been crucial players in this unfolding drama. I, too, have played a role in this debate by taking Moulthrop's challenge to heart, although I did so some years before he articulated exactly what I had been doing.

Specifically, I believed (and still do) that it is necessary to intervene in the technologies we use for research and teaching. Thus, having tinkered with programming early on, it was natural for me to reconfigure Open Source platforms to allow me to build software and learning environments that did not separate "play and reflection" (Moulthrop 2005, 211). Moulthrop defines intervention as follows: "a practical contribution to a media system (e.g., some product, tool, or method) intended to challenge underlying assumptions or reveal new ways of proceeding" (Moulthrop 2005, 212). But he also insists that such a contribution involves a "substantial, productive engagement with code" (Moulthrop 2005, 212). It is not enough, he claims, to simply alternate between play and reflection: "We must also play on a higher level, which means that we must build" (Moulthrop 2005, 212). Thus, I take both Ulmer's challenge to *invent* electracy and Moulthrop's call for *intervention* as parallel tracks that form the bridge between play and reflection, ludology and literacy, in a new *inter/vention*.

This book contributes to the invention of electracy (and constitutes an intervention) in two key ways. First, it traces its path across a number of digital and rhetorical domains: informatics (history of computing), hacker heuretics, ethics/rhetoric, pedagogy/learning, virtual space (ergodic play), and monumentality (games as experience engines). Second, it introduces play as a new genre of electracy (allied with, but an alternative to, the "mystory" genre)—as the "ludic electrate transversal" (which is rendered in the tracing of the axis across the path listed above). In other words, it broadens the mystorical genre by including the ergodic (Aarseth 1997). For mystory and play the goal is the same, namely, the invention of electracy, but they reach it by different means—through ludic and ergodic means in the present/contemporary cycle of experience and reflection (Moulthrop 2005). We are adding to the repertoire of electrate practices in order to understand and demonstrate how play invents electracy. We participate in the invention of the institutional practices of electracy, as Ulmer would say, practices that are heuretic in nature. Play is the bridge, and the transversal accomplishes the engineering of this bridge.

Electracy

This book seeks to position the ludic as a postliterate position that is informed by a new heuretic approach to learning known as electracy. The concept of electracy was first developed and introduced by Gregory Ulmer to describe and capture the skills and competencies that are required to master the new media-rich world in which we live. In his book *Internet*

Invention: From Literacy to Electracy, Ulmer writes that electracy is relative to orality and literacy as a new apparatus (a social machine, part technological, and part institutional) that "is to digital media what literacy is to print" (Ulmer 2003, xii). Ulmer traces the origins of electracy back to early nineteenth-century Paris, where new forms of entertainment emerged as public discourses in the wake of the Industrial Revolution and the new sociopolitical and cultural conditions that it created. In *Avatar Emergency*, Ulmer writes, "Electracy dates from the rise of the industrial city, beginning in the nineteenth century. The new recording technologies invented in the modern city, most of them institutionalized in some forms and modes created by Entertainment, functioned to help citizens to adapt to industrialization" (Ulmer forthcoming, 4).

Just as agents seeking to express themselves in alphabetic writing need to be literate, that is, master the discourses and conventions of writing, egents who seek to express themselves in digital media need to be electrate. In popular discourse, both academic and otherwise, the term *digital literacy* is frequently used to describe the skill set that new digital media require. This is not simply a matter of what some might claim to be terminological convenience. It is a dangerous grammatological misappropriation on the part of the Literati that, in a very real Foucaultian sense, attempts to name and relegate new digital media forms as subjugated practices to the old print media discourses and its established literate institutions. In *Of Grammatology*, Jacques Derrida argues that writing is not merely a reproduction of speech (Derrida 1974). The very act of writing in itself strongly influences how knowledge is constructed. Taking his cue from Enlightenment philosopher Jean-Jacques Rousseau, in the following passage, Derrida revitalizes writing anew: "Writing is at the North: cold, necessitous, reasoning, turned toward death, to be sure, but by that tour de force, by that detour of force which forces it to hold on to life. In fact, the more a language is articulated, the more articulation extends its domain, and thus gains in rigor and in vigor, the more it yields to writing, the more it calls writing forth" (Derrida 1974, 226).

Similarly, in today's complex digital world, we must understand new media expressions and digital experiences not simply as more technologically advanced forms of "writing" that can be understood and analyzed as "texts" but as artifacts in their own right with their own discrete and generative impacts on the creation of knowledge in our time. Resistance to change, and the desire on the part of the establishment to subjugate new forms of expression, is nothing new. In *Orality and Literacy: The Technologizing of the Word*, Walter Ong appropriately reminds us that writing itself has been subjected to the very same forms of resistance and subjugation throughout history.

Most persons are surprised, and many distressed, to learn that essentially the same objections commonly urged today [1982] against computers were urged by Plato in the *Phaedrus* (277-7) and in the *Seventh Letter* against writing. Writing, Plato has Socrates say in the *Pheadrus*, is inhuman, pretending to establish outside the mind what in reality can only be in the mind. It is a thing, a manufactured product. The same of course is said of computers. Secondly, Plato's Socrates urges, writing destroys memory. Those who use writing will become forgetful, relying on an external resource for what they lack in internal resources. Writing weakens the mind. (Ong 1982, 78)

This passage from Ong illustrates how writing came under fire during two very important apparatus shifts in human history. The first shift was from orality to literacy. The second shift is in process, the shift from literacy to electracy. These shifts, however, should not be confused with what Thomas Kuhn describes in *The Structure of Scientific Revolutions* as paradigm shifts (Kuhn 1962). Orality did not go out of vogue or cease to exist when literacy emerged; similarly, literacy will not disappear or be replaced by electracy. People still go to church on Sundays to hear God's word. Political speeches are still regarded as a benchmark by which politicians are measured. At universities around the country, forensics programs and debate teams are still doing what they have always done, and parents and grandparents are still telling stories to their children and grandchildren. Similarly, writing will not lose its importance or prominence either. To the contrary, people write more today than ever before. With the digitization of writing, however, it has morphed into a variety of new media and genres due in large part to its simplicity and portability. Writing is a lightweight and persistent technology that is highly adaptable in nature. Digital writing today spans everything from traditional forms of writing such as books and essays to short text messages and online chat and everything in between. What has happened during the process of the digitization of writing is that it has escaped its traditional forms and arenas, and thus the literate apparatus as conceived by the ancient Greeks is no longer sufficient to account for all its forms and permutations. Therefore, writing can no longer be a privileged form of expression now that so many other expressive forms exist in the digital space.

Early on, Ulmer was drawn to Derrida's new way of reading/analyzing texts, *deconstruction*. It was, however, Derrida's way of reconceiving how texts are produced (grammatology) that fascinated Ulmer. In *Applied Grammatology*, Ulmer focuses on how "Derrida systematically explores the nondiscursive levels—images and puns, or models and homophones—as an alternative mode of composition and thought applicable to academic work, or rather, play" (Ulmer 1985, xi). The word play in Derrida's thought has been one of the main criticisms of his work over the years, but for Ulmer this is its main value. Juxtaposing serious academic work and play, rather blurring the boundary between these two registers of work, astonished Ulmer. Here's Ulmer: "I say I was astonished because it is one thing to engage in wordplay, but another thing to sustain it and extend it into an epistemology, into a procedure that is not just a tour de force but that is functional, replicable. This Writing, however, is not a method of analysis or criticism but of invention" (Ulmer 1985, xii). What we see here is Ulmer's notion of invention as a conductive logic that follows from play. Word play (or puncepts in this case) is easily expandable to all forms of ludic activities because it is inventive in nature. That is, to play means to invent by heuretic means. When we play, we don't always have a particular goal in mind or some winning condition to reach. A lot of the time, humans play because we enjoy it and because we wish to see where it takes us.

We also play in order to game the system that plays us, which is to say that we are as much players as being played. Ulmer recognizes the urgency of our condition as subjects of the institutionalization of play, something Derrida calls "sure play" (Derrida [1966] 1978, 292), which sets us in a dynamic tug-of-war between "art and instrumentalism" (Ulmer 2003, 3). To counter this dialectic, Ulmer sets up his EmerAgency: "a consultancy 'without portfolio' . . . an umbrella organization gathering through the power of digital thinking all the inquiries of students around the world and forming them into a 'fifth estate,' whose purpose is to witness and testify, to give voice to a part of the public left out of community decision making, especially from policy formation" (Ulmer 2003, 1). For Ulmer, "the dilemmas of the practical world are fundamentally resistant to policies that neglect the human question" (Ulmer 2003, 2). Thus, Ulmer invites us to blur the boundary between the realm of abstraction/poetic imagination and the realities of human suffering. His is a "poetry *applied*" (Ulmer 2003, 4), and the EmerAgency is "the basis for the inference system of a digital apparatus" (Ulmer 2003, 4).

In order to begin to understand what electracy means, it is helpful at this point to consider Ulmer's apparatus table and the various constituents that come together to form the electrate apparatus with which this book is concerned (see table 1.1). According to Ulmer, "the point of making the table is to help understand, by analogy, what is happening in the present conditions of cultural shift (using as analogy for the present

Table 1.1
An Overview of Gregory Ulmer's Apparatus Theory

Apparatus	Orality	Literacy	Electracy
Practice	Religion	Science	Entertainment
Procedure	Ritual	Method	Style
Institution	Church	School	Internet
State of mind	Faith	Knowledge	Fantasy
Behavior	Worship	Experiment	Play
Philosophy	Mythology	Epistemology	Aesthetics
Ground	God	Reason	Body
Ontology	Totem	Category	Chora
Mode	Narrative	Argument	Figure
Axis	Right/Wrong	True/False	Pleasure/Pain

Source: Ulmer 2009.

moment what we know about the shift from orality to literacy)" (Ulmer 2009).

According to Ulmer, the *practice* of electracy is entertainment. He situates this constituent relative to religion and science as the predominant practices of orality and literacy, respectively. In this book, I am blurring the boundaries among the three by positioning entertainment with its new electrate practices as a meta-practice that eclipses both religion and science. In chapter 2, for instance, I look at the historical development of informatics, traditionally considered squarely within the practice of science, as entertainment in which electrate practices were invented. In modernity, science and technology served to awe and inspire people, whether it be engineering feats such as iron bridges or "iron horses" that connected peoples and lands that had historically been separated and isolated, or "electronic brains" that could beat the human brain in the game of games, Chess. Even in our postmodern world where the unabridged enthusiasm for progress through reason and logic has come under increasing scrutiny, Carl Sagan's wildly popular TV series, *Cosmos* (Sagan, Druyan, and Sotor 1980), and numerous other popular science programs serve as examples that science still entertains us today. NASA's televised and widely watched lunar landing in 1969 is another example where science emerged as the prime entertainment moment of the entire twentieth century. In the same vein, religion (and the spectacles associated with it) has always had entertainment aspects to it. From the heroic tales of David and Goliath and Moses's exodus from Egypt in the Old Testament, to the trials and tribulations of the ancient gods in Norse or Greek mythology, to the spectacle of the modern day televangelists, so well depicted by actor and director Robert Duvall in his film *The Apostle*, religion entertains as much today as it did in historic times (Duvall 1997). In chapter 3, I bring the three apparati—religion, science, and entertainment—together through an analysis of the Free- and Open Source software movement of the 1980s and 1990s and the form of evangelism that they employed in order to spread and gain acceptance for their new electrate modes of invention.

The *procedure* of electracy, Ulmer maintains, is style. He contrasts this with ritual and method, which constitute the procedures of orality and literacy. Church services or political speeches have more or less rigid procedural rituals associated with them. Even storytelling around the campfire adheres to certain rituals where the audience remains quiet and in listening mode while the storyteller controls the discursive situation and can use his or her voice and body as he or she pleases to achieve narrative special effects. In the literate apparatus, the procedure of science is the method. The method is what makes science reliable and reproducible. The method is that which produces true or false results, the benchmark against which science is measured. Academia teaches its students methods that they can employ to achieve sound results. Electracy, in contrast, operates on style, the domain of aesthetics. Ulmer explains in a 1998 interview in *PMC*: "My pedagogy aims at helping students notice, map, and enhance their own image of wide scope (their own learning style—with the term style marking the aesthetic quality of the thinking)" (Weishaus 1998). As one of the five canons of classical rhetoric, style has historically resisted the methodological logic of containment. Methods allow us to contain something in order to teach it. Style resists such appropriation. As Dick Hebdige has noted, "the tensions between dominant and subordinate groups can be found reflected in the surfaces of subculture—in the styles made up of mundane objects which have a double meaning" (Hebdige 1979, 2). Style "signals a Refusal" (Hebdige 1979, 3). Style "is the area in which opposing definitions clash with most dramatic force" (Hebdige 1979, 3).

Each apparatus, Ulmer continues, produced its own *institutions*. Within orality, religions invented the place of worship: the temple, church, or mosque. In literacy, practitioners founded the place of learning: the school, university, or laboratory. And in the literate apparatus, we have the place of entertainment: the theater, the circus, and the Internet. In his work with electracy, especially in his most recent trilogy of books, *Internet Invention* (2003), *Electronic Monuments* (2005), and *Avatar Emergency* (forthcoming), Ulmer focuses primarily on the Internet as the institution in which electracy is practiced and invented. Other writers and theorists, such as Brenda Laurel in *Computers as Theatre* (Laurel 1991) and Janet Murray in *Hamlet on the Holodeck* (Murray 1997), have made the connections between digital and historical institutions of entertainment. In chapter 2 of this book, I investigate the formation of the current institutions of electracy, the digital computer and the Internet, through a historical analysis of informatics and science as entertainment; but unlike traditional histories, mine is a *conductive* history.

State of mind is Ulmer's fourth apparatus constituent. Within the oral apparatus, faith constitutes the predominant state of mind. To have faith means to believe without proof or absolute knowing. On the other end of the spectrum, in literacy, knowledge represents the agent's state of mind. Knowledge is built on proof, and proof is generated through observation and reason, method, and empirical facts. The spiritual person believes without knowing. The scientific person does not believe without proof. For the electrate person, Ulmer suggests, fantasy is the state of mind by which experiences and meanings are created. Fantasy exists in the human mind as something that is both connected to, and separate from, the constraints of the world around us. Fantasy allows us to escape those constraints, to see ourselves and the world unabridged.

Behavior constitutes how practice is conducted within Ulmer's three apparati. In orality, he says, behavior is characterized by worship. In literacy, the predominant behavior is experimentation, while the electrate behavior is play. Play, Ulmer contends, is the action that bestows electracy on the human agent. Throughout this book, play, particularly within digital environs, is the central line of investigation into the invention of electracy. Historically, play as a *heuretic* behavior has received surprisingly little attention from scholars within the arts and sciences. This is rather interesting given that play is such an integral part of both human and animal behavior. It is through the act of playing that both humans and animals first learn about the opportunities and limitations of their world. Furthermore, play is one of the oldest forms of entertainment. Long before the ancient Greeks invented the Olympic Games, and the Romans had instituted the coliseum as the arena for competitive games, native peoples from all cultures had invented a myriad of games to entertain themselves. In 1938, Dutch historian and cultural theorist Johan Huizinga opened his now famous book, *Homo Ludens*, with the following passage:

A happier age than ours once made bold to call our species by the name of *Homo Sapiens* [Latin for "wise man" or "knowing man"]. In the course of time we have come to realize that we are not so reasonable after all as the Eighteenth Century, with its worship of reason and its naive optimism, thought us; hence modern fashion inclines to designate our species as *Homo Faber*: Man the Maker. But though *faber* may not be quite so dubious as *sapiens* it is, as a name specific of the human being, even less appropriate, seeing that many animals too are makers. There is a third function, however, applicable to both humans and animal life, and just as important as reasoning and making—namely, playing. It seems to me that next to *Homo Faber*, and perhaps on the same level as *Homo Sapiens*, Homo Ludens, Man the Player, deserves a place in our nomenclature. (Huizinga [1938] 1955, ix)

In *Homo Ludens*, Huizinga identified and discussed play as a formative element of human culture from historic times until the present day. Huizinga's work received renewed attention around the turn of the twenty-first century when it spawned a name for the new field of academic inquiry known as *ludology*, or game studies (more on this below). One of the main goals of my work is to contribute to the field of ludology through both a broader understanding of Huizinga's "Man the Player" and the rhetorical lenses of Gregory Ulmer's electracy apparatus theory. The other main goal, of course, is to contribute to the field of rhetoric by linking it to ludology through the behavior of play as a heuretic rhetorical strategy.

Philosophy may actually seem most evident in the literate area of the apparatus table because epistemology emerged as the dominant means of producing and studying knowledge. Earlier oral cultures relied on mythologies as the foundation of their individual and collective worldviews. As literacy took hold, knowledge became a goal in itself, and philosophy claimed itself as epistemic (i.e., the sole producer and purveyor of knowledge). Epistemology, along with the power base that politicized who controlled knowledge, became not just a form of philosophy but a literate machine cranking out philosophical dogma. In electracy, however, philosophy has had to relinquish its hold on this machine. The arts, and visual/auditory modes of delivery of knowledge, become part and parcel of philosophical understanding. Aesthetics allows philosophy to divest itself of literate shackles, of narrow-minded thinking, and print-based archives where philosophy feels most at home. Postmodern aesthetics set up the mechanisms for calling literate philosophy into question.

The three apparati of orality, literacy, and electracy are, according to Ulmer, *grounded* in God, reason, and body, respectively. In religion, God is the supreme deity, the foundation from which everything flows. In literacy, reason is that which constitutes the basis for human judgment, whereas in the electrate apparatus, body and self serve as the filter from which understanding of the world is derived. Ulmer posits, "The key point for us is that in the electrate image the individual body functions as filter, selecting from a flood of raw data what counts as real" (Ulmer forthcoming, 15). With his newest book, *Avatar Emergency*, Ulmer's trajectory of thinking on electracy now includes the critical shift from literacy to electracy as well as theorizing how avatar (i.e., the digital prosthetic body) functions "as the site of a new dimension of identity formation" (Ulmer forthcoming, 3). Theory, however, is not the sole purpose of avatar, in Ulmer's view. As with electracy, avatar represents and enacts "the invention of practices forming the skill-set needed by citizens to become native to electracy, as science and engineering are to the invention of the technology and equipment" (Ulmer forthcoming, 3). Furthermore, "the player–avatar relation is associated with the history of practical reason and the virtue of prudence, or good judgment" (Ulmer forthcoming, 4). However, the history of practical reason is bound up with the history of violent acts, acts by those whose standards for good judgment led to genocide and bloody revolutions. Central to Ulmer's aim in reconfiguring the apparatus of reason is reintroducing the human question into the equation.

The *ontologies* in Ulmer's apparatus theory concern theories of being and are represented by the concepts of totem, category, and chora. According to Ulmer:

Any apparatus supports a metaphysics, referring to the mode of (categorial) organization functioning at every level, in every dimension of the lifeworld. A context for our project is the assumption that we are working within an historical shift, fashioning a new coherence out of the dissolution of "essence" (literate metaphysics) in every sphere of experience, just as literacy fashioned a new coherence out of the dissolution to "totem" (think of Aristotle's taxonomies). (Ulmer forthcoming, 140)

Of course, the apparatus itself is a category system, but one that functions analogically. It is a matrix that gives us a visual sense of the cultural shifts by which each ontology may be marked. In oral cultures, totem is to ontology as symbol is to language. Literate culture installs analytics as its primary mode of being, and ontology becomes a matter of species/genus analytics. We define and therefore something *is*. We define it in relation to something else, and the relationships in a category system become *how* it exists, whereas electracy converts this categorical relationship into what Ulmer calls (after Plato) the *chora*, a spatial filtering system of "our identity that sorts the world of our experience into a pattern of coherence" (Ulmer 2003, 101). In *Avatar Emergency*, Ulmer explains: "Plato's chora is a 'strange' kind, neither intelligible nor sensible, but 'generative,' a space or region that functions as a receptacle within which Being and Becoming (ideal forms and material embodiments) interact" (Ulmer forthcoming, 17).

The *modes* by which practices are conducted in the different apparati in Ulmer's thinking are narrative, argument, and figure. Eschewing linear logic of the narrative and the deductive and inductive logic inference methods from literacy, Ulmer prefers conductive logic, which "puts into logic the aesthetic operations of images" (Ulmer 2003, 10). And figures/images retool logic with the affective dimension, what he calls the pain/pleasure axis. According to Ulmer, "The purpose of flash reason is to develop the rhetorical practice that allows users within the apparatus to take full advantage of the equipment and forms becoming available for everyday use. . . . What the written verb 'to be' is to literacy, these image tools are to electracy. Literacy augmented the experience of idea (thinking); electracy augments the experience of affect (feeling)" (Ulmer forthcoming, 16).

In an attempt to visualize the dimensionality of the three social machines, Ulmer has proposed the following *axis* configuration (figure 1.1). As with every abstraction such as this, there is a distinct danger of reductionism. However, properly viewed, it is evident that Ulmer's thinking is far from reductive. The level of abstraction in his treatment of the axis as an organizing principle is actually a welcome relief that serves to bring into clear focus the bigger picture of his project.

Within the oral apparatus, he claims, the predominant dimensionality is that of right and wrong. Religions, with their morality and ethics, operate on this binary, as do other narrative traditions in many cases. From Aesop's fables and Dr. Seuss's books to the present-day Hollywood drama, we can clearly observe narratives that are constructed in such a way as to instill or problematize concepts of right and wrong in the audience. The literate apparatus intersects orality at a 90-degree angle and operates on the binary of true and false. Every constituent of the literate apparatus concerns the question of right and wrong in some form or another. The Aristotelian worldview, which the Enlightenment and Modernity inherited, was founded on the literate axis of true and false. This binary defines science as a truth-seeking activity that is distinctly different from orality.

Electracy, as the new and emerging social machine, is situated at a 45-degree angle to the oral and literate axis. Ulmer calls it a *transversal*, which is a term borrowed from mathematics, meaning a line that intersects a system of lines. The electrate transversal connects the experiences of pain and pleasure, or sadness and joy, and is situated squarely (so to speak) within a Nietzschean affirmative life-aesthetic. For Ulmer, "Nietzsche's insight, his changed attitude, is against the ascetic values of the entire Western tradition, the rejection of 'life' as it is, including its pain and suffering, the 'spirit of revenge' against the passage of time, and the

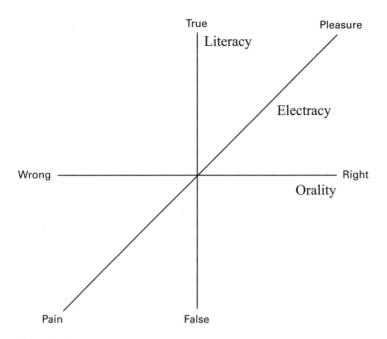

Figure 1.1
Gregory Ulmer's electracy transversal.
Source: Courtesy of Gregory Ulmer.

like. Against this 'nihilism' Nietzsche says 'yes' to his own life, in its embodied finitude, whose materiality affords in recompense the capacity to be affected, to possess a moment of happiness, an event of joy" (Ulmer forthcoming, 120).

In short, Ulmer's transversal axis is also thoroughly embedded in the question of human value, of human life. He explains: "Nietzsche is 'existential' in making his own life a test of his philosophy. One of his maxims is to look for *that secret point at which the aphorism of thought intersects with the anecdote of life*" (Ulmer forthcoming, 121).[1] This book is devoted to the ludic transversal, which I take to be an instance of Ulmer's electrate transversal. In very simple terms, play is understood as an activity in which the human agent seeks to experience pain or pleasure. In competitive games, losing definitely constitutes a painful experience for most people, whereas winning constitutes the opposite. In more exploratory games, where there is no discreet winning condition, pain and pleasure are constituted by other individual determinants that are constructed by the player through the ludic experience itself. In the final chapter of this book, I return to a much more in-depth treatment of the ludic transversal and how it can aid us in our quest to invent electracy.

Conducting Ludology

What I have been tracing are lines of argument for how this book distinguishes itself from both rhetoric and ludology via Ulmer's electracy. It should be stated, however, that my aim is not to undermine the history of rhetoric or ludology or the contemporary research that situates itself at the intersection of rhetoric/games or ludology/narrative. These debates have shaped their respective fields in extremely productive and exciting ways. The primary trajectory of this book is one that straddles these centrifugal divergences: (1) the splits that have defined how we study rhetoric as play and how we play rhetorically, and (2) the rift in game studies that pitted ludology against narratology in the race to establish a discipline focused on play. In order to *conduct* ludology and rhetoric into their new electrate trajectory, it is necessary to identify how the dominant logics, deduction and induction, have obstructed (thus far) a way out of this impasse. According to Gonzalo Frasca, the term *ludology* gained favor very swiftly in the past decade.

Contrary to what has been claimed, the term "ludology" has not been coined neither by Espen Aarseth (3, 11) [nor] by myself (20). According to research performed by Jesper Juul, the term was used as early as in 1982, albeit scarcely and with a different meaning. However, the expression seems to have started gaining acceptance around 1999, after my publication of "Ludology meets narratology," which was followed in the year 2000 by Jesper Juul's "What computer games can and cannot do," presented at the third Digital Arts and Culture (DAC) conference. My article proposed using the term "ludology" to describe a yet non-existent discipline that would focus on the study of games in general and videogames in particular. It was a call for a set of theoretical tools that would be for gaming what narratology was for narrative (8). This need was shared by a large number of researchers, so the word caught on. (Frasca 2003)

Markku Eskelinen marks the inception of the narratology/ludology debate with the publication of Espen Aarseth's (1997) groundbreaking book *Cybertext* (Eskelinen 2009, 208). But, he suggests, the debate really took shape (and heated up) "with the publication of the first issue of *Game Studies* in 2001 (www.gamestudies.org), especially the papers by [Jesper] Juul (2001) and Eskelinen (2001a) in that issue" (Eskelinen 2009, 208). Quite rightly, Eskelinen argues that this debate has exhausted itself insofar as each of the major players in the debate has moved on. Frasca moved on to "game rhetoric and serious games, Juul (2004) to the interplay of rules and fiction and casual games . . . [Henry] Jenkins (2007) to transmediality and Eskelinen (2006) to transmediality and to the perspectives ludology offers to ergodic literature and literary studies" (Eskelinen 2009, 209), in particular his dissertation from which this historical analysis is drawn: *Travels in Cybertextuality: The Challenge of Ergodic Literature and Ludology to Literary Theory* (Eskelinen 2009). In fact, Ian Bogost organized a rematch of the debate at Georgia Institute of Technology in the fall of 2009 called "How to Think about Narrativity and Interactivity," and featured speakers were Espen Aarseth, Janet Murray, and Fox Harrell ("How" 2009). I organized a group of students and faculty to attend the colloquium, and we were struck by the consistent message (especially between Aarseth and Murray) that this narratology/ludology debate was a thing of the past. Nevertheless, it has certainly shaped the field of game studies and allowed it to emerge as a major player among academic disciplines, both literary and scientific. My book does not take issue with this history so much as contributes to opening another trajectory for game studies: electracy.

The question for game studies, which has forged the ludology practice by distinguishing itself from literate practice (and too frequently, I believe, allies itself with the scientific tradition), is how *conducting* ludology might reroute the field altogether. In short, my book bypasses the literacy/ludology debate in order to link ludology and rhetoric through electracy. There are, in my view, compelling reasons for why this is necessary. Play is an activity not founded in literacy, ethics, or any such thing. It is an activity that exists alongside of those things. Faith and science are two socially constructed machines, whereas play is a third thing that moves around those two traditions. I am not concerning myself with such foundations and traditions in this book, except insofar as play must be circumscribed, and defined, as a singularity outside these grand narratives. Ulmer lends us the concepts and intellectual framework to talk about play as an electrate praxis. Ironically, it seems that much of the current game studies research comes out of the scientific tradition, playing by the rules of that tradition by establishing models and taxonomies, and by drawing conclusions about games and player actions based on deductive and inductive methods.

It is important to acknowledge that deduction and induction are not logically flawed means of arriving at conclusions. Nor do I mean to say that game studies scholars have "sold out," so to speak, by crafting arguments and studies based in traditional research methods. On the contrary, game studies must find whatever means possible to establish the parameters and portals of useful insights in order to extend those boundaries that have contained (and crippled) its progress toward legitimacy. However, we must not limit ourselves to the rules, or winning conditions, of the academic game. We have an obligation to play, and playing means playing out of bounds, in the gaps, over the chasm that no deductive or inductive logic can traverse.

The year 1997 saw the publication of two key books in this short history of game studies. Brian Sutton-Smith, an education scholar, published *The Ambiguity of Play* (Sutton-Smith 1997), and Espen Aarseth published *Cybertext: Perspectives on Ergodic Literature* (Aarseth 1997). Clearly Aarseth's book became a major catalyst in establishing the field of game studies. As my dissertation supervisor, Aarseth also guided me toward the academic field of humanistic informatics, where the genesis of this book originated. Sutton-Smith's book is promoted as offering "the components for a new social science of play" (book jacket), while Aarseth's is touted as defining "a new aesthetics of cyborg textuality" (book jacket). Each in its own way offers a bridge from science and literature to the study of play as a distinctly different realm. Sutton-Smith invokes rhetoric throughout his study, while Aarseth brings in an amazing array of textual (both print and digital) artifacts that he then examines in the light of his cybertextual theory. Both books have become iconic touchstones in game studies, although Aarseth's has spawned a generation of diverse and prolific extensions of his thought (most notably Markku Eskelinen and Raine Koskimaa's coedited series of essay anthologies begun in 2000, *CyberText Yearbook*).

Of course there have been seminal works prior to 1997, especially research that concerns what Sherry Turkle terms *Life on the Screen* (Turkle 1995). Many of us working in Internet environments (both synchronous and asynchronous) in those days published about the connections between play and writing (Haynes and Holmevik [1998] 2002; Holmevik and Haynes 2000). Thus, there are no clean divisions between studies that theorized, or empirically studied, sociocultural life online and research in game studies "proper," whatever that is. In the intervening years, journals have been born (gamestudies.org, *Games and Culture*), anthologies collected and published, conferences and symposia (DAC, DiGRA) held, blogs created (WaterCooler Games, Ludology, etc.), and industry exhibitions now partner with academic researchers (GDC, SIGGRAPH). So, tracing the proliferation and explosion of published research in game studies is not the focus of this book; rather, my aim here is to merely point to the most recent books (literate treatments of electrate research) and explain briefly how this book is distinct from that work.

No doubt there are any number of books and publishers devoted to new media and game studies, but no one press is more committed to publishing such research than the MIT Press. Between 2004 and 2011, the MIT Press published no fewer than twenty books that have all influenced my work in various ways.[2] My purpose in this brief review of publications in game studies and new media is to highlight both a commitment to this emerging field as well as the literate engagement still important to the concept of play. Obviously, my book is intended to contribute to both. But I am not engaging this prior scholarship as in a competition among literati; I am playing *through*. And I am helping invent electracy at the intersection of play and the human question. This is not to say that these scholars listed are not thoroughly engaged with community, the individual, and play as activism for improving the human condition. They most definitely are. Play is the arena in which we all work. The work/play dichotomy is at stake in all of this serious scholarship, as well as in such authors' commitment to publish research *about* play. Perhaps my playing *through* this field means that it is also important to locate play within a *praxis*, the purest form of play. Thus, electracy, I argue, is both the best apparatus to understand games and play, as well as the best means of inventing play as praxis. Taking my cue from Ulmer, who deconstructs reasoning by deductive and inductive logic, I aim to *conduct ludology* into a new phase. *Playing through* is a form of conduction, as an electrical charge plays through its network of transmitters.

This book does, to some extent, take issue with Ulmer's concept of "dimension pollution" about deliberative reason (Ulmer forthcoming, 11). I suggest that deliberative reason can take place in game spaces and that time is not necessary for deliberative reason. Games can allow for this collapse of time and space. Therefore, in solidarity with Ulmer's "flash reason," I aim to contribute to his argument for flash reason but by way of play and games. The traditional arcade games, for example, are all about "flash reason." They are all about the "twitch." Being in a raid in *World of Warcraft* means consistently adapting to and being aware of one's surroundings. You have to make split-second decisions that cannot always be deliberative, and training yourself to make such quick decisions is a feature of this kind of "flash reason." Your avatar in the game becomes the site for this.

Widescope

Gregory Ulmer's project, although both theoretically complex and intellectually ambitious, can be understood as an effort to "approach electracy by trying to invent it (what I call 'heuretics'—the use of theory to invent forms

and practices, as distinct from 'hermeneutics' which uses theory to interpret existing works)" (Ulmer 2003, 4). For Ulmer, "the goal is not to adapt
digital technology to literacy (anyway, that is happening as a matter of
course) but to discover and create an institution and its practices capable of
supporting the full potential of the new technology" (Ulmer 2003, 29). To
help us invent these new electrate skills that are needed in the age of digital
media, Ulmer proposes a new heuretic genre that he calls Mystory. Mystory
was first introduced in *Teletheory: Grammatology in the Age of Video* (Ulmer
1989) and should be pronounced my'stry, a grammatological construction
that is meant to differentiate it from existing literate forms of knowledge
production such as history, that is, HIS-story. Mystory, according to Ulmer,
does for electracy what the argumentative essay does for literacy. It focuses
on the agent and his or her own experiences as opposed to asking the agent
to seek understanding outside of his or her own. History tells us how others
shaped the world around us, whereas the mystory tells us how we came to
be shaped by our experiences of being in that world.

To more fully understand how the mystory accomplishes this, it might
be helpful here to consider what the German philosopher Martin Heidegger sets forth in his highly influential work from 1927, *Being and Time*
(Heidegger [1927] 1962). Heidegger's thinking centers around one seemingly simple question of what it means to be, *dasein*. Heidegger begins his
treatment of this subject by rejecting Immanuel Kant's notion that space
and time are equally important principles in the way humans organize
our world. Space, he said, is almost insignificant; time is the mystery. He
connects time and human existence as the one fundamental dimension
that can begin to explain the question of *dasein*. Heidegger then goes
on to explore how being is really a process of becoming, that we *are* by
virtue of being in the process of becoming that which we have not yet
become. Heidegger rejects the old Aristotelian notion that there is an essence of man founded on reason and logic. This is an abstraction, he says.
What comes first is Man's own existence, and that existence is inexplicably linked to time and our own projections of what we seek to become in
the future.

Ulmer's mystorical genre revolves around some of the very same principles. It is first and foremost a reflexive and self-directed exercise that is
designed to help us understand how we came to be and, more important,
what we might become in the future. The mystory helps us uncover Heidegger's mystery of being and time as it pertains to our own *dasein*. In
the mystory, Ulmer asks us to consider our relationship to four different

discourses that, he contends, are instrumental in shaping who we are. These discourses are *career, family, entertainment*, and *community history*. In *Internet Invention*, the textbook he wrote on the mystory genre and its place in the invention of electracy, Ulmer explains: "The five parts of the book [*Internet Invention*] reflect the steps of composing a mystory. Students map or document their situations or relationship to each of four institutions: Career field or major; Family; Entertainment; community History (as taught in school or otherwise commemorated in the community" (Ulmer 2003, 6). These four discourses represent what Ulmer calls the "popcycle" into which we are interpellated. Interpellation is a concept that comes from the French Marxist structural theorist Louis Althusser and refers to the process by which individuals are "hailed" into certain subject positions. "In our context," Ulmer says, "interpellation may be understood as the provisional acceptance of the default or ready-made images and themes of the popcycle" (Ulmer 2003, 247). When the *egent*, as Ulmer calls it, has mapped his or her relationship to each of the four discourses, typically as websites or other digital artifacts, the final task is to link them in such a way that a pattern emerges. "The pattern," he reveals, "emerges not at the level of meaning or theme (these may be derived or inferred from the pattern). Rather, the pattern forms at the level of repeating signifiers—words and graphics" (Ulmer 2003, 6). Ulmer's focus on the signifier is important to note here. Contrary to claims made by some structuralist theorists who maintained that the signifier is independent, and therefore superior to the signified, the poststructuralist position taken by Ulmer sees them as inseparable but not united. The pattern that emerges through the mystorical exercise produces what Ulmer calls an emblem that "evokes the look and feel of [the] mystory" (Ulmer 2003, 246). "*What resembles, assembles,*" he says in typical playful style, the emblems of the wide scope (Ulmer 2003, 271).

I started this book by relating my own experiences with games and computer programming as a way to lead into the central theme of this work. Although it is not strictly a mystory by an Ulmerian definition, it does explain a lot about where I am coming from and what I attempt to do in this book. I am a player first and always have been. I don't make any excuses for that or try to compartmentalize it from my professional and academic interest in games and play. Work and play for me are both situated along the ludic transversal, which is an instantiation of the electrate dimension. My career discourse has also been largely influenced by play and games. Between 1995 and 2004, I spent most of my professional time on the development of game technology for educational use, and I published two books on that subject, the edited collection *High Wired* in 1998 and *MOOniversity* in 2000, both with Cynthia Haynes. In 1996, I took a job as a visiting assistant professor in the Department of Humanistic Informatics at the University of Bergen, where I later earned my PhD. It was a very small department at that time, and Espen Aarseth and I taught most of the classes. Both of us had a longstanding interest in games. I can fondly remember many evenings spent around his kitchen table playing Bungie's then-new, real-time strategy game *Myth* over a LAN. I distinctly remember thinking about how nice it would be to one day make a living from working with such games in academia. A few years later, in 1998, when Aarseth founded and organized the first Digital Arts and Culture (DAC) conference, I was introduced to a group of new scholars, most of whom were graduate students at the time and who also shared a unique interest in new digital media and games. In the years that followed, the DAC conference served as an intellectual platform from which many careers were launched and games theorized. In 2000, I was fortunate enough to chair that conference. If I were to suggest a wide scope for myself, then, based on those signifiers that have assembled me, it would have to be something that expresses the playful journey, the adventure. Knowing that there is a goal or destination, but not necessarily knowing exactly what that might be or how to get there is what sets us on the path to discovery. That is my starting point for the sort of invention I am concerned with in this book. In the age of electracy, play can and does facilitate invention. I know this because I was there when play invented the field of ludology.

The wider scope of this book is to propose not a new *genre*, which is a term that is inexplicably linked to the literate apparatus, but a new *heuretic*, in which play acts as a conductor for the invention of electracy. Play is a metabehavior that touches on every constituent in Ulmer's electracy apparatus theory. *Entertainment* continues to be one of the main reasons that people play games. Even the concept of serious games, which has gained traction in recent years, founds its primary appeal to "education" through entertainment. *Style* and image logic, as opposed to ritual and method, afford the player aesthetic experiences that inspire new practices. The *Internet* becomes the institution in which the digital game is situated. Multiplayer and social-media games, for example, do not make sense outside of the institutional frame of the network. *Fantasy* is a dominant state of mind in which many players of many digital games find themselves. *Play* as behavior runs through the entire apparatus as the most significant cultural shift to invent electracy. *Aesthetics* encompasses the artistic/ creative impulse from which play, both the material/physical and digital platforms of play, is pervasively attuned. The digital *Body*, the avatar, acts as the site for electracy formation. *Chora* is the generative game space in which Being and Becoming melt together through what Aarseth called in *Cybertext* "ergodic activity" (Aarseth 1997). *Figure* names image logic as the most significant mode that conducts meaning within graphically enriched games. Finally, the digital game affords us experiences in which the *axis* of pain/pleasure, sadness/joy can be traversed through immersive interaction.

Ulmer's mystory genre forms a loose heuretic metaframework for the organization of this book in the way that it draws our attention to the "crossing of discourses that has been shown to occur in the invention process" (Ulmer 1994, xii). Through a mapping of play as invention across the four mystorical discourses that constitute the "popcycle" of digital gaming, that is to say, the institutions that interpellate us into the subject position of the gamer or player, I seek to uncover how the invention of electracy is facilitated through the apparatus constituents of each. For the *career discourse*, Ulmer asks us in *Internet Invention* to focus on "an important discovery or a (founding) invention" (Ulmer 2003, 21) within the career domain. In response, I have dedicated chapter 2 (Hacker Noir) to an analysis of the invention of the digital computer and the emergence of a new type of electrate inventor, the hacker. In chapter 3 (Choral Code), I address the *community history discourse* through a study of hacker heuretics, specifically with regard to how a more playful practice of invention, which is uniquely different from the literate scientific practice, conducts electracy via a subversive *choral* code. The *entertainment discourse* is addressed tangentially in chapter 4 (Venture) and chapter 5 (Intervention), wherein I foreground early digital games as rhizomatic experience generators in which entertainment and learning morph through subversive strategies and deconstruction into forms of electrate practices. Chapter 6 (Ludic Ethics) touches on Ulmer's *family discourse* by way of ethics. The family is the first institution in which ethics is learned and internalized, and in the context of this book, I am using it as a metaphor for the gaming community and the subject positions into which players are interpellated. Is there a particular ethics associated with digital gaming; if so, how does it configure behaviors that conduct electracy? In chapter 7 (Burning Chrome), I direct my focus back to the wide image, and I look at the "signifiers" that have emerged in previous chapters in an attempt to assemble how play signifies a new heuristic for the invention of electracy and also how they have assembled my own emblem (figure 1.2) as it emerged through the mystorical and conductive research and writing process of this book.

Figure 1.2
Burning chrome.
Source: Courtesy of Richard Berry.

2 Hacker Noir

There still exists among ourselves an activity which on the technical plane gives us quite a good understanding of what a science we prefer to call "prior" rather than "primitive," could have been on the plane of speculation. This is what is commonly called "bricolage" in French.

—Lévi-Strauss, *The Savage Mind*

The French anthropologist Claude Lévi-Strauss provides us with an excellent starting point for our journey into the ludic dimensions of electrate invention. In his well-renowned work, *The Savage Mind* from 1966, Lévi-Strauss introduces us to the *bricoleur*, which he says is a term that describes someone who "works with his hands and uses devious means compared to those of a craftsman" (Lévi-Strauss 1966, 16). The word originates from the old French verb *bricoler*, which in English means to putter or tinker. It was always, he explains, "used with reference to some extraneous movement: a ball rebounding, a dog straying or a horse swerving from its direct course to avoid an obstacle" (Lévi-Strauss 1966, 16). Lévi-Strauss contrasts the *bricoleur* with the engineer or craftsman in that "the 'bricoleur's' means cannot . . . be defined in terms of a project" (Lévi-Strauss 1966, 17). "The 'bricoleur,'" he notes, "is adept at performing a large number of diverse tasks; but, unlike the engineer, he does not subordinate each of them to the availability of raw materials and tools conceived and procured for the purpose of the project" (Lévi-Strauss 1966, 17). The bricoleur's first step to invention, says Lévi-Strauss, is retrospective.

He has to turn back to an already existent set made up of tools and materials, to consider or reconsider what it contains and, finally and above all, to engage in a sort of dialogue with it and, before choosing between them, to index the possible answers which the whole set can offer to his problem. He interrogates all the heterogeneous objects of which his treasury is composed to discover what each of them could "signify" and so contribute to the definition of a set which has yet to materialize but which will ultimately differ from the instrumental set only in the internal disposition of its parts. (Lévi-Strauss 1966, 18)

The *bricoleur*, in Lévi-Strauss's definition, provides us with a very useful conceptualization of the electrate inventor. It is someone who, metaphorically speaking, works with his or her hands, that is to say, someone who *creates through the act of re/making*, as opposed to the engineer or craftsman who creates through deliberative reason founded in scientific literacy. Another interesting concept for our purposes here is what Lévi-Strauss calls *heterogeneous objects*, which he says constitutes the bricoloeur's means. "The set of the 'bricoleur's' means," he writes, "cannot . . . be defined in terms of a project. . . . It is to be defined only by its potential use" (Lévi-Strauss 1966, 17).

I must point out here that it is certainly not my intention to argue that scientists and engineers do not share at least some of the bricoleur's approaches to, and strategies for, invention. For many decades now, scholars in science and technology studies (STS) and related fields such as sociology of science and history of technology, and cultural studies, for instance, have presented compelling cases and arguments for how science and technology is not necessarily just a product of what we normally associate with scientific methodologies and deliberative reason. Bruno Latour and Steve Woolgar became influential proponents for social constructionism, an epistemological framework for understanding how science and technology is shaped and in turn shapes us through interactions and practices that extend well beyond what we normally think of as the site for scientific and technological invention (Latour and Woolgar 1979). Actor-network theory, developed in the 1980s and 1990s by Bruno Latour, Michel Callon, John Law, and others, expands on this theoretical trajectory through the introduction of nonhuman agency as a player in the invention process (Latour 1987; Bijker et al. 1989). Bruno Latour carries this line of thinking even further in *We Have Never Been Modern* (1993), in which he takes issue with the modernist notion, perhaps most famously articulated by C. P. Snow in *The Two Cultures* in 1959 at the eve of modernism, that there existed a great divide between nature and culture, between the sciences and the humanities (Snow [1959] 1993). Although we can certainly find traces of similar modernist sentiments in Lévi-Strauss's juxtaposition of the bricoleur and the engineer, I would argue, with Latour, that for our purpose here, "we should be talking about morphism. Morphism," he says, "is the place where technomorphisms, zoomorphisms, phusmorphisms, ideomorphisms, theomorphisms, sociomorphisms, psychomorphisms, all come together. Their alliances and their exchanges, taken together, are what define the *anthropos*" (Latour 1993, 137).

It turns out that "man" is always already a morph-anthropos, a kind of morphamphibian being—one foot in play, the other foot playing. Derrida tosses Lévi-Strauss a proverbial ball by injecting free play into the binary itself:

> If one calls *bricolage* the necessity of borrowing one's concept from the text of a heritage which is more or less coherent or ruined, it must be said that every discourse is *bricoleur*. The engineer, whom Lévi-Strauss opposes to the *bricoleur*, should be the one to construct the totality of his language, syntax, and lexicon. In this sense the engineer is a myth. . . . The notion of the engineer who supposedly breaks with all forms of *bricolage* is therefore a theological idea; and since Lévi-Strauss tells us elsewhere that *bricolage* is mythopoetic, the odds are that the engineer is a myth produced by the *bricoleur*. (Derrida [1966] 1978, 285)

In effect, Derrida's deconstruction of these categories of player (engineer and *bricoleur*) constitutes a clever hack—both are of the "species of *bricoleurs*," and thus "the very idea of *bricolage* is menaced and the difference in which it took on its meaning breaks down" (Derrida [1966] 1978, 285).

Latour's idea of the interplay of morphisms as that which defines the *anthropos* (Greek, human being) and Derrida's re/visioning of Lévi-Strauss's *bricoleur* dovetails well with Gregory Ulmer's notion of the body or avatar as the site for electrate invention and gives us a solid theoretical basis from which to begin thinking about the hacker as a ludic electrate inventor.

Hacker Noir

For most people, the word *hacker* is synonymous with that of a clever nerd who uses his or her wizardly computer skills for devious purposes. In some cases, those purposes are permissible within the confines of the law, in other cases they are not. Sometimes they are not even devious at all. In this book, I do not wish to draw, as so many writers have done, a clear distinction between the hacker as a hero or as a villain because what I am really interested in is the morphism, the amalgamation of the two, and how it is configured through the playful, subversive behaviors that both archetypes so clearly display. In other words, whatever their ultimate motives might be, the ludic elements of their electrate practices are of primary interest to us here.

The term *hacker* rose to prominence in the 1980s at a time when computers and digital networks began to penetrate the public discourse in earnest.

Against the dystopian visions of George Orwell's novel *1984*, of a society in which the individual is subjected to complete control and surveillance and an increasing discomfort by the threat of a nuclear holocaust set in motion by man's loss of control of the very technologies that were put in place to help and protect us (Orwell 1949), the hacker emerges as the new John Wesley Hardin, a morphism of outlaw and folk hero on the "digital frontier." In Stanley Kubric's magnum opus, *2001: A Space Odyssey* (Kubric 1968), the movie-going public was introduced to artificial intelligence in the form of the super computer HAL 9000, who in an act of self-preservation shows that "smart" machines are capable of committing murder. Back in 1968, computers were still a novelty for most people, but by the 1980s and the arrival of the personal networked computer on the scene, the dangers of thinking machines and the clever wiz kids who possessed the skills to manipulate them were no longer science fiction. The film *WarGames* from 1983 captures this very scenario against a backdrop of the ultimate Cold War nightmare of weapons of mass destruction out of control. David, a young hacker and video gamer played by Matthew Broderick, hacks into what he believes to be an online supercomputer belonging to a game development company, and engages in a game of Global Thermonuclear War. "Do you want to play a game," the computer asks in a voice suspiciously reminiscent of HAL from *2001* (*WarGames* 1983). The video gamer gleefully accepts the challenge. It soon turns out that the stakes of this particular game are much higher than what David could ever have anticipated. The computer he is playing against belongs to the top-secret military organization War Operations Plan Response, and the ensuing events threaten to set off World War III. The central question that runs through the film is, "Is it a game or is it real?" (*WarGames* 1983). The answer, of course, is that it is both.

In literature, the 1980s cyberpunk scene became an important outlet for the cultural construction of what I have termed *hacker noir*. William Gibson's short story *Burning Chrome* (1986a) and his much-celebrated Sprawl trilogy of books (*Neuromancer* [1984], *Count Zero* [1986b], and *Mona Lisa Overdrive* [1988]) brought with them a new and much darker form of hacker. Gibson's hacker noir is suspended somewhere between the 1970s and 1980s punk disillusionment and a Phillip K. Dick–inspired futuristic vision of a high-tech Sprawl where people's struggle to survive pulses to the rhythm of the opportunities and dangers of an omnipresent digital matrix.

A year here and he still dreamed of cyberspace, hope fading nightly. All the speed he took, all the turns he'd taken and the corners he'd cut in Night City, and still he'd seen the matrix in his sleep, bright lattices of logic unfolding across that colorless void. . . .The Sprawl was a long strange way home over the Pacific now, and he was no console man, no cyberspace cowboy. Just another hustler, trying to make it through. (Gibson 1984, 5)

Inspired, perhaps, by these and other fictional representations of the hacker noir, journalists and other nonfiction writers in the late 1980s and early 1990s began to portray stories of real-world hackers noir. In his book *The Cuckoo's Egg*, astronomer, Unix systems administrator, and self-styled cybersleuth Clifford Stoll relates how he tracked down and helped bring to justice German hacker Marcus Hess, who in the late 1980s had been breaking into various U.S. research and military computer installations in order to obtain sensitive intelligence for the Soviet KGB (Stoll 1989). In another influential book from around the same time, *Cyberpunk: Outlaws and Hackers on the Computer Frontier*, *New York Times* journalists John Markoff and Katie Hafner exposed the cyberexploits of hackers Kevin Mitnick and Robert Tappan Morris (Hafner and Markoff [1991] 1995). Morris, author of the famous Internet Worm that infected and replicated itself to an estimated 6,000 Unix machines across the United States on November 2, 1988, was in many ways the personification of the computer wiz kid from the film *WarGames*. He was a clean-cut first-year Cornell University doctoral student in computer science from a well-to-do family, and his father, ironically enough, was a chief scientist working on computer security for the National Security Agency. Morris later explained that his intentions had never been malicious. "The goal of this program," he said, "was to demonstrate the inadequacies of current security measures on computer networks by exploiting the security defects that [he] had discovered" (Morris 1991). Morris didn't think he had done anything bad by writing and releasing his Worm onto the Internet. In his view, it was a fun and innovative way of drawing attention to a perceived problem while employing and perhaps showing off his computer systems and coding skills. In the public discourse, the story took a very different and much darker direction. A reporter for Channel 8 News in Boston had the following narrative to present to TV viewers that night:

Life in the modern world has a new anxiety these days. Just as we've become totally dependent on our computers, they are being stalked by saboteurs. Saboteurs who create computer viruses. The defense department, universities, and research centers are still recovering tonight from a computer virus that brought a nationwide network [the Internet] to a standstill. [. . .] The suspect," the reporter concludes, "a dark genius." (Ten O'clock News 1988)

Another "dark genius" who found himself the target of increasing public interest at the time was Kevin Mitnick, the California hacker whose much-publicized arrests in 1988 and 1995 for various cyber-related crimes propelled him to the very top of hacker noir fame. Mitnick's many hacking exploits, while certainly serious enough in many instances, cannot however account for the cult status that he later achieved. The credit for that must largely go to journalists like John Markoff and others who, through their persistent and carefully crafted narratives of the hacker noir—like writers of old Westerns—created legends that quickly eclipsed the men they sought to depict.

Although stories and narratives about the darker sides of hacking are certainly fascinating reading and, as I have pointed to above, largely defined the hacker in the public discourse, there is another side to this that is even more interesting to us in terms of electrate invention. That is the story of hackers as present-day *bricoleurs* whose skills and heuretic methodologies helped subvert and reinvent the very process of digital invention. Steven Levy's book *Hackers* is a wonderfully passionate, yet remarkably honest, account of what he perceives to be the true unsung heroes of the computer revolution ([1984] 1994). These heroes were not the scientists or engineers working within well-defined scientific research projects that were firmly situated in the literate apparatus, but rather they were *bricoleurs*, players, and upstarts who worked with what was at hand because it was fun to create and re-create technologies that suited their needs and represented their visions for how things should be. The following sections of this chapter focus on how their entertainment of choice, the digital programmable computer, came to be.

Inventing a Universal Machine

Early attempts to "program" machines to perform automated tasks can be traced back at least to the Industrial Revolution of the late seventeenth and early eighteenth centuries. The perhaps best-known example of such an early programmable machine is the *Jacquard Loom* invented by the French silk weaver Joseph-Marie Jacquard (1752–1834) in 1801. The Jacquard Loom was an automatic weaving machine that could be programmed to automatically weave any pattern in fabric. Data about various patterns were encoded as holes or the absence of holes on pasteboard cards. When a series of these cards was fed into the machine, it would mechanically read the punched cards and automatically reproduce the patterns that had been encoded onto them. Some of the most intricate and complex patterns woven by Jacquard Looms could take tens of thousands of cards to produce. While the Jacquard Loom was a programmable machine that bore no resemblance to traditional calculating machinery whatsoever, it was nevertheless an early example of a programmable machine that was, in many historians' opinion, a significant precursor to the programmable computer itself (Goldstine 1972).

Another often-cited inspiration for the development of digital programmable computers is attributed to the British mathematician Charles Babbage (1791–1871), who in 1833 devised a sophisticated mechanical calculator that could be programmed to automatically perform scientific computations (Lee 1994a). Babbage called his machine the *Analytical Engine*. The ideas for the machine grew out of an earlier project, the *Difference Engine*, which he had worked on since 1823. In his autobiography, Charles Babbage describes how his life-long pursuit of automatic calculating machinery began (Williams [1985] 1997).

One evening I was sitting in the rooms of the Analytical society at Cambridge, my head leaning forward on the table in a kind of dreamy mood, with a Table of logarithms lying open before me. Another member, coming into the room, and seeing me half asleep, called out, "Well, Babbage, what are you dreaming about?" To which I replied, "I am thinking that all these Tables might be calculated by machinery." (Babbage 1864, 42)

Unfortunately, due to the limitations imposed by the tool-making art of the early nineteenth century and problems of funding caused in part by his somewhat eccentric personality, Babbage was never able to successfully complete the Analytical Engine. Thanks in large part to the writings of Lady Ada Lovelace, daughter of the illustrious British poet Lord Byron, however, the ideas and concepts of the machine were passed down through history.

Lovelace (1815–1852) had become interested in mathematics at an early age, and after she met Babbage in 1834 and learned of his work, she too became fascinated with his research into automatic calculating machinery. She was one of the few people at the time who were able to understand and explain Babbage's work. In one of her many notes she eloquently sums up the concept of the machine with the following words: "We may say most aptly that the Analytical Engine weaves algebraic patterns just as the Jacquard-loom weaves flowers and leaves" (Toole 1998, 696). Lovelace is also credited with coming up with the idea for an algebraic coding system with which to "program" the still-theoretical machine. Her theoretical thinking went far beyond just mathematical calculations, however, something that is clearly evidenced in another of her notes:

Again, it [the Analytical Engine] might act upon other things besides numbers, were objects found whose mutual fundamental relations could be expressed by those of the abstract science of operations, and which should be also susceptible of adaptations to the action of the operating notation and mechanism of the engine. . . . Supposing, for instance, that the fundamental relations of pitched sounds in the science of harmony and of musical composition were susceptible of such expression and adaptations, the engine might compose elaborate and scientific pieces of music of any degree of complexity or extent. (quoted in Toole 1998, 694)

Lovelace's significant theoretical achievements in the area of machine programming have led some to erroneously dub her the world's first computer programmer (Rheingold [1985] 2000). Although there are conceptual similarities between her work and the computer programming systems devised in the twentieth century, there is no historical evidence to suggest any direct linkages between the two. Nevertheless, in the history of computing machinery, especially as it relates to the art of programming, Lady Ada Lovelace remains one the most prominent figures of all time. In 1979, the U.S. Department of Defense named a new programming language *Ada* in her honor.

The digital programmable computer, unlike computing and data processing machinery of previous eras, and indeed one might say every other type of machinery, was a universal machine. It was essentially capable of solving *any* problem that could be adequately conceived of and described in an algorithmic manner. In 1937, the British mathematician Alan Turing published the now-famous article "On Computable Numbers," in which he formulated many of the modern computer's theoretical underpinnings (Turing 1937, 230–265). In this article, Turing addressed the question of unsolvable mathematical problems known as Hilbert's "Entscheidungsproblem." He was able to prove the existence of such problems by devising a theoretical machine (Turing machine) that was, in effect, capable of solving any computable (i.e., solvable) mathematical problem. While the Turing machine and the theory behind it was an important factor in the conceptualization of the universal machine, it was not until World War II that the first prototypes of what we today consider the modern computer started to emerge.

In wartime Germany, under the cloak of Hitler's Nazi regime, a young engineer named Konrad Zuse invented what many historians now believe to be the world's first fully functional digital programmable computer (Ceruzzi [1998] 2003). The machine, known as the Z3, was based on Zuse's earlier work with electromechanical calculators dating back as early as 1934. With the outbreak of the war in 1939, young Zuse was drafted into military service, but he managed to work on the Z3 off and on until the machine became operational in 1941. As Zuse explains, German aviation authorities took an immediate interest in the Z3 and realized that it could be a valuable tool in aircraft design.

Unlike aircraft stress, wing flutter results in critical instability due to vibration of the wings, sometimes in conjunction with the tail unit. Complex calculations were needed in order to overcome this design problem. [. . .] I achieved a breakthrough using my equipment for this calculation. Unfortunately the Aircraft Research Institute had not been given a high enough priority for me to be released from military service. (Lee 1994b)

The Z3 was lost during an Allied bombing raid on Berlin in 1944, but by this time Zuse was already hard at work on his next machine, the more powerful and improved Z4. As Allied forces closed in on Berlin in the late winter and spring of 1945, Zuse was forced to suspend his work in the city and move the Z4 around what was left of Nazi Germany in an attempt to avoid capture. He was successful in his escape, and the machine eventually ended up in the small Alpine village of Hinterstein, where the next chapter in the Z4 saga unfolded. During the war years, Zuse had, as we shall soon see, also become interested in problems related to the programming of his machines. He says:

One aspect became clear to me in view of all this research between 1936 and 1946. Some means was necessary by which the relationships involved in calculation operations could be precisely formulated. My answer was "Plankalkül"—today it would be termed an "algorithmic" language. (Lee 1994b)

Far from the inferno of war in Berlin, in what had once been a stable in the pastoral Bavarian countryside, Zuse and his team managed to restore the Z4 to its working condition, and work on the Plankalkül began in earnest. While some historians hold that Plankalkül was the world's first high-level programming language (Giloi 1997), it was not, according to Zuse, "conceived as a means of programming the Z4 or other computers available at the time." He says, "Its true purpose was to assist in establishing consistent laws of circuitry, e.g. for floating point arithmetic, as well as in planning the sequence of instructions a computer would follow" (Lee 1994b). Nevertheless, Zuse did use it for specific programming purposes. One of the first applications that he wrote using Plankalkül was, in fact, a Chess-playing program. "I remember mentioning to friends back in 1938 that the world chess champion would be beaten by a computer in 50 years time" (Lee 1994b). We know today that he was not much off in his prediction and that he himself had a lot to do with its realization. Although he was clearly ahead of his time, Zuse's remarkable achievements were not generally known or acknowledged until many years later. Germany had lost the war, and, as we know, victors write the history.

In the United States, there were chiefly two separate developments that contributed to the invention of the digital programmable computer. The first took place at Iowa State College under the direction of John Vincent Atanasoff (1903–1995) and his young graduate student Clifford Berry (1918–1963), who between the years of 1939 and 1942 designed, built, and tested what would later be known as the world's first wholly electronic digital computer, the Atanasoff–Berry Computer (ABC). In an interview from 1972, Atanasoff recalls:

In the fall of 1939—and Clifford's understanding was so good that we will just repeat history, now, and say that, although Clifford came to work in September, that by the end of the year we had a prototype, a demonstration of a prototype doing calculations in this way, according to the methods which I had previously conceived. Clifford Berry was a good mechanic, which was an essential part of the thing. He could do electronic works freely with his hands, but his technique was equally as good as his digital manipulation—manual manipulation. He was very orderly. So I had no problem. Clifford Berry and I would sit out and we'd talk about how we might do things, so then Clifford would do them and there wasn't any need of any drawings, any large amount of drawings, or special designs. Things just went together rapidly in his hands. (Atanasoff 1972)

Atanasoff and Berry's collaboration offers a highly educational glimpse into the often-veiled invention process of what we, with Derrida, may call *science bricoleurs*.

The other main American development took place at the University of Pennsylvania's Moore School of Electrical Engineering. In the summer of 1943, the U.S. Army Ordnance commissioned a team of Moore School engineers headed by J. Presper Eckert and John W. Mauchly to build a high-speed computer for the production of ballistic firing tables. Two years later, in the fall of 1945, the team presented Electronic Numerical Integrator and Computer (ENIAC), the world's first electronic digital computer. While Konrad Zuse's electromechanical machines and Atanasoff and Berry's electronic ABC represented important innovations with regard to computing machinery, the ENIAC was the first real prototype for the digital programmable computer we know today. It was highly complex and versatile and could crunch numbers with far greater speed and accuracy than any other calculating machine of its time. Yet for all its speed, ENIAC had to be manually reconfigured in order to solve different computational problems. The machine had several large plug boards on which the "programmers" created physical binary representations of the algorithms they wanted to run.

For each new program, they had to go through a tedious and error-prone process of physically rewiring these plug boards. The process of building the ENIAC taught the engineers a lot about the potential of high-speed digital computers. In 1945, Eckert and Mauchly had a series of discussions with renowned mathematician John Von Neumann of Princeton University's Institute for Advanced Study, and together they came up with the idea of using a "memory" to store data and computational instructions inside the machine itself (Von Neumann architecture). This later became known as the *Stored-Program Concept* and was the foundation for the development of all the software technologies that followed (Aspray 1990).

The Beginnings of Computer Programming

In the early days of computer programming, algorithms were typically coded directly in binary. This was a tedious and error-prone process, so the first larger computer programs were instead written in octal, a numbering system of base eight, which made the transition between our decimal system and the computer's binary system somewhat more manageable (Hopper 1981). As the digital programmable computer became more widespread, a number of other programming systems were also adopted. One of the most popular of these was the assembly system that implemented mnemonic codes like ADD and MUL to substitute certain machine instructions and thereby make the code easier for humans to read and write. Another problem that frequently occurred when manually translating programs into machine-readable form was the introduction of errors. Even the slightest mistake could corrupt the entire program; as a result, the programmer often had to spend much time finding and correcting the problem. As long as the computer was primarily being used for scientific computations and, furthermore, carefully tended to by a staff of highly skilled mathematicians doing the programming work, coding in octal or assembly, for example, was a feasible way of utilizing the (by today's standards) sparse machine resources because of its isomorphic relationship to machine code. However, during the 1950s, as the computer was increasingly being applied to other areas such as business data processing, for instance, this scheme became more problematic.

Around 1950, when the Eckert–Mauchly Computer Corporation started selling its Universal Automatic Computer, better known as UNIVAC, one way the company remedied this problem was by providing a system for easier programming. The system, Short Code, was written by John Mauchly in 1949, and it was the first serious attempt to give the "programmer an actual power to write a program in a language which bore no resemblance whatsoever to the original machine code" (Hopper 1981, 9).

In 1951, mathematician Grace M. Hopper (later Rear Admiral in the U.S. Navy) also started to look into this problem. Hopper was already among the veterans in the fledgling field of modern computing and had considerable experience in computer programming dating back to projects she had worked on during the war. Her point of view was that "you could make a computer do anything which you could properly define" (Hopper 1981, 13). So, why not let the computer automate the entire code translation process? The solution that she came up with in May 1952 was the *compiler*, a program that took as its input another program and gave as an output a machine-readable or binary version of that program.

The advent of the compiler revolutionized the art of computer programming. It was able to translate code into binary quickly and accurately; consequently, programmers no longer had to think like a machine when formulating solutions to the problems they wanted to solve. Instead they were able to focus on the more abstract principles and mechanisms that constituted the algorithmic solution to their problems. The new "automatic" programming scheme pioneered by Hopper, combined with efforts to create pseudo-coding systems such as Short Code, eventually led to what we know as high-level programming. Another equally important "side effect" of the compiler was creating the potential for commercial software. People cannot easily read programs distributed in binary form, so a compiled program is an excellent safeguard for intellectual property such as algorithms. Although the compiler made all this possible very early on, software development for commercial gain did not take off until at least a decade later. During these early years, the money was in hardware—software was mostly an incentive to drive hardware sales.

From the late 1950s onward, an increasing amount of research went into the development of high-level programming languages. It created a whole new understanding of what digital computers could do. By extension, it also spawned a whole new field of research. What had previously been considered to be "applied mathematics" would henceforth be known as "computer science."

A programming language is, in essence, a set of natural language–like statements coupled with mathematical and operational rules for how to formulate problems that a computer can solve. With the aid of such languages, the once arcane and error-prone art of coding for computers became much simplified. Problems could now be formulated using an English-like, abstract syntax where the programmer focused on the logical solution to

a problem rather than the technical oddities of binary coding and translation. Two of the most widespread programming languages of all time,
FORTRAN (FORmula TRANslation, 1957) and COBOL (Common Business
Oriented Language, 1959), first came into existence during the late 1950s.
Another less widespread, yet highly influential, programming language
named ALGOL (ALGOrithmic Language, 1960) was also born during these
early days of high-level programming languages. Together these three languages formed the nucleus that shaped the direction that computer science
would follow for many years. Even more pertinent for our discussion here,
they became the foundation for the programming tools that generations of
hackers have used ever since.

Within a few short years, there were programming languages for scientific computation, data processing, simulation, artificial intelligence, and
many other areas of application. While the trend early on leaned heavily
toward the proliferation of special-purpose languages, the search for the
general-purpose programming language became the primary focus of the
science and engineering efforts toward the end of the decade. The desire to
conceive unifying and general-purpose programming concepts arose partly
out of a more mature understanding of the modern computer as a truly universal machine. In part it came as a response to a notion that software development in the late 1960s had reached a state of crisis (Naur and Randell
1969). The outcome of the debates surrounding these issues was, on the one
hand, the new field of Software engineering and, on the other, a general
consensus about the importance of general purpose programming tools.

The first steps that led to the idea of the general-purpose programming
language took place ten years earlier. Early programming language development was predominantly platform specific (i.e., IBM was making FORTRAN
for its hardware, and Univac was making FLOW-MATIC [and later COBOL]
for its systems). In 1958, therefore, an international committee of research
scientists met in Zurich, Switzerland, with the goal of creating a universal, platform-independent language that could serve as a standard for the
publication of algorithms. While the original ALGOL 58 specification was
important in its own right, it was the refined ALGOL 60 two years later that
would become one of the most important milestones in the early history of
programming languages. Although ALGOL was for all intents and purposes
a language for scientific computations, it clearly demonstrated the benefits
of code portability and unifying language constructs.

ALGOL was so important because it was an international and collaborative research effort. Many of the luminaries of early computer science started
their careers in the ALGOL research community, and several of the language

projects that continued to lead the field into the 1970s and 1980s had their origins in ALGOL. One such language was Simula, developed by Kristen Nygaard and Ole-Johan Dahl at the Norwegian Computing Center in Oslo, Norway, between 1964 and 1968. Simula was originally an ALGOL-based language for discrete-event simulations, but with the increasing emphasis on generality, it was later revised into a full general-purpose programming language. Simula is notable because it was the first language to introduce the concepts of object-oriented programming, which became the dominant paradigm in computer programming in the 1990s (Holmevik 1994, 2004). Another important language that grew out of the ALGOL research community was Pascal, written by Niklaus Wirth of the Swiss Federal Institute of Technology in Zurich between 1968 and 1972. Pascal became perhaps the most important educational programming language of the 1970s and 1980s, and it was the first programming language that I was introduced to when I started studying computer science at the university.

By the 1970s, general-purpose programming languages had become the mainstay of computer science. During the next ten years, most of the development efforts in programming language design would be directed not so much toward the creation of new concepts as toward the refinement of the principles of generality. The one language that perhaps more than any other managed to capture the spirit of universal applicability was C, a language designed by Dennis M. Ritchie of Bell Labs between 1969 and 1973. C was developed in close relation to the Unix operating system, and for this reason it quickly became a favorite development tool among programmers in many fields.

In the 1980s, the focus shifted once again toward new theories. During this time, concepts such as object-oriented programming, modularity, and the reuse of code became the focal points for the research and development efforts. While object-oriented programming had first been introduced in Simula back in the 1960s, languages such as Smalltalk, C++, and Java actually brought them out into the world and established the object-oriented paradigm that dominated the computer science field around the turn of the twentieth century.

Code Jockeys

By tracing this history and linking it to electracy and ludic intervention, my aim is to foster a broader understanding of the computer as a "digital sandbox" out of which any number of amazing creations can arise. Seeing the computer as a ludic space in this way affords us a better opportunity to understand how it came to hold such a fascination for hackers and how they ended up making it their own unique bricolage.

In the 1960s, computers were becoming commercially available in greater numbers. Companies such as Sperry Rand Univac, IBM, DEC, and others offered systems that for the first time were within the financial reach of universities and research institutions. That allowed students a chance to experience and work with the new and exciting computer technology. In *Hackers*, Levy examines how one such group of students at the Massachusetts Institute of Technology (MIT) became so fascinated with the computer that it completely consumed their lives (Levy [1984] 1994). The first MIT hackers were young, male students who shared a deep fascination for computers and the things they could do. To these men, the computer represented something far more than a mere tool to achieve other goals. To them, the computer itself was the goal. In his study of the early MIT hackers, Levy reveals that they not only shared a common interest in computers, but that they also shared a community of values and cultural traits. Over the years, the hackers have played the part of both villains and heroes as I have discussed above, and their contributions to the history of software, both in their darker and lighter incarnations, have been both profound and unmistakable. Their approach to invention was that of the *bricoleur*. They did not code in order to produce academic papers or programming standards or to make money, necessarily. They coded simply because they loved doing it and because they thought it was fun and challenging. According to the *New Hacker's Dictionary* (Raymond [1993] 1996), which grew out of the venerable "Jargon File" compiled by the hackers themselves (Raymond 2011), hacking as it relates to computers might be understood as "an appropriate application of ingenuity. Whether the result is a quick-and-dirty patchwork job or a carefully crafted work of art, you have to admire the cleverness that went into it" (Raymond [1993] 1996). Richard Stallman, whom Levy in 1984 affectionately dubbed "the last of the true hackers," notes that hacking as a phenomenon isn't even necessarily connected to computers or programming. Stallman relates the following amusing story from a restaurant visit in Korea in 2000:

I went to lunch with some GNU fans, and was sitting down to eat some tteokpaekki, when a waitress set down six chopsticks right in front of me. It occurred to me that perhaps these were meant for three people, but it was more amusing to imagine that I was supposed to use all six. I did not know any way to do that, so I realized that if I could come up with a way, it would be a hack. I started thinking. After a few seconds I had an idea. First I used my left hand to put three chopsticks into my right hand. That was not so hard, though I had to figure out where to put them so that I could control them individually. Then I used my right hand to put the other three chopsticks into my left hand. That was hard, since I had to keep the three chopsticks already in my right hand from falling out. After a couple of tries I got it done. Then I had to figure out how to use the six chopsticks. That was harder. I did not manage well with the left hand, but I succeeded in manipulating all three in the right hand. After a couple of minutes of practice and adjustment, I managed to pick up a piece of food using three sticks converging on it from three different directions, and put it in my mouth. It didn't become easy—for practical purposes, using two chopsticks is completely superior. But precisely because using three in one hand is hard and ordinarily never thought of, it has "hack value," as my lunch companions immediately recognized. Playfully doing something difficult, whether useful or not, that is hacking. I later told the Korea story to a friend in Boston, who proceeded to put four chopsticks in one hand and use them as two pairs—picking up two different pieces of food at once, one with each pair. He had topped my hack. Was his action, too, a hack? I think so. Is he therefore a hacker? That depends on how much he likes to hack. (Stallman 2002)

For the hackers of the early 1960s, however, computers were not easily accessible. The machines of the day were typically large mainframe systems that did not allow for exclusive individual use. Because of the heavy investments made in these machines, it was paramount that they be used to the maximum capacity at all times. For this reason, batch processing was the order of the day. In a batch processing system, computer programs and data were prepared off-line and then fed into a queue of tasks that the computer would then carry out. The MIT hackers viewed batch processing as an oppressive system that kept them out and limited their opportunity to use the computers that held such fascination for them. Many of them still managed to gain access to the computers late at night, however, when no one else was around.

During the daytime if you came in, you could expect to find professors and students who didn't really love the machine, whereas if during the night you came in you would find hackers. Therefore hackers came in at night to be with their culture. And they developed other traditions such as getting Chinese food at three in the morning. And I remember many sunrises seen from a car coming back from Chinatown. It was actually a very beautiful thing to see a sunrise, cause' that's such a calm time of day. It's a wonderful time of day to get ready to go to bed. It's so nice to walk home with the light just brightening and the birds starting to chirp, you can get a real feeling of gentle satisfaction, of tranquility about the work that you have done that night. (Stallman 1986)

The concept of time-sharing was invented in order to make more efficient use of a computer's resources, and in universities it significantly improved the students' access to computers. Time-sharing was built around the idea that users share the CPU's resources. This is done by way of an operating system that divides the CPU's total power among all users so that each user gets the feeling of having the entire machine to themselves. With the advent of time-sharing, a truly interactive approach to computer programming could be adopted, and this was something that suited the hackers perfectly.

In the 1950s and 1960s, computer software was not generally commercially available. Typically, the computer makers would commission or write software for their own systems. This software was then provided as part of the computer system that was purchased. Software was, in other words, something that was not sold separately and, as such, didn't have much of a market value of its own. The value of the software laid in the total solution that computer vendors could offer to augment their hardware systems. In many cases, this meant programming languages and compiler systems that users could employ to develop their own software solutions.

Programming was a novel activity with which only a few people had much experience. In this embryonic environment, the hackers coded for fun to see how far they could go and how they could impress their friends and peers with ever more ingenious and elegant programs. The code they wrote was freely circulated among the members of small hacker groups, and anyone could make changes to anyone else's code. Hackers didn't necessarily think of making a living from programming computers or pursuing an academic career in computer science. For come casual observers, they were wiz kids who could do things with computers few others could even imagine; for the majority, however, they were viewed as socially inept outcasts. To the hackers, none of this mattered much. In their own eyes, they belonged to an avant garde—elite code warriors who had conquered the mighty computer and bent it to their will.

From the 1960s onward, the hackers developed a collaborative model of software development where anything from code fragments to entire computer programs were considered community property and freely shared among its members. At the core of this gift economy was the source code. A computer program in readable form is called a source code. Anyone who knows the syntax of the particular programming language in which the program is written can usually read and understand what the program does. With the right tools and knowledge, they can change and adapt the program to their own particular purposes.

Because the computer has no concept of what the source code means, it must be translated into machine-readable binary form before it can be used. The compiler is a computer program that was developed for the express purpose of rapid automatic translation of source code into binary code. As I have mentioned, by doing this, the compiler opened up the concept of proprietary software. When the source code is sent through a compiler and translated into computer-readable binary form, it is no longer possible to read it. Nor is it possible to change it unless the source code is available. This means that the programmer can keep the source code to themselves and only give others access to the finished binary versions of programs. In the limited market for commercial software that existed in the 1960s, proprietary software was still largely an unfulfilled promise, but that was about to change.

Silicon Visions

In 1971, Intel introduced the microprocessor—also called the "computer on a chip." With the advent of the microprocessor, the hackers' dream of having personal computers at their disposal suddenly became a possibility. For some, the personal computer came to represent the ultimate tool for giving people access to the power of computer technology. For others, it promised the realization of the long-awaited desire to have a computer of one's own.

The first real personal computer was the Altair, introduced in 1974. It was not the result of multimillion dollar research-and-development efforts. To the contrary, it was in essence a pragmatic attempt to meet a growing demand among hackers and computer hobbyists for a small, low-cost personal computer. Recalling Lévi-Strauss, we might understand the Altair as a bricolage, cobbled together from existing parts and components that had been collected and selected by hackers "on the principle that 'they may always come in handy' " (Lévi-Strauss 1966, 18). When the Altair was introduced in 1974, the machine aimed for a small but enthusiastic market of hackers and electronics hobbyists. The Altair was offered as a kit that had to be carefully assembled, and this in itself limited its market potential. However, the Altair clearly demonstrated that one could build small personal computers at a fraction of the cost of other commercially available systems. This heralded the beginning of the personal computer era.

In 1977, several companies, including Apple Computer, Radio Shack, and Commodore Business Machines, began to offer personal computers. Unlike the Altair, these machines were all complete computer systems that could be put to use without consumer assembly, but there was hardly any software available for them. For the hackers, this didn't pose much of a problem because they could easily write their own software. The vast majority of new computer users, however, would need to purchase software; this suddenly created a new and tempting market.

Among the first applications to open up the market for commercial personal computer software were computer games. The success of the early arcade computer games in the 1970s had clearly demonstrated that the home computer market for these types of applications could be substantial, and companies like Atari, Commodore, and others jumped on the bandwagon. Suddenly there was a demand for talented and highly skilled programming, which was common among hackers. The typical hacker interests and lifestyle was ideally suited for computer games programming, and during this time period the host of new computer game companies absorbed many of them. For readers who are interested in learning more about early digital game systems, I recommend the platform study *Racing the Beam: The Atari Video Computer System* by Nick Montfort and Ian Bogost (Montfort and Bogost 2009).

As more and more computers found their way into homes and small businesses, it became ever more apparent that software could become the new growth sector in the computer industry. Two people who realized this early on were Bill Gates and Paul Allen. In the 1970s, when the first personal computers became available, Gates was a student at Harvard University, but with all the exciting developments going on, it wasn't long before he dropped out to start his own software company, Microsoft, in 1975. Microsoft's first product was a version of the BASIC programming language for the Intel microprocessor family used in most personal computers at the time.

Microsoft was not the only actor in the early personal computer software business. In 1979, a small and unknown company named Software Arts Inc. introduced a program called VisiCalc. It would change the computer industry in more ways than one. As the first spreadsheet program, VisiCalc opened up a whole new application area for personal computers by putting the power of financial planning directly into the hands of ordinary users. More important, however, is that VisiCalc also represented the beginning of a change in people's perception of the value of software versus hardware. Because VisiCalc was originally only available on the Apple 2 computer, many people bought this machine simply to be able to use the VisiCalc program. What's more, VisiCalc offered functionality and features that were not even available on mini computers and mainframe systems at the time; this drove home the point that the personal computer was not only a toy for hackers, hobbyists, and home gamers, but also a serious business tool. Although VisiCalc was the first software program to achieve such a defining status, other programs would follow. One example is Aldus PageMaker (1985), which together with the Apple LaserWriter printer (1985) created "desktop publishing." PageMaker was made possible by the introduction of Apple Computer's Macintosh model in 1984. The graphical user interface of the Macintosh enabled software makers to explore design-related applications, such as desktop publishing. Again we see that people began to buy Macintoshes just to be able to use the PageMaker program. Software was becoming more important than the hardware on which it ran.

As with most other computer manufacturers in the 1970s, the personal computer took IBM by surprise. Since well before World War II, the company had been far and away the dominant manufacturer of data processing and calculating machinery. Their mainframe systems were tailored to the business markets, and hardly anyone in blue suits paid any attention to what was happening at the grassroots level. Thus, when the first personal computers—the Altair and subsequently the Apple 2—appeared on the scene, IBM did not see them as any threat to their hegemony. The relative quick success of these small and inexpensive systems, however, soon alerted IBM to the fact that future market opportunities might lay in personal computing. For this reason, a new division of IBM was established in Boca Raton, Florida, to build and manufacture an IBM personal computer.

Apple's success with the Apple 2 model propelled the little startup company to the forefront of the rapidly growing personal computer industry. The Apple 2 not only benefitted from the clever designs of its creator, Stephen Wozniac, but far more important was the fact that hundreds of independent programmers and small software companies provided a large base of software for it. The Apple 2 was, in effect, the first computer to demonstrate the power of open standards for both hardware extensibility and software.

When the first IBM PC was introduced in 1981, it was, unlike the IBM's other computer systems, specifically designed to embrace the open standards concept. It was built around an open standards hardware architecture much in the same way the Apple 2 had been five years earlier, and this allowed third-party developers to provide PC users with a host of add-on technologies that IBM alone could not, or would not, have done. More important, however, its system software was also intended to adhere to open standards. When the PC was created, its designers wanted to get the operating system from an already established vendor. This led IBM to Bill Gates and Microsoft. While Microsoft at the time did not have an operating system that it could sell, Gates immediately realized what a golden opportunity had just knocked on his door. He promised IBM that he would deliver an operating system for the PC, and with that deal Microsoft embarked on one of the most remarkable business adventures in history—one that would make Gates the richest man in the world.

The deal between Microsoft and IBM over the PC operating system known as MS-DOS (Microsoft Disk Operating System) is now legendary lore, and it sealed the fate of the personal computer software industry for many years to come. By controlling the PC's operating system, Microsoft suddenly had both a major source of income to further the company's growth and complete control over the standards on which new software was created. The alliance between the IBM PC and Microsoft's MS-DOS software soon became a serious competitor to Apple Computer and its line of Apple 2 machines. In the early 1980s, Apple therefore began development of a new computer that would meet this competition and help the company maintain its role as a market leader. The result of Apple's effort was the Macintosh, introduced in 1984. The Macintosh personal computer, with its groundbreaking graphical user interface, was a major achievement and a milestone in the history of modern computing. Still, it failed to make the impact that its creators had hoped for. With the Macintosh, Apple had forgotten its own open standards lesson that had served the company so well with the Apple 2. The Mac was a closed, proprietary system in both hardware and software. The first Macintosh models did not have any hardware expansion capabilities, and the operating system, despite its elegant and user-friendly concepts, was considered cumbersome and hard to write programs for. Although Apple had some success with the Macintosh, the IBM PC and Microsoft had gotten the upper hand.

Due to the PC's open standards, a new generation of computer manufacturers began to appear on the stage in the 1980s. These so-called clone-makers built personal computers that for all intents and purposes were copies of IBM's PC. The IBM-compatible clones soon became IBM's most serious competitors. They could offer personal computers with the same MS-DOS as the IBM PC, thus allowing their machines to run the same software as the PC, and they could sell their machines at a much lower cost. Although the low cost of these clone PCs certainly contributed to their popularity, their running Microsoft system software, and therefore taking advantage of the rapidly growing software base for the PC, mattered most to new computer buyers. As Microsoft strengthened its grip on the personal computer software market in the 1990s with its Windows operating systems, its only real competitor, Apple, fell further and further behind. The Windows systems were close imitations of the Macintosh's graphical user interface, and this, in effect, eliminated the competitive edge that Apple had over Microsoft. By the end of the decade Microsoft had secured a near monopoly on the computer software market—the vast majority of computers made in the world at that time were Windows machines.

As we begin the second decade of the twenty-first century, Microsoft's dominance in the technology market place is on the decline, while Apple (by 2010), like the mythical Phoenix, has reinvented itself once more to become the world's most valuable technology company. The *New York Times* called it "one of the most stunning turnarounds in the business history for Apple, which had been given up for dead only a decade earlier" (Helft and Vance 2010). The *Times* went on to conclude that much of the reason for this is that "consumer tastes have overtaken the needs of business as the leading force shaping technology," and "the click-clack of the keyboard has ceded ground to the swipe of a finger across a smartphone's touch screen" (Helft and Vance 2010). Under Steve Jobs's visionary leadership after his return to the company in 1997, Apple has once again become a world leader when it comes to innovation in consumer electronics. With groundbreaking innovations such as the iPod, iPhone, and iPad, as well as services such as the iTunes Store, the iOS App Store, and more, Apple is reinventing the way we create, distribute, and use entertainment in the twenty-first century. If we take a theoretical perspective, we can say that Apple's resurgence over the past decade signifies an ever-growing importance of entertainment in our culture. This is what Ulmer calls the practice of electracy. Furthermore, it was the very institution of electracy—namely, the Internet—that made it all possible. Last, the consumer behavior that drives it all is one of play, both in the playful way that we interact with these devices and services, but also in terms of the applications that we use. In early 2011, eighteen of the twenty top-grossing applications in Apple's online App Store were games, with the top spot going to the game *Angry Birds*. One thing that most people don't know is that Apple also owes a large part of its success to the OS X operating system, which uses the open-source kernel Darwin and builds on BSD Unix. I will return to the history of the BSD operating system in the next chapter.

Hacking a Social Media

I began this chapter by describing the hacker figure as a bricoleur, someone who works with what is available to create new and exciting possibilities because he or she finds that interesting and entertaining, and because of a personal need or desire to make those possibilities reality. As their communities grew bigger and more widespread, hackers wanted more convenient ways to communicate with one another. Today, we can see the transformative power of the communication technologies, the foundations of which were built by hackers, going far beyond what they could possibly have foreseen. The role of social communication technologies such as Facebook and Twitter in the Iranian uprising following the elections in the summer of 2009, or during the peaceful revolution in Egypt in early 2011, where the embattled government shut down the country's Internet services in a futile attempt to prevent people from communicating with one another and organizing protests, shows clearly that social media and digital communication technologies in general are poised to play a vital role in shaping the human condition in the twenty-first century.

Long before Facebook and Twitter came along, however, hackers were already busy creating spaces for electrate practice and invention. In the closing sections of this chapter, I will examine the history of a few of the most influential social communication technologies that the hackers invented. If we go back to the mid-1990s, software made Gates the richest man in the world. His software empire stretched to all corners of the globe, and Microsoft products influenced people's lives in ways that only a handful of technologies have done. Only twenty years earlier, few would have predicted that something like this could happen—that software would become such a powerful technological and socially transformative force. The collaborative code-sharing communities of the hackers seemed to have all but disappeared in the face of the new and all-encompassing commercial software industry. Under the shiny surface of commercialism, however, a new generation of hackers was forming a new movement. Linked together via the Internet and the World Wide Web, this was a global movement vastly bigger and more resourceful than prior hacker communities had ever been. Many in the new hacker generation were born after the advent of the personal computer, but they were still driven by the same fascination for computer programming that had characterized the first hackers thirty years earlier.

The hacker movement existed, like any other subculture, in a state of opposition to a main dominating culture. For the first generation of hackers, the opposition was directed at what they considered the oppressive and exclusionary mainframe culture. For the new generation of hackers in the 1990s, the opposition more and more came to be directed at Microsoft and what was perceived as the company's imperialistic attempts to control and dominate software development with technically inferior products. The hackers had a cause to rally around, and now they needed the means to fight back against software imperialism. The project that these hackers flocked to was the GNU/Linux operating system. GNU/Linux represented interesting programming challenges as well as an alternative to Microsoft's Windows operating systems. Linked together via the Internet and aided by collaborative tools such as email, Usenet, Internet Relay Chat, and the World Wide Web, the new global hacker movement of the 1990s embarked on a formidable project: to create a new Unix-based operating system that could change the world.

The history of the GNU/Linux project and the new hacker movement as a force for new electrate invention is covered in detail in the next chapter. In the final sections of this chapter, however, I want to cover some of the important developments that helped build the infrastructure for communication and collaboration among hackers on the Net from the mid-1980s until the turn of the twenty-first century.

By 1990, the Internet was a mature infrastructure for worldwide communication and exchange of information. The Unix-based TCP/IP protocols, first deployed on the ARPANET in 1982, had become the ubiquitous standard for facilitating traffic across the digital data network. Combined with the growing popularity and affordability of Unix-based systems in the 1980s such as AT&T, Unix, BSD, Sun OS, and others, this led to a rapid network expansion that accelerated into the 1990s. Although the inventors and designers of the ARPANET had conceived of the network as primarily a system for resource sharing, entrepreneurial users and developers soon found that it could also be an excellent system for messaging and communication of a more social kind. A good number of these communication-oriented network applications that have been the mainstay of electronic communication over the past twenty years came about as "unsanctioned hacks." A good case in point is email.

In 1971, Ray Tomlinson came up with the idea of using the ARPANET to send electronic mail messages to users in remote locations. The idea of using computers to send electronic messages was not that revolutionary in itself. By the time Tomlinson started working on email in late 1971, users of time-sharing systems had already had the ability to send electronic messages to one another for some time. The significance of the new email system, however, was that electronic messages could now be sent across a network of remote computers, thus eliminating geographical barriers in the communication between people. Sending messages to colleagues in the room next door had a certain but somewhat limited usefulness; however, sending messages to colleagues half a world away and getting immediate responses opened up a whole new set of possibilities. Yes, email, like most of the other technologies that I discuss in this book, was very much a hacker creation. According to Tomlinson himself, he created it "mostly because it seemed like a neat idea . . . there was no directive to 'go forth and invent e-mail'" (Jordan 2008, 3). Email was, in other words, a neat hack that Tomlinson did because he enjoyed the challenge. This becomes even more apparent when Tomlinson explains how the system was implemented. At the time, he had written a simple file-transfer protocol named CPYNET that would act as a bridge to carry data from one computer to another, and this provided the infrastructure that he needed to implement an electronic mail system. He explains:

I had two programs. One was called SNDMSG, which was used for composing messages to be put in the mailbox of another user in a time-shared computer. There were versions of SNDMSG from Berkeley and MIT, but I recoded it. Another program was an experimental FTP program. I wrote a version to act as a server, another to act as a client, to specify what should be transferred, then send the data of the file to the other computer. I took those two programs and put them together with some glue software, the sticky stuff. Rather than getting the source from a file, you'd get the source from the buffer of the editor. And instead of simply writing the file at the remote end, you would append the characters to the mailbox file. The new message would follow the earlier message that would already be there.

And then there's a thing that everyone remembers, or associates with e-mail, which is the @ sign, which gave the editor a way to specify the recipient. You had to have a way of separating the user and the computer name. In English the @ sign is obvious, in other languages it isn't. But being the only preposition on the English keyboard, it just made sense. (Festa 2001)

The development of email, or network mail as it was called at the time, happened to coincide with the design and implementation of the ARPANET file-transfer protocol, and when word about Tomlinson's experimental email system got out, the decision was made to include it for general use on the ARPANET. In this manner, email came to be a standard feature in the early days of the ARPANET, and its success was almost instantaneous. In 1973, it was estimated that 75 percent of all traffic on the ARPANET was email (Hafner and Lyon [1996] 2006).

The first electronic email-based communities on the ARPANET grew up around mailing lists of various sorts. Since then, email systems have been refined and expanded on numerous times by many programmers, but from the users' point of view, little has changed since Tomlinson's original conception of electronic network mail. To this day, email remains a convenient and flexible medium to communicate with colleagues and stay in touch with friends and family.

Although email has remained a vital medium of communication among hackers, other media have also been used extensively. The perhaps most popular and influential one in the 1980s and early 1990s was Usenet, also called NetNews or simply News. Like most of the technologies mentioned in this book, Usenet was not created because some government agency or commercial software developer thought there would be a need for it. It happened simply because a group of dedicated graduate students wanted to make it happen.

The idea that was to become Usenet was born in 1979 by Duke University graduate students Tom Truscott and Jim Ellis. Feeling excluded and left out from the ARPANET, they decided to create their own "General Access Unix Network" with the aim of connecting people with a common interest in Unix. Steven Daniels, a graduate student at Duke who wrote the first C-based News program (A News), explains:

We (or at least I) had little idea of what was really going on on the ARPANET, but we knew we were excluded. Even if we had been allowed to join, there was no way of coming up with the money. It was commonly accepted at the time that to join the ARPANET took political connections and $100,000. I don't know if that assumption was true, but we were so far from having either connections or $$ that we didn't even try. The "Poor man's ARPANET" was our way of joining the Computer Science community and we made a deliberate attempt to extend it to other not-well-endowed members of the community. (Hauben and Hauben 1997, 41)

With the help of Steve Bellovin, a graduate student from the neighboring University of North Carolina at Chapel Hill, the group soon had a small experimental network running among Duke University (duke), University of North Carolina at Chapel Hill (unc), and the Physiology Department of the Duke Medical School (phs). The News software ran on Unix machines linked together by homemade 300-baud autodialer modems. The system was designed so that an article or news item posted from one of the network nodes would propagate to other nodes whenever the autodialer opened a connection. In this way, Usenet would automatically synchronize all the information in the network and make it available to users in a timely and organized manner. The first public presentation of Usenet was made in January 1980 at the academic Usenix meeting in Boulder, Colorado. The response from the conference participants was overtly positive, and this encouraged the group to go on and create a public release of the Usenet software for general distribution at the 1980 Usenix summer meeting. Documentation accompanying the distribution stated that, "[a] goal of USENET has been to give every UNIX system the opportunity to join and benefit from a computer network (a poor man's ARPANET, if you will)" (Hauben and Hauben 1997, 41).

To the surprise of its creators, Usenet grew slowly at first, but when the University of California at Berkeley joined the network by 1981, the expansion rate increased exponentially as links to the ARPANET began to appear in numbers. Between 1979 and 1988, the number of Usenet nodes grew from 3 to more than 11,000, and the newsgroups hosted within were no longer limited to just Unix discussions; they now spanned a vast array of subjects (Hauben and Hauben 1997, 44). For hackers who might have found themselves as outsiders in their real-world communities, Usenet and electronic bulletin board systems (BBS) that began to appear at the same time (Christensen and Suess 1989) provided important escape hatches into new digital communities where they could connect with like-minded individuals who understood their vocations and with whom they could share their interests. In the case of Linux, which I discuss in depth in the next chapter, the news group comp.os.minix, for instance, was an exceedingly important community in the early days as Linus Torvalds began to conceive of and implement his new operating system. Later on, other news groups as well as mailing lists would fulfill similar functions and help bring more people into the thriving Linux community.

Whereas email and Usenet proved to be flexible and powerful asynchronous modes of communication, various chat systems became popular media for online synchronous communication. Chat systems in various forms had existed on ARPANET and other networks since the early days, but during the 1980s their popularity and use grew to such an extent that systems administrators became seriously worried about the load they presented on network traffic. A rapidly growing number of people found online chatting to be not only fun and useful but also highly addictive, and thus the use of chat systems continued unabated. One of the best-known chat systems on BITNET in the 1980s was Relay, a program written by Jeff Kell of the University of Tennessee–Chattanooga in 1985. It became a smash hit that propelled online chatting to even greater volumes. As a result, by 1987, Relay was on the verge of becoming a victim of its own success, not primarily due to the network or CPU load but because of an increasing number of unruly users who logged in "just to play" and cause problems for the system administrators (Kell 1987).

In the 1990s, the most popular chat program was Internet Relay Chat, generally known as IRC. Jarkko Oikarinen, a systems administrator at the University of Oulu in Finland, wrote the original IRC in the summer of 1988. At his job he had a lot of free time, and he spent part of this time running OuluBox, a public-access BBS system at the university. According to Oikarinen, the ideas behind IRC were inspired by a desire to make the university's BBS more useful by adding "USENET News-kind of discussion and groups [. . .] in addition to real time discussions and other BBS related stuff" (Oikarinen 2011). In the development, he also borrowed ideas and concepts from both BITNET Relay Chat, the Unix person-to-person Talk utility. After the first IRC server was up and running on his local machine, Oikarinen sent copies of IRC to friends at other universities in southern Finland, and pretty soon the new chat program had a good-sized user base among students and academics in Finland. Encouraged by the success at home, Oikarinen says he then "contacted some friends [. . .] through BITNET Relay and asked if they would try this program. Internet connections did not yet work from Finland to other countries, so they could not connect to the Finnish network" (Oikarinen 2011). The recipients of IRC set up their own chat servers and passed along copies to their own friends. In this manner, the IRC program spread quickly, and soon new IRC chat servers were popping up all over the Internet.

IRC first gained international fame during the Persian Gulf War of 1990–1991 when hundreds of users tuned into IRC channels such as #peace to hear real-time reports from ordinary people in and around the war zone. The news that was mediated via IRC had a real personal, authentic, and down-to-earth quality to it that in great part contributed to the growing fascination with IRC. In the summer of 1990, there were thirty-eight IRC servers. During the war, peak usage went up sharply from 100 to 300 simultaneous users. The system continued to grow and spawn new networks such as Undernet, DalNet, EFnet, and others. Another major peak occurred in 1996 when id Software released its highly anticipated first-person shooter game Quake. The IRC channel #quake saw more than 1,500 users, which made it the largest and most active channel on all the IRC networks. By the end of the 1990s, IRC served more than 50,000 users. Although the competition from new chat and instant-messaging systems was becoming fiercer, IRC still continued to serve as an important meeting place for hackers and others interested in free and open source software. IRC was a social medium before we knew what such a thing might be, and its legacy lives on today in other forms.

Hacktivism

"Information Wants To Be Free," proclaimed Stewart Brand (creator of the Whole Earth Catalog [1968] and the WELL [Whole Earth 'Lectronic Link,

1984]) at the first Hacker's Conference in the fall of 1984 (Brand 1988, 202). Brand organized the conference in response to the book *Hackers*, which I discuss earlier in the chapter. With that simple and catchy slogan, Brand captured the spirit of hacker thinking and rhetorical tactics in the 1980s and beyond. Today, hacking remains a subversive form of free-play that decenters and disrupts established structures of knowledge and information with regard to access, influence, control, and ownership. Hacker noir, then, must also encompass the new electrate forms of activism that accompanied it. "Hacktivism" is often used to describe this confluence of hacking and activism that targets political power structures for socially engaged goals.

In 1996, a group calling themselves the Critical Art Ensemble (formed in 1987) published the book *Electronic Civil Disobedience and Other Unpopular Ideas* as a "a launch point for debating the nature of power and resistance in the information age." Two years later, the Electronic Disturbance Theater, another loosely organized group of individuals, began experimenting with new electrate forms of electronic civil disobedience as virtual sit-ins in the form of client-side denial-of-service (DoS) attacks, facilitated by a Java applet known as the Zapatista FloodNet. The protests targeted the websites of the Mexican federal government and President Ernesto Zedillo, and they were conducted in support of the revolutionary left-wing Zapatista Army of National Liberation, named after the Mexican revolutionary Emiliano Zapata (1879–1918). In an interview in the *Hacktivist* e-zine in 1999, Ricardo Dominguez, a member of the Electronic Disturbance Theater, explains:

FloodNet performs automatic reloads of the site in the background, slowing or halting access to the targeted server. FloodNet also encourages interaction on the part of individual protesters. Net surfers may voice their political concerns on a targeted server via the "personal message" form which sends the surfer's own statement to the server error log. Additionally, a mouse click on the applet image (containing a representation of the targeted site), sends a predefined message to the server error log. . . . You begin to see President Zedillo's web site reloading, every 3 to 7 seconds on three different frames. The more people come, the faster it reloads. This creates a disturbance, a symbolic gesture that is non-violent. It doesn't break a server necessarily since many such as the Pentagon are quite robust and expect millions of hits. But FloodNet does create a sense of solidarity, what I would call "community of drama" or a community joined by the magic stick. It also creates a mirror, that brings real criminal acts into view. (Fusoco 1999)

Another early and influential group with ties to hacktivism is the Cult of the Dead Cow (cDc), founded by a group of young hackers in Lubbock, Texas, 1984. In 1999, cDc formed the subsidiary group Hactivismo, and in 2001 they published a manifesto, the Hactivismo declaration, in which they announced: "We are hackers and free speech advocates, and we are developing technologies to challenge state-sponsored censorship of the Internet" (Hactivismo 2001).

While these hacker groups helped define the concept of hacktivism in the 1990s and early 2000s, hacktivists remained largely fringe elements of society with limited influence outside of the politically and socially conscious hacker circles. That all changed when Assange and Wikileaks burst onto the scene in October 2006. Assange began hacking under the handle Mendax in 1987, and with friends he formed the group International Subversives. In the late 1980s and early 1990s, Assange became one of the leading figures in the emerging underground hacking community in Melbourne, Australia. Like so many other hackers of the day (e.g., Kevin Mitnick), Assange first experienced hacker noir through phone phreaking and social engineering. In the book *Underground*, to which Assange contributed research, Suelette Dreyfus writes:

Back in early 1988, Mendax was just beginning to explore the world of hacking. He had managed to break through the barrier from public to private section of PI, but it wasn't enough. To be recognised as up-and-coming talent by the aristocracy of hackers such as The Force and The Wizard, a hacker had to spend time inside the Minerva system. Mendax set to work on breaking into it. . . . Sometimes Mendax went to school. Often he didn't. The school system didn't hold much interest for him. It didn't feed his mind the way Minerva would. The Sydney computer system was a far more interesting place to muck around in than the rural high school. (Dreyfus and Assange 1997)

At the time Assange was active in the Melbourne underground hacker community, no one could predict that he would one day become one of the world's most famous, and infamous, hackers. Today Assange sees himself as a publisher and a journalist, and he wants to distance himself from his past. In an interview with Forbes.com in 2010, he said: "That was 20 years ago. It's very annoying to see modern day articles calling me a computer hacker . . . . that hacker mindset was very valuable to me. But the insiders know where the bodies are. It's much more efficient to have insiders. They know the problems, they understand how to expose them" (Greenberg 2010).

The insider who, allegedly, would help propel Assange to international fame was Private First Class Bradley Manning. Freedom of information, as I have mentioned, has always been one of the most treasured causes of the hacker movement, and there is no other hacker in history who has been able to release as much classified and secret information as Assange. While his methods may have changed, obtaining and publishing secret information was still his number-one ambition and priority.

During 2010, Assange's organization, WikiLeaks, published a treasure trove of secret and classified intelligence documents pertaining to the Iraq and Afghan war efforts, as well as diplomatic cables that U.S. authorities alleged were illegally obtained from Manning, an insider who had been stationed in Iraq in 2009. Manning was summarily arrested, and Assange soon found himself in legal troubles as well when two Swedish women subsequently accused him of rape in the summer of 2010. The hacker-turned-publisher was on the run, and he and his organization found themselves more and more isolated as banks, Internet service providers, and other entities cut their ties to WikiLeaks in an effort to distance themselves from the man who had defamed and embarrassed the world's superpower. In subsequent months there was a rush of hacktivism in support of Assange and WikiLeaks. Hacker groups like LulzSec and Anonymous quickly grabbed the attention of the public and the media through a flurry of hacking attacks on institutions and companies across the United States and abroad. Many of these were in retaliation for the way the authorities had responded to Assange, WikiLeaks, and Manning. Some attacks, like the massive compromise of Sony's Playstation Network in April 2011, were most likely perpetrated by more nefarious hackers who were swept up in the renewed public interest in hacking in general.

Note, here, that hacker noir's return to the public eye in 2011 also helped bring down Britain's biggest-selling newspaper, the *News of the World*. The renewed public attention to hacking, not seen since the 1980s, revealed that journalists for the British tabloid had for years actively used one of the oldest tools on the hacker's repertoire, phone phreaking, as a way to obtain information from the phones of celebrities, murder victims, and even casualties of war. The *News of the World* scandal and WikiLeaks alike show that hacker noir has become part of who we are today. Some will argue that WikiLeaks serves a nobler purpose than the tabloid journalists who manipulated the phone messages of a murdered girl in order to boost their sales. Hacker noir, however, makes no distinction or moral judgment because human nature makes room for both. Information wants to be free, and we need to look beyond these dichotomies of good and evil if we want to truly understand what this means in an electrate reality where entertainment now shapes our identity more than ever before.

In this chapter, I have looked at some of the most important developments in the first fifty years of the history of software as they pertain to the creation of playgrounds for electrate practice. Unlike the notion of the special purpose machine born out of the Industrial Revolution, the modern computer as it materialized after World War II was a truly universal machine.

Once people realized the significance of this concept, software became one of the most important areas of research and development within the new fields of computer science and engineering. The invention of the compiler and the first high-level programming languages in the 1950s made computers more accessible and helped open up commercial markets. Throughout the 1960s, much of the scientific research on software was directed toward the development of general purpose tools and concepts. At the same time, students, who for the first time were able to become involved with computers, developed a whole new hacker culture devoted to programming. The 1970s and 1980s were the time when computers became machines for everyone. This was made possible by the invention of the microprocessor and the personal computer, but software such as computer games, word processors, spreadsheets, desktop publishing, and more was the true driving force behind its popularity. In the late 1990s and 2000s, the computer morphed into yet another type of device, this time with a focus on communication. The evolution of the Internet and its uses was driven to a significant degree by advances in the software communication technologies associated with it. Most of these technologies were developed by the group of people whom I previously referred to as hackers.

When Steven Levy wrote his book about the hackers of the 1960s and 1970s, he was talking about local hacker groups who really didn't have much contact with one another or a common sense of community (Levy [1984] 1994). The Internet changed all that. Communication technologies such as email, Usenet, IRC, and the World Wide Web brought hackers together in communities that spanned the globe and fostered a self-conscious movement that made significant and lasting impacts on technology, society, culture, and economy. In the 1980s and early 1990s, these communities were typically found on BBS communities, in Usenet news groups such as *comp.os.minix* and *comp.os.linux*, on email discussion lists, or in online chat environments such as IRC. Open source projects, which are hacker communities unto themselves with their own infrastructure, goals, and ambitions, interconnected with one another in a rhizomatic way to form a common frame of reference and understanding of themselves and their place within the emerging electrate apparatus. Most important, however, what emerged out of *hacker noir* (the literate and electrate conjunction of cyberpunk culture, computer science, and ludic hacking) is the acknowledgment that hackers were also largely responsible for the development of the very infrastructure of the Internet, the Unix-like operating systems that drove it all, which we shall see in the next chapter, Choral Code.

3   Choral Code

That chorography is more grammatological than deconstructive does not reduce the impossibility of the program: the method of no method (the possible impossible). How to practice choral writing then? It must be in the order neither of the sensible nor the intelligible but in the order of making, of generating. And it must be transferable, exchangable, without generalization conducted from one particular to another.
—Gregory Ulmer, *Heuretics: The Logic of Invention*

In *Heuretics*, Ulmer is concerned with the concept of place and its relation to invention. He observes that in historical works and accounts of technological innovation, the metaphor of the *frontier* is often evoked as a means to describe the site of invention and the creative activities that take place there. He notes, "Vannevar Bush (who proposed the Memex library-in-a-desk before hypermedia technology existed) made such an allusion with his call for a 'new profession of trailblazers, those who find delight in the task of establishing useful trails through the enormous mass of the common record'" (Ulmer 1994, 26-27). In the same vein, Ulmer makes an allegorical reference to Charles Mercer, who in 1964 wrote about the French Foreign Legion in Africa as "*pioneers* who open a new country. We are the rugged, primitive laborers who do the hardest work." Mercer wrote: "We are the visionaries who see wonderful possibilities in the future. . . . Every path we have [built] bears the pain of our men. It is they who have opened the way for civilization to come into the heart of this savage country" (Mercer 1964, 255). In the 1980s and 1990s, terms such as *frontier* and *pioneer* were frequently used to describe the emerging Internet as a new form of digital frontier—a vast and still largely unexplored *cyberspace*, to use William Gibson's terminology. "The computer," then, Ulmer surmises, "is responsible for the most recent 'frontier of knowledge' [. . .] bringing into existence a virtual if not a literal new world" (Ulmer 1994, 27). We don't hear these terms used so much anymore because the Internet has now become all but commonplace, but writing about these phenomena at the time, Ulmer expresses a distinct sense of unease with the associations and categorical imperatives that they evoke. With reference to Francis Bacon and the understanding of scientific enlightenment as attuned to spatial concepts of discovery/invention and colonization, Ulmer warns that the "metaphor of 'frontiers of knowledge' is ubiquitous, a reflex, a habit of mind that shapes much of our thinking about inquiry" (Ulmer 1994, 24). In order to arrive at a different understanding of invention and its relation to place, Ulmer proposes *chorography* as a new way to deconstruct the myth of the frontier. He explains:

The strategy of chorography for deconstructing the frontier metaphor of research is to consider the "place" and its "genre" in rhetorical terms—as a *topos*. The project is then to replace *topos* itself (not just one particular setting but *place* as such) with *chora* wherever the former is found in the *trivium*. In order to foreground the foundational function of location in thought, choral writing organizes any manner of information by means of the writer's specific position in the time and space of a culture. (Ulmer 1994, 33)

Chorography, thus, is a "resonance for a rhetoric of invention concerned with the history of 'place' in relation to memory" (Ulmer 1994, 39). Ulmer's approach to chora is inspired by Derrida, who in turn derived the concept from Plato's *Timaeus*. For Plato, the *chora* (Khôra) is the metaphysical space in which the ideal forms are stored, whereas *topos* is the physical and situated space where instances of these eternal truths are manifested. In Ulmer's thinking, chora comes to represent a personal space that conflates place and memory. He chooses chorography as the "heuretic approach to inventing a 'method' useful for this 'world' [the *frontier* re/visioned as *chora* which] takes into account the present state of imagination and curiosity" (Ulmer 1994, 27). Fantasy, as I discuss in chapter 1, represents the state of mind in Ulmer's electrate apparatus theory.

Code is the chora with which I am concerned here. It is at the same time a memory (writing) and the mise-en-scène, that which stages the enactment of electrate praxis, "in the time and space of a culture" (Ulmer 1994, 33). This code represents the writing, complete with its embedded rhetorical strategies and objectives, what Ian Bogost has called *procedural rhetoric* (Bogost 2008) and which Ulmer seems to have anticipated in *Heuretics*. Code is also the enactment that follows when you execute the code in a cultural and temporal context. Choral code connects the place of invention (virtual) with the function of memory and meaning (also virtual). As memory, choral code prescribes possibilities; it does not determine actions. Rather, it enables and empowers egents, whom we will call players (or hackers), to define as many outcomes as they can find ways to use the code's program. Through its realization, choral code jams the literate apparatus' "hermeneutic code and its drive to reduce enigmas to truth" (Ulmer 1994, 106). The code, while precise, structured, and algorithmic in its source form necessitated by the computer's strict binary regimen, morphs (*a la* Latour) from a continuous stream of zeroes and ones into a chora of vast metaphorical and actual possibilities when activated. It becomes what we, with Paul Virilio, might understand as a *dromospheric space* where electronic speed (Dromos; Virilio 1997) causes dimensionality to collapse, and flash reason becomes a conductor for electrate invention that is simultaneously and perpetually conceived, realized, experienced, and re/conceived.

In *Heuretics*, Gregory Ulmer defines the term *heuretic* as the branch of logic that treats the art of discovery or invention. "Part of working heuretically," he says, "is to use the method that I am inventing while I am inventing it" (Ulmer 1994, 17). I maintain that this is precisely what hackers are doing. They work within the chora of the code that they are creating while concurrently forging new methods for inventing code itself. Chorography, Ulmer says, is an "impossible possibility" (Ulmer 1994, 26), but so were many of the innovations of difference that the hackers have given us.

The Code

Computer operating systems are innovations of difference. As Richard Stallman, self-appointed leader of the free software movement in the 1980s and 1990s, points out: "With an operating system you can do many things; without one you cannot run the computer at all" (Stallman 1999, 55). For this reason, operating systems have continued to occupy the imagination and creative talent of hackers up until the present day. The case studies in this chapter attempt to frame the concept of choral code through a historical analysis of the Unix operating system and its derivatives BSD and GNU/Linux. The history of these systems is significant because it illustrates how hackers have appropriated a technology that was originally developed for scientific research purposes and made it their own playground through heuretic re/invention.

I start the treatment with an overview of the early history of time-sharing systems. Due to their hands-on character, these systems caught the attention of hackers early on, and many of the principal actors in this story cut their first teeth on the experimental systems that were being pioneered at places like MIT in the 1960s. The main focus of my analysis, however, is a treatment of the development of the BSD and Linux variants of Unix spanning almost three decades from the mid-1970s until 2000. In the course of creating these two systems and related software, hackers have situated themselves as a community with shared interests, values, ethics, and goals that are manifested through the philosophy of free software and the concept of open source. Through their appropriation and adaptation of Unix technology, and with the help of the Internet, hackers have also forged new heuretic models of collaborative development that by the turn of the century were making serious inroads into how digital technologies are *re/visioned* by their users.

During the 1950s, advances in digital computing not only produced faster and more versatile hardware, they also spawned a new area of research centered on the development of software solutions ranging from operating systems to programming languages. Still in its infancy, digital computing posed an endless array of interesting challenges both of a practical engineering nature and of a more theoretical and intellectual nature. One of the challenges that rose to prominence around 1960 was the question of how computers could be used in ways that took better advantage of both the technical advances that had been achieved and that were better suited to face new problems and challenges in the emerging area of software engineering.

In the 1940s and 1950s, the predominant mode of using computers was through a method known as batch processing. This scheme had been used with punch-card data processing machinery since the late nineteenth century and meant in essence that users interacted with the machine in an asynchronous fashion. A user had to prepare her data—for example, a computer program—in advance, and then take it to the computer, where it was placed in a queue. She then had to wait to obtain the results until the computer had worked its way through all prior jobs in the queue. This could take hours or even days. For a programmer, batch processing posed several significant problems. For example, if the computer encountered a bug while running a program, it would stop and return an error message. The programmer would then have to take the program back to her office, fix the problem, return to the computer, and run it through the batch system again and again until the program finally ran properly.

Although batch processing was the order of the day in the 1950s, alternative models did exist, if only in very experimental ways. Between 1946 and 1951, a group of engineers and scientists working under the direction of Jay Forrester at MIT had developed Project Whirlwind, a digital computer using a groundbreaking random-access magnetic-core memory technology that Forrester had invented. Whirlwind was originally intended to be a general-purpose flight simulator for the U.S. Navy, but over time it evolved into what became, in essence, the world's first real-time general-purpose computer (Redmond and Smith 1980). By 1960, technical advances such as the transistor-based TX-0 computer developed at MIT's Lincoln Lab in late 1957, in combination with CRT-type monitors, further demonstrated the promise of real-time digital computing. With the technical opportunities at hand, it didn't take long for the MIT research scientists to start thinking about ways to implement software solutions to make real-time computing a reality. What took place during this process was the beginning of a new paradigm in the way people use computers. That paradigm would be known as time-sharing. What's more, time-sharing creates the condition of possibility for the chora to exist in a *dromospheric* space where the generative writing practice (hacking and coding) redistributes writing/code across time and space differently.

John McCarthy, one of the pioneers behind the concept of time-sharing, explains that, "by time-sharing, I meant an operating system that permits each user of a computer to behave as though he were in sole control of a computer, not necessarily identical with the machine on which the operating system is running" (McCarthy [1983] 1996). McCarthy had first started thinking about time-sharing as early as the fall of 1957, when he first arrived at MIT's Computation Center in Cambridge, Massachusetts. In a memo from January 1959, McCarthy outlines his thoughts on the benefits and implications of such a system. He begins by saying that the goal is to develop "an operating system for it [IBM 709] that will substantially reduce the time required to get a problem solved on the machine" (McCarthy 1959, 1). He goes on to say that, "I think the proposal points to the way all computers will be operated in the future, and we have a chance to pioneer a big step forward in the way computers are used" (McCarthy 1959, 2). In light of this, it is interesting to note that today's emerging *cloud computing* technologies have a long and fascinating history behind them, much longer in fact than most people realize.

McCarthy's ideas were met with enthusiasm among his colleagues at MIT, and over the next couple of years the research scientists there worked on various ways to implement a system in which users could share the use of one computer. Much of this early work involved hardware modifications to IBM machines on which the time-sharing system was implemented, something that required a close collaboration with IBM. The first tangible result of the efforts to build a time-sharing operating system was the Compatible Timesharing System (CTSS), so named because it had to be compatible with existing batch-processing systems that were also in use at the time.

CTSS was developed under the direction of Fernando J. Corbató of MIT's Computation Center and first unveiled in the fall of 1961. By 1965, CTSS had been implemented to run on a modified IBM 7094. It could support thirty simultaneous users and clearly demonstrated that computers could be utilized much more efficiently and creatively when users were allowed to work with the machine in real time.

Due largely to the success of CTSS and the promise of time-sharing, in 1963 MIT established Project MAC (Multiple Access Computers/Man and Computer), whose main focus was to further the research and development in this area. A significant portion of the funding came from the U.S. Department of Defense's Advanced Research Projects Agency (ARPA [now DARPA]). The project had two prongs, one of which was the development of a new time-sharing operating system dubbed Multics (Multiplexed Information and Computing Service) led by Corbató. Multics was an ambitious research project where "one of the overall design goals is to create a computing system which is capable of meeting almost all of the present and near-future requirements of a large computer utility" (Corbató and Vyssotsky 1965). It was designed to be a true time-sharing system, and in order to be as platform independent as possible, the whole operating system was to be implemented in a new high-level programming language from IBM called PL/1. Other cutting-edge features included virtual memory and support for multiple processors. In 1964, the MAC team chose a GE-645 machine from General Electric (GE) for the first implementation of Multics. A year later, Bell Labs decided to acquire the same type of machine and subsequently became involved in the Multics project with MIT and GE. Although the project now had significant resources at hand, the development did not progress as quickly or as smoothly as they had hoped. The choice of PL/1 as the implementation language slowed down the progress partly because it was harder than expected to implement it on the GE-645 and partly because it took much longer than anticipated to produce a decent compiler for it. Several times the Multics project came close to cancellation, and in April 1969, Bell Labs decided to withdraw from the project altogether. A few months later, in October 1969, an early version of Multics finally became operational ("Multics History" 2011). Although Multics never became a widely used system, as a research project it was an important stepping stone in operating system design. Many of the key features and concepts found in later systems were invented and first appeared in Multics, and several of the project members later went on to become key figures in computer science. Two of those people were Bell Labs researchers Ken Thompson and Dennis Ritchie.

After Bell Labs withdrew from the Multics project, Thompson, Ritchie, and a few others began searching for ways to create an alternative to the Multics operating system. Ritchie explains:

What we wanted to preserve was not just a good environment in which to do programming, but a system around which a fellowship could form. We knew from experience that the essence of communal computing, as supplied by remote-access, time-shared machines, is not just to type programs into a terminal instead of a keypunch, but to encourage close communication. (Ritchie [1979] 1996)

Throughout 1969, Thompson in particular spent a good deal of time experimenting with design and implementation of core components of a new operating system. These included a hierarchical, Multics-like file system, an assembler for implementation of programs, a command interpreter (shell), and a small set of utilities such as copy, print, and delete for easy file manipulation. During this time, Thompson also wrote the game *Space Travel* (a simulation of the movement of stars and planets in the solar system) that served as "an introduction to the clumsy technology of preparing programs for the PDP-7" (Ritchie [1979] 1996). The ludic element as behavioral practice in the electrate apparatus surfaces here in a tangible site of invention. The game reflects that choral space facilitates, clumsy or not, the hacking, play, and invention that form the language of this *conductive* history that I am writing.

With these basic components in place, Thompson then brought in Doug McIlroy and Dennis Ritchie, who were also interested in programming languages. Based on their feedback, he rewrote the system a couple of times in PDP-7 assembly (Cooke et al. 1999). A new operating system was taking shape, but according to Ritchie, it was "not until well into 1970 that Brian Kernighan suggested the name 'Unix,' in a somewhat treacherous pun on 'Multics,' [that] the operating system we know today was born" (Ritchie [1979] 1996).

The earliest versions of the Unix operating system (V1-V3) were written in assembler. This ensured that the system was fast and responsive, but it was not particularly portable because its code was highly machine-specific. Another drawback of the assembly language used in the early implementations of Unix, according to Ritchie, was that it did not have any mechanisms such as loader and link-editor, which meant, among other things, that one could not make use of libraries. Every program had to be complete in itself, and this led to a significant code redundancy (Ritchie [1979] 1996). In an effort to surmount these problems, Thompson first attempted to reimplement the system in a language called BCPL. He says, "I thought [it] was a fairly straight translation, but it turned out to be a different language so I called it B, and then Dennis took it and added types and called it C" (Cooke et al. 1999, 60). With the advent of C, Thompson and Ritchie had a development tool that supported both high-level portability and modularization and low-level efficiency through the incorporation of assembly code. Thompson says, "We tried to rewrite Unix in this higher-level language that was evolving simultaneously. It's hard to say who was pushing whom—whether Unix was pushing C or C was pushing Unix" (Cooke et al. 1999, 61). The first C implementation of Unix was released as version V4 in 1973.

Although Unix was developed in the setting of a traditional research laboratory, namely AT&T's Bell Labs, its creation had many similarities with that of a hacker system. According to Ritchie, "It was never a 'project'; it was not designed to meet any specific need except that felt by its major author, Ken Thompson, and soon after its origin by the author of this paper, for a pleasant environment in which to write and use programs" (Ritchie 2000). Perhaps for this very reason, Unix quickly became the system of choice for hackers, programmers, and system administrators alike. It was open and minimalist, yet powerful and flexible. It allowed its users complete access to the inner workings, but it also had a rigorous permission system in place that ensured the necessary stability needed in a multiuser environment. In combination with Dennis Ritchie's C programming language, Unix became an ideal environment for program development, but, perhaps more important, it became one of the most portable operating systems ever made. In the continuation of this analysis, I focus on two of the systems that came about because of Unix: BSD and GNU/Linux.

Heuretic Invention

The origins of the Berkeley Software Distribution, commonly known as BSD, can be traced back to the fall of 1973, when Robert Fabry, a professor at the University of California at Berkeley, learned about Unix from a conference presentation by Thompson and Ritchie. This was the first public presentation of Unix, and Fabry became so interested that he approached the developers to obtain a copy (McKusick 1999). Berkeley was, at the time, in the process of acquiring a new PDP-11 mini computer, and Fabry felt that Unix would be a perfect match for that machine. His reasoning for wanting Unix was quite pragmatic. Due to antitrust restrictions imposed on AT&T by the U.S. government, in which the company was not allowed to benefit commercially from non-telephony-related inventions, AT&T had to sell Unix at a very low cost. Furthermore, for an additional $99, academic and government institutions could obtain a license to the system's source code. Compared with the competition, Unix was also a highly cost-efficient system to run and maintain. Whereas the cost per user on a typical mainframe multiuser system could easily reach $50,000, the cost per user on a mini-system running Unix could be as little as $5,000 (Leonard 2000).

After Unix version V4 was installed at Berkeley in 1974, it quickly began to outpace the existing batch-processing system in terms of popularity, especially among the students. It was not, however, until Thompson, himself a graduate of the University of California at Berkeley, arrived to spend the 1975–1976 academic year as a visiting professor in the computer science department that a more genuine interest in the inner workings of the system arose. During his tenure at Berkeley, Thompson worked on a revision of the system dubbed V6, and, perhaps more important, he taught Unix. For many, learning Unix directly from the master was a revelation. Fabry recalls, "We all sat around in Cory Hall and Ken Thompson read code with us. We went through the kernel line by line in a series of evening meetings; he just explained what everything did. [. . .] It was wonderful" (Leonard 2000). Not surprisingly, students in particular became fascinated with Unix through Thompson's teachings. One of those students was Bill Joy, who had just started his undergraduate studies at Berkeley in the fall of 1975.

Thompson's presence at Berkeley in the mid-1970s was an important catalyst for the BSD development that later ensued. On the one hand, he helped create an intellectual environment in which to study and learn the Unix system; on the other hand, as an accomplished programmer and hacker, he became a model and a source of inspiration for aspiring young programmers like Joy and others. A good example of Thompson's practical influence at Berkeley was a Pascal system that he "had hacked together while hanging around the [PDP] 11/70 machine room" (McKusick 1999, 32). As with any other hack, the system had plenty of room for improvements, something that Joy soon discovered. He was at the time involved in a student-programming project using Thompson's Pascal system. Joy explains:

I tried to write the thing in Pascal because Pascal had sets, which Ken Thompson had permitted to be of arbitrary length. The program worked, but it was almost 200 lines long—almost too big for the Pascal system. I talked to Thompson to figure out how I could make the Pascal system handle this program. Chuck Haley and I got involved in trying to make the Pascal system handle it, but the thing was wrong because it was building the entire thing in core. So I got sucked in, got department help, and built some hope of receiving enough support eventually to pay for this program to work under Pascal. (Joyce 1984, 58)

According to McKusick, over the course of the year, Joy and Haley "expanded and improved the Pascal interpreter to the point that it became the programming system of choice for students because of its excellent error recovery scheme and fast compile and execute time" (McKusick 1999, 32). Chuck Haley earned his PhD for his work on the revised Pascal system and left Berkeley. For Joy, however, it was only the beginning.

After Thompson returned to Bell Labs in 1976, Joy began to take more and more interest in the Unix kernel. He had all the source code available, and in the true hacker spirit, he soon began to make little improvements, additions, and enhancements here and there. By this time, word of the improved Pascal system had gotten out, and requests for it started to come in. Therefore, he decided to put together a distribution of Unix containing the Berkeley enhancements. The distribution became known as the Berkeley Software Distribution (BSD) and was built and released by Joy in early 1977.

In the context of this study, the history of BSD is particularly interesting because of the way it illustrates a development model for, and the evolution of, a large collaborative software project. While Ulmer's heuretics cue individual invention, it also translates in the electrate apparatus in the Institution category. Recall that the shift is

Church (orality)—> School (literacy)—> Internet (electracy).

These programmers/hackers were rewriting the Institution by undoing its dependence on the containment of knowledge within proprietary, scientifically anointed spheres of power. The basis for BSD was, as I have mentioned, the Unix source code written mostly by Thompson. As such, BSD was not, at least in the beginning, an operating system in itself. It was, as the name implies, a distribution of Unix that included certain additions and enhancements developed by the hackers at Berkeley. In the early days, the most notable additions were Joy and Haley's improved Pascal system, and an early version of a small editor that later morphed into a Unix mainstay tool for text manipulation—vi (McKusick 1999). The Berkeley hackers' motivation for creating BSD was, in other words, not part of a scheme to replace Unix or even create a new operating system. By experimenting and playing with the code, they had come up with certain enhancements that they thought were clever and useful. When others in turn came to the same conclusion, sharing the fruits of their work was simply the natural thing to do. In 1984, Steven Levy dubbed this the "hacker ethic," which I take up in greater detail in chapter 6.

Over the next few years, Joy produced several new releases of BSD. With each new release, new features and enhancements were added, so that over time BSD came to have its own distinct flavor. In hindsight, perhaps the most significant of these additions was the inclusion of the TCP/IP protocols, which appeared in 4.2BSD in 1983. TCP/IP networking was added to BSD at the behest of ARPA, which was interested in using the system as a standard for computers on the emerging ARPANET, the precursor of the Internet. ARPA's reasoning was that it would be much more practical to standardize the network on software rather than hardware, and BSD, being an essentially free academic product, fit the bill perfectly (McKusick 1999). On Fabry's initiative, in 1980, a working group named Computer Systems Research Group (CSRG) was established to develop an enhanced version of the then current 3BSD for the ARPA community. Fabry hired Joy as the project leader, and with the backing of ARPA and the organizational framework of the CSRG, BSD's popularity increased steadily.

Although every copy of BSD was shipped at a nominal cost complete with source code, contributions and feedback from the user community were, according to Joy, sparse at first (Leonard 2000). He held code destined for inclusion in the distribution to a very high standard, and he maintained strict control with every aspect of the project, and this may well have discouraged people from contributing. Among his colleagues and peers he earned a reputation for being both an arrogant and a brilliant hacker. Marshall McKusick says, "Bill's very good at taking something, [. . .] saying, 'OK, this is what I have, this is where I want to get to, what's the shortest path from here to there?' His code was ugly, unmaintainable, incomprehensible, but by golly it only took him two weeks to do an incredible amount of functionality" (Leonard 2000).

Arrogance and brilliance are character traits that hackers know and value. Joy's many and substantial contributions to BSD in the late 1970s and early 1980s elevated him to stardom within the hacker community. Without knowing it, he came to represent the kind of personality that has shaped many people's perceptions of BSD developers ever since. When once asked how he had accomplished some particularly clever piece of coding, he remarked in the proverbial hacker way, "Read the protocol and write the code" (Leonard 2000). Alexander Galloway, in *Protocol: How Control Exists after Decentralization*, suggests, however, that protocols often produced "negative influences" and are established within a "patchwork of many professional bodies, working groups, committees, and subcommittees, this technocractic elite toils away, mostly voluntarily, in an effort to hammer out solutions to advancements in technology. Many of them are university professors . . . [and] this loose consortium of decision makers tends to fall into a relatively homogenous social class: highly educated, altruistic, liberal-minded science professionals from modernized societies around the globe" (Galloway 2004, 122). As Galloway argues, the significance of such large-scale, but homogenous, collaboration is in its formative departure from interpretation. Whereas before HTML protocol is invented, "protocol had very little to do with meaningful information. Protocol does not interface with content, with semantic value. It is . . . against interpretation. But with [Tim] Berners-Lee comes a new strain of protocol: protocol that cares about meaning" (Galloway 2004, 139). It is my contention, however, that this is where we see the productive confrontation between heuretics and hermeneutics, not the founding moment of what Galloway calls *tactical standardization* (Galloway 2004, 143). In other words, this is the engineer/bricoleur myth taken to its most negative extreme. But Joy's arrogance and brilliance is not the point. Nor is it necessary to situate protocol as the apotheosis of "anti-diversity" (Galloway 2004, 142). It is, rather, evidence of another aspect in Ulmer's electrate apparatus: *Axis*. Galloway's account follows Orality (Right/Wrong) and Literacy (True/False). We are following Electracy (Pain/Pleasure).

In the spring of 1982, Joy left Berkeley to cofound a new company, Sun Microsystems, and the BSD project was eventually taken over by Marshall McKusick, another Berkeley graduate student. McKusick was much more pragmatic and open to input from the user community, and during his tenure, BSD evolved into what was essentially the first large-scale example of what people would later call an open source project. He says, "The contribution that we made was in developing a model for doing open-source software. . . . We figured out how you could take a small group of people and coordinate a software project where you have several hundred people working on it" (Leonard 2000).

The collaborative model that the BSD group pioneered was one of layers. At the center of the project sat a core group of people whose job it was to oversee the project's overall goals and directions. The middle layer consisted of trusted contributors who had access to the official source code repository and had permission to commit changes to that repository. The outer layer consisted of programmers who only had access to read code in the source repository. These people could submit bug reports and suggestions for improvements, but they did not have the privilege to make changes to the source code directly.

BSD and AT&T Unix had coexisted peacefully and shared a mutually beneficial research and development environment from the very beginning, but when the AT&T monopoly was broken up in 1984 and the company began efforts to commercialize Unix, the ties between the two began to weaken. In 1992, when the University of California, along with BSDi, a spin-off company from its Computer Systems Research Group, began selling a commercial version of BSD, AT&T sued over copyright infringements. What AT&T had not taken into account, however, was that due to the long and close collaboration with the BSD group, their own commercial Unix system also contained massive amounts of code from BSD, most notably the BSD TCP/IP stack. The University of California promptly countersued AT&T for the same copyright violations. After a prolonged court battle, the case was finally settled in 1994. BSD was allowed to continue their distribution, but they had to remove certain files and could no longer use the trademark Unix. A new release called 4.4BSD was promptly put together, and under the terms of the lawsuit settlement, anyone using this as a basis for new BSD-based distributions was out of harm's way legally.

Perhaps the single most important event in the computing world in the 1980s was the popularization of the personal computer. By the end of the decade, these affordable machines had reached a level of power and sophistication that promised to give mini-systems such as DEC's VAX series or Sun's professional workstations serious competition. Incidentally, the first effort to create a Unix-like operating system for personal computers was made by Microsoft as early as 1980. The system Microsoft developed, called XENIX, was based on AT&T's Unix System V and was intended for 16-bit microprocessors. When the company, a year later, eventually decided to develop their own operating system called MS-DOS for the IBM PC, the XENIX effort was stranded until 1983 when a new company known as the Santa Cruz Operation (SCO) entered the stage with a system called SCO XENIX for Intel 8086- and 8088-based PCs ("History of the SCO" 2011). While SCO in the 1980s established itself as a big Unix player in the microcomputer arena, the BSD camp was firmly planted in the world of mini machines. By 1990, however, more and more people were lamenting the fact that there was no BSD available for PC. One of those was BSD developer Bill Jolitz. He felt that the BSD porting efforts were not keeping up with the times, and together with his wife, Lynne, Jolitz proposed to undertake the job of porting BSD to the PC. The initial release of the system, dubbed 386BSD, happened on March 17, 1991 (Chalmers 2000). It was a bootable but very rudimentary BSD system, and there were many outstanding issues that had to be fixed and worked out before it would be truly useful. Over the next year, the Jolitzs worked hard on a more feature-complete release, and on July 14, 1992, they could proudly announce:

We are pleased to announce the official release of 386BSD Release 0.1, the second edition of the 386BSD operating system created and developed by William and Lynne

Jolitz and enhanced further with novel work and contributions from the dedicated 386BSD User Community. Like its predecessor, 386BSD Release 0.0, Release 0.1 comprises an entire and complete UNIX-like operating system for the 80386/80486-based AT Personal Computer. (quoted in Chalmers 2000)

Because 386BSD was released entirely on the Internet via FTP, according to McKusick, "within weeks [it] had a huge following" (McKusick 1999, 43). The Jolitzs had expected a few hundred downloads of the system, but in all there were more than 250,000 (Chalmers 2000). Although the Jolitz's BSD port was both well designed and functional, they did not manage to keep up with the inevitable flood of bug reports and other contributions garnered from the ever-expanding user community. They also had their day jobs to consider, and for this reason, work on 386BSD revision did not proceed as fast as many users wanted. When the much-revised version 1.0 finally appeared in December 1993, much of the initial momentum had been lost. In the time that had passed between the initial and the final releases, the idea of Unix on the PC had spread like wildfire across the Internet, and several more players emerged in the arena. Three of these came from the BSD world.

The first one, NetBSD, was formed in early 1993 by a group of avid 386BSD users who were particularly interested in system portability and multiplatform support. Their vision was to make a BSD distribution that would run on as many computer platforms as possible, and appropriately they chose the slogan "Of course it runs NetBSD" ("Portability" 2011). Between 1993 and 2010, the NetBSD project released thirty-six versions of their system, and by 2010 it was running on fifty-three different platforms ("NetBSD" 2011). In the mid-1990s, the NetBSD project split in two with the formation of a new group calling themselves OpenBSD. The principal aim of OpenBSD was to improve the security of the BSD system and at the same time make it easier to use for inexperienced system administrators. The third, and perhaps most influential, spin-off from 386BSD was called FreeBSD. The project was started by Jordan Hubbard and others in 1993 in response to what they felt were the Jolitz's reluctance and inability to handle and incorporate feedback from 386BSD users (Hubbard 2011). When the Jolitzs refused to accept their contributions, the FreeBSD group simply decided to build their own distribution, the first of which was released in December 1993. Although the various BSD-based distributions for the PC enjoyed a reasonable amount of popularity in the 1990s, they totally paled in comparison with another and quite unexpected challenger, Linux. The remainder of this chapter is devoted to the history of the Linux operating system and how it took the PC Unix market by storm in the 1990s and gave a whole generation a new perception of how to develop, market, and distribute software.

Between 1977 and 2000, BSD evolved from a one-man hack to a Berkeley-centered cooperative effort to a distributed collaborative endeavor involving thousands of hackers and programmers all over the world. Along the way, it contributed significant portions of code and technical design features to almost every other Unix-like operating system in existence, helped foster the Internet, and pioneered a collaborative open source model of software development. The historical significance of BSD runs across all these dimensions, and yet it all comes down to one thing. In his essay, "Twenty Years of Berkeley Unix," longtime BSD hacker and distribution maintainer McKusick sums it up with the following words: "The history of the Unix system and the BSD system in particular had shown the power of making the source available to the users. Instead of passively using the system, they actively worked to fix bugs, improve performance and functionality, and even add completely new features" (McKusick 1999, 40).

The locomotive for the resurgence of the collaborative software development model in the 1990s was the creation and evolution of the Linux operating system. It represents the hacker movement's perhaps greatest achievement, not in technical terms, but because it captured the imagination of a whole new generation of hackers, computer users, and journalists alike. As we have seen, with the advent of batch processing, time-sharing, and collaborative hacking, the parameters of choral code became much broader (and more porous) than one would perhaps think. The shift from literacy to electracy across the entire spectrum of Ulmer's electrate apparatus table begins to materialize. In addition, Stuart Moulthrop's notion of "intervention" as scholarship is being gathered up in my *conductive* history of the apparatus. For Linux broke the mold of both the development process and choral code.

Re/vision

In order to adequately understand the story of Linux, we need to go back to the mid-1980s and examine the developments that made it all possible. On September 27, 1983, Richard Stallman, a long-time hacker of MIT's Artificial Intelligence Lab, posted an announcement to the Usenet newsgroups *net. unix-wizards* and *net.usoft,* which came to mark the beginning of a life-long project that Richard Stallman still carries on to this day.

Starting this Thanksgiving I am going to write a complete Unix-compatible software system called GNU (for Gnu's Not Unix), and give it away free to everyone who can use it. Contributions of time, money, programs and equipment are greatly needed. To begin with, GNU will be a kernel plus all the utilities needed to write and run C programs: editor, shell, C compiler, linker, assembler, and a few other things. After this we will add a text formatter, a YACC, an Empire game, a spreadsheet, and hundreds of other things. We hope to supply, eventually, everything useful that normally comes with a Unix system, and anything else useful, including on-line and hardcopy documentation. (Stallman 1983)

Having been raised in the academic code-sharing environment of MIT, Stallman had come to regard the ongoing commercialization of software with great skepticism and distrust. As he saw it, the traditional gift-sharing economy of software engineering was gradually being replaced by a commercial proprietary model designed to take away programmers' access to code and the ability to freely share computer programs. Prompted by MIT's decision in 1982 to move from its own Incompatible Time-sharing System (ITS) operating system to DEC's new proprietary VAX system, Stallman decided it was time to do something to slow this trend. He says:

The answer was clear: what was needed first was an operating system. That is the crucial software for starting to use a computer. With an operating system, you can do many things; without one, you cannot run the computer at all. With a free operating system, we could again have a community of cooperating hackers—and invite anyone to join. And anyone would be able to use a computer without starting out by conspiring to deprive his or her friends. (Stallman 1999, 55)

In January 1984, Stallman quit his job at the Artificial Intelligence Lab to begin the GNU project. He felt that this was a necessary move in order to ensure that MIT could not lay claim to, or place restrictions on, GNU. The name GNU, says Stallman, "was chosen following a hacker tradition, as a recursive acronym for 'GNU's Not Unix' " (Stallman 1999, 56).

In his Usenet announcement, Stallman said that GNU, to begin with, would consist of a "kernel plus all the utilities needed to write and run C programs." Being the core of the operating system, the kernel might have seemed like an obvious place to start; but as it turned out, it would, in fact, be the last piece of the puzzle to fall into place. Instead, Stallman ended up starting at the opposite end by writing an editor called GNU Emacs that could be used to implement the other pieces of the system (Chassell 2001). This editor was based on a macro collection known as Emacs (Editor MACroS) that Stallman had written in 1976 ("GNU Emacs" 2011). In view of the future prospects for GNU, Stallman's decision to start off with Emacs instead of the kernel was shrewd because it meant that the project could deliver something useful almost right away. Whether Stallman was consciously aware of this at the time or whether it was the result of lucky circumstances is not entirely clear. What seems quite clear, however, is that had he followed his original intentions as outlined in his Usenet posting, the GNU project might never have gotten off the ground. A kernel by itself has almost no practical use. A fully featured, state-of-the-art editor that could be ported and used freely on any type of Unix, and Unix-like system, however, was a different proposition altogether.

The first version of GNU Emacs was put up for distribution via FTP in early 1985. Because many people did not have Net access at that time and because Stallman was trying to make a living from writing and distributing free software, he also set up a small distribution business that sold the program on tape for $150 a copy. GNU Emacs became an almost instant hit with users, and soon the tape distribution business became too much for Stallman to handle alone. The success of GNU Emacs also brought more volunteers to the GNU project, and it was therefore decided to form a tax-exempt charity organization that would act as an institutional framework for GNU and its various activities. The Free Software Foundation (FSF), as the organization was called, was incorporated in October 1985 with Robert Chassell as founding director and treasurer. Stallman's aim with GNU was to create a free alternative to Unix that he could "give away to anyone" (Stallman 1983). From this and other early references, it is clear that he wanted the software to be *gratis*. More important, however, he also wanted GNU to be free in the sense that anyone could use, copy, modify, and redistribute it. Chassell explains, "Richard set the original goals, which was to create a system that wasn't even necessarily as good as Unix but somewhat like Unix with the condition only that it be free and not restricted" (Chassell 2001).

To achieve this goal, GNU needed a license, a binding legal document that would set forth the terms and conditions for using the software. The license that the SFS eventually came up with was called the GNU General Public License (GPL), and it would become perhaps the most important document ever written by the free software movement ("GNU General Purpose License" [1989] 2007). In the GPL, users of GNU software are guaranteed the rights to use, copy, modify, and distribute, and programmers who write the software are protected from companies or individuals who may want to use their code in proprietary software. If anyone makes a modification and redistribution of software under the GPL, they are required by the license to give users of the derivative software the same rights they originally had. This concept was dubbed *copyleft*, and it was designed to prevent free software from ever becoming proprietary and closed source. Furthermore, the GPL became an important instrument in fostering the self-sustained growth of the free software community because programmers were required to share their modifications with the community from which they gotten it in the first place.

"The easiest way to develop [the] components of GNU," says Stallman, "was to do it on a Unix system, and replace the components of that system one by one" (Stallman 1999, 62). Thus, after he had finished the GNU Emacs editing environment, Stallman immediately cast his eyes on what he identified as the next major component, the developer tools. These were the tools needed to actually implement the remaining parts of the system and included most notably a compiler, a debugger, and a set of libraries. Early in the project, Stallman had made some attempts to get permission to use certain existing compiler tools for GNU, but when these efforts eventually stranded, he decided to go ahead and write the compiler himself. C was the language of choice on the Unix platform, so a C compiler was what he wrote. The GNU C Compiler, popularly known as GCC, was first released in beta form in March 1987, with the following official 1.0 release on May 23 ("GCC Releases" 2011). More than perhaps any other component of the GNU system, GCC has been the major driving force in the creation of free and open source software. Over the years, it has been ported to nearly every Unix system in existence, and thus it has provided programmers with a familiar, multiplatform programming environment that not only saved them thousands of dollars in licensing fees but also allowed them to make modifications and additions for their own particular needs and challenges. Today GCC is known as the GNU Compiler Collection; in addition to Stallman's original C compiler, it now also contains front ends for several other popular programming languages such as C++, Objective C, Fortran, and Java ("GCC Releases" 2011).

Although Stallman was exceedingly important in jump-starting and driving the GNU project in the mid-1980s, a growing number of other contributors also joined the ranks. While many of these people made valuable contributions to the project, FSF had a hard time getting volunteers to take on development of major remaining GNU components. Chassell explains:

We had lots and lots of volunteers. I think at that time the number of people volunteering to some extent or another may have been a few hundred. It's hard to estimate because when you think in terms of how these people got involved, well, if someone sends a patch to Emacs which lots of people did, I think of them as a volunteer, but what we were concerned with, what was more important over the next seven or eight years, was getting things done that volunteers wouldn't do. (Chassell 2001)

Such is the nature of Ulmer's EmerAgency as well. It is useful to interject here that Egents (players) form a community, a "consultancy 'without portfolio'" (Ulmer 2003, 1). The chorus of egents has, however, a task beyond what Stallman envisioned, namely, "how to improve the world" (Ulmer 2003, 1). As Ulmer explains, "Wittgenstein once said that even if we could solve all the technical or scientific problems, we would still leave the human question untouched. The EmerAgency approaches public or community problems in terms of this human question, from the perspectives of the humanities and liberal arts" (Ulmer 2003, 1). What Ulmer saw in his own upbringing, his mystory, was a "tension, contradiction, dialectic between art and instrumentalism" (Ulmer 2003, 2). Ulmer cuts through this dialectic in a stark way: "What I intuited in that argument was that art in its purest form had a contribution to make to the practical world. To put it now more strongly: the dilemmas of the practical world are fundamentally resistant to policies that neglect the human question. Nor is it a choice between two different approaches, but the interdependence of arts and sciences" (Ulmer 2003, 2). The conductive link to Stallman's efforts is that the GNU acted as an EmerAgency comprising conflicts about problem solving and the role of play and hacking in problem solving. But I believe, at its core, that these hackers also wanted to reinject the human question back into the equation, as we will see shortly.

An example of a component that the volunteers, according to Chassell, were reluctant to take on was the GNU C library, a set of common functions and procedures that defines the system calls and other basic facilities. This was a major undertaking that the FSF felt had to be approached, designed, and implemented in a systematic and thorough way in order to produce a truly useful resource that would stand the test of time. For this reason, they decided that the best course of action would be to hire a programmer, Roland McGrath, rather than be dependent on a volunteer effort. Nevertheless, contributions from volunteer programmers continued to be important for the GNU project throughout the 1980s. Chassell says:

People did develop on their own especially things like little utilities because they aren't huge projects, or people could add to a project that was well started like Emacs and GCC, but they wouldn't start it on their own because it was too big. So part of the psychology of all this is that it's easy to have people start and work on and even complete small projects, but big projects are more difficult. (Chassell 2001)

By 1990, the GNU system was almost complete to the point where it could be used by itself. The only major missing part was the kernel, the core of the system on which all the other components would run. At the time, Carnegie Mellon University had developed a promising and free microkernel called Mach, and it was decided to implement the GNU kernel as a collection of servers running on top of Mach to implement file systems, network protocols, file access control, and other vital operating system features. In the finest hacker naming tradition, the kernel was named HURD, which in reality is a pair of mutually recursive acronyms, where on the first recursive level, the acronym HURD stands for "HIRD of Unix-Replacing Daemons," and, on the second level, the acronym HIRD stands for "HURD of Interfaces Representing Depth." If we look at the recursive nature of the name, we'll see that what it actually represents is an infinite loop. Incidentally, that is also what came to characterize the whole GNU HURD project. From the start, HURD was a highly ambitious project that aimed to create the best and most advanced kernel available. Needless to say, accomplishing such a feat would not be done in a day, and for this reason the project dragged on and on throughout the 1990s. Chassell explains:

I think that Richard and others got seduced by the promise of the GNU HURD, and it went directly contrary to what he had said in various policy statements earlier, which was that anything used by a free software GNU system needs only to be almost as good as Unix. It just needs to be a suitable replacement. But the theory behind the HURD was that it would actually be better, and there is a major driving force in people writing code to write stuff that's better. It's a real personal motivator, and I think part of what happened with the GNU HURD is that people got motivated to do something that was really better and as far as I can figure out, the GNU HURD in theory is at least still better than any contemporary operating system. (Chassell 2001)

When HURD was first presented publicly at a conference organized by the FSF in 1996, it was immediately met with skepticism among the hackers. Eric Raymond, who was also at the conference, remembers talking to Keith Bostic, a fellow hacker from the BSD community, during a conference break:

Keith gives me this sort of troubled look and says, "So what do you think?" I looked at him and I said what he was thinking. I said, "It's beautiful, it's elegant, it's elaborate, it's ornate, it's huge and it's going to be killed on performance." Both of us looked at the HURD design and we said in effect this is not practical engineering, this is computer science masturbation. That was also, quite symbolically, the first time I met Linus Torvalds. (Raymond 2001b)

For the Fun of IT

Unbeknownst to the GNU people and just about everyone else, in 1991, a 21-year-old computer science student at Helsinki University in Finland named Linus Torvalds started developing his own operating system. At the university, Torvalds had been introduced to Unix, and in his spare time he had started playing with a small Unix-like system called Minix that enjoyed a fair amount of popularity at the time. Minix was a free Unix clone for personal computers written by Dutch computer science professor Andrew Tanenbaum and first introduced in January 1987. It was designed to teach students about operating system design and principles, and for this reason it also came complete with source code. The rising popularity of Minix was clearly manifested in the Usenet news group comp.os.minix, where users from all over the world gathered to discuss the system, report bugs, and suggest improvements. When Torvalds' feedback and suggestions for improvements of Minix went largely unanswered by Tanenbaum, he thus decided to take matters into his own hands. Postings on comp.os.minix suggests that he had started thinking about doing his own operating system sometime in the spring and early summer of 1991, but it wasn't until August that year that he made his intentions clear in a post to the comp.os.minix newsgroup.

Hello everybody out there using minix -

I'm doing a (free) operating system (just a hobby, won't be big and professional like gnu) for 386(486) AT clones. This has been brewing since april, and is starting to get ready. I'd like any feedback on things people like/dislike in minix, as my OS resembles it somewhat (same physical layout of the file-system (due to practical reasons) among other things). I've currently ported bash(1.08) and gcc(1.40), and things seem to work. This implies that I'll get something practical within a few months, and I'd like to know what features most people would want. Any suggestions are welcome, but I won't promise I'll implement them:-)

Linus (torva. . .@kruuna.helsinki.fi) (Torvalds 1991a)

As opposed to the GNU HURD and Minix kernels, which were both based on a modern microkernel design, Torvalds's kernel, later was named Linux, was based on a more traditional monolithic design. Most operating systems up until that time, including Unix, VMS, MS-DOS, and others, were monolithic designs where process management, memory management, i/o, and file handling were all contained in one single monolithic file. The hacker Torvalds's motivation for building his kernel on a monolithic design had primarily to do with concern for efficiency and the processing power of the personal computers for which he targeted his system. A monolithic kernel, even though it was not state of the art in system design was, in Torvalds's opinion, simply faster and more efficient than a microkernel for small personal computers. He says, "I am a pragmatic person, and at the time I felt that microkernels (a) were experimental, (b) were obviously more complex than monolithic Kernels, and (c) executed notably slower than monolithic kernels" (Torvalds 1999). Tanenbaum, the computer science professor, however, was not impressed when he later learned about Linux. In his view, it represented "a giant step back into the 1970s" (DiBona et al. 1999, 222), something he explains by adding, "[it's] like taking an existing, working C program and rewriting it in BASIC. To me, writing a monolithic system in 1991 is a truly poor idea" (DiBona et al. 1999, 222). In a posting to the comp.os.minix newsgroup in January 1992 titled "Linux is obsolete," he attempted to put Torvalds in his place: "As most of you know, for me MINIX is a hobby, something that I do in the evening when I get bored writing books and there are no major wars, revolutions, or senate hearings being televised on CNN. My real job is a professor and researcher in the area of operating systems. As a result of my occupation, I think I know a bit about where operating systems are going in the next decade or so" (DiBona et al. 1999, 222). In characteristic hacker style, Torvalds shot back that very same night:

Re 1:   you doing minix as a hobby—look at who makes money off minix, and who gives linux out for free. Then talk about hobbies. Make minix freely available, and one of my biggest gripes with it will disappear. Linux has very much been a hobby (but a serious one: the best type) for me: I get no money for it, and it's not even part of any of my studies in the university. I've done it all on my own time, and on my own machine.

Re 2:   your job is being a professor and researcher: That's one hell of a good excuse for some of the brain-damages of minix. I can only hope (and assume) that Amoeba doesn't suck like minix does. (DiBona et al. 1999, 223)

Linus Torvalds, obviously, would not be deterred by professorial criticism, and in the middle of September 1991, shortly after the initial announcement on comp.os.minix, he released Linux version 0.01 on the Internet. Torvalds had asked people for feedback on things they wanted to see in a new operating system, and in a posting to the comp.os.minix news group on October 5, 1991, he went one step further and asked people to send him contributions that he could include in the Linux system. He opened his post with the following words: "Do you pine for the nice days of minix-1.1, when men were men and wrote their own device drivers? Are you without a nice project and just dying to cut your teeth on a OS you can try to modify for your needs? Are you finding it frustrating when everything works on minix? No more all-nighters to get a nifty program working? Then this post might be just for you:-)" (Torvalds 1991b). The Minix hackers must really have been ready for a change of pace because Torvalds soon had a small and dedicated following. By Christmas 1991, in the span of just four months, Linux had reached version 0.11. One could already hear the echoes of what would become the mantra of open source development in the 1990s: release early and often. Unlike Stallman and the older hackers whom I have presented in this chapter, Linus Torvalds, born in 1969—the same year ARPANET was first commissioned by the U.S. Department of Defense—grew up with the Internet. For him it was a natural arena in which to operate and find collaborators. While BSD had been largely a Berkeley-centered effort that proliferated mostly in academia due to its focus on mini machines such as the PDP and VAX, Linux found its primary audience among PC hackers on the Internet. As the system became more and more functional through frequent releases and updates, it began to gain momentum, and its user base soon numbered in the thousands. Unlike Unix, BSD, Minix, and other systems written by hackers in academia or by professional computer scientists like Tanenbaum, Linux was simply a hack written by a hacker for hackers. In response to Torvalds on comp.os.minix, he stated that "I still maintain the point that designing a monolithic kernel in 1991 is a fundamental error," and he added tongue-in-cheek, "Be thankful you are not my student. You would not get a high grade for such a design" (DiBona et al. 1999, 225).

The Linux operating system that Torvalds invented in 1991–1992 was a very simple system that might very well have faded into obscurity. It had a working kernel, just a few essential utilities and tools, and it only ran on Intel X86 hardware. By 1998, however, Linux had become a well-known player in the operating systems world. It had morphed into a major multiplatform OS that had captured a good portion of the server market and was starting to make inroads into the lucrative desktop market. How did this happen? How does one explain the Linux phenomenon of the 1990s? There is no simple answer, and the reasons are as complex and manifold as the operating system itself. Part of the answer, no doubt, is found in the resurrection of the open source concept by, among others, the BSD group and the Free Software Foundation in the 1980s and since then manifested through the hard and dedicated work of thousands of hackers all over the world. Important parts of the answer must also be sought in the remarkable growth of the Internet itself, the economic dot.com boom in the latter part of the 1990s, and the commercialization efforts within the Linux community at that time. I also believe one must seek answers in the 1990s growing dissatisfaction with the increasingly monopolistic behavior of Microsoft combined with the lure of anti-establishment hacker subculture, as I mentioned in the previous chapter. In concluding this chapter, however, the focus is on one significant reason behind Linux' success; it was a technology built on the hacker movement's successful adaptations of the time-tested

Unix technology and was enhanced and expanded on by its own users in an intricate collaborative effort.

In his autobiography, Linus Torvalds describes himself as an accidental revolutionary (Torvalds and Diamond 2001). I believe this is a good characterization. When he started hacking Linux in the early 1990s, Torvalds had no intention of creating a major new operating system that, by the end of the decade, would compete head to head with commercial and industrial strength heavyweights. All he wanted to do was to hack and learn Unix and to create what in his mind would be a better version of Minix that he could play with on his PC. What he didn't realize, however, was that by developing the Linux kernel, he had incidentally also filled in the missing piece of the GNU puzzle. Initially, Torvalds had released Linux under a license that forbade people to make profit from it. That license, however, was soon replaced with the well-publicized GNU GPL, according to Torvalds, because the GNU's GCC compiler he had included in Linux used the GPL (Torvalds 1999). By licensing Linux under the GPL, he not only adopted GNU's free software philosophy that encouraged people to use, copy, modify, and redistribute his system, he also tied Linux to the whole GNU OS framework. Linux was more than just a realization of Stallman's GNU OS, however. Components such as the X Windows system developed at MIT were added early on, as were numerous other components from BSD. Spawned by the successful application of the collaborative open source development model as demonstrated in the case of Linux, the mid-1990s saw a host of new projects develop that would boost Linux's usability and popularity even further. Among these were the K Desktop Environment (KDE), the Apache web server, and many others. These projects were started chiefly by hackers who had found Linux to be an excellent environment in which to do and promote development for both open and proprietary Unix-like systems.

In the early days of 1991–1992, people who wanted to try Linux had to go on the Internet, find and download all the components that were needed, build the disk file system by hand, and compile and install the software file by file. I can remember downloading hundreds of files and trying to build a Linux file system from scratch on my PC. For a hacker it was certainly a fun thing to do, but it was clear even to me that any widespread adoption would be significantly hampered by the complex setup and configuration process. In 1993, therefore, an early Linux adopter from the comp.os.minix news group, Peter MacDonald, decided to put together a Linux distribution that would be easy to install for new users. Characteristically he called his distribution Softlanding Linux Software (SLS). With SLS, users got an easy-to-use installation program that took them step by step through the process of installing Linux on their system. In addition to the basic Linux system that consisted of the kernel, the shared libraries, and basic utilities, users could also easily install any number of optional software packages such as the GNU development tools, Emacs and other editors, networking and mail handling software, the X Window System, and more. For convenience, this and other distributions that followed could also be bought on CD-ROM for a nominal cost. With fairly easy-to-install distributions such as SLS, one of the major thresholds for wider adoption of Linux had been surmounted, and Linux was fast becoming an operating system also for nonhackers. During the 1990s, the Linux distribution business grew by leaps and bounds. Carried forth by volunteer efforts such as SLS, Slackware, and Yggdrasil in the first half of the decade, to major commercial Linux distributors such as Red Hat, S.u.S.E., Caldera, and Mandrake toward the end of the decade, Linux became the most successful and widely recognized hacker effort of its time. More than an operating system, Linux became a collaborative patchwork stitched together by the philosophy of free software and the concept of open source.

In this chapter, I have explored code as *chora*, a site for the hacker movement's successful adaptation and reengineering of technology. Hackers not only took existing operating systems technology, refined it, and produced their own systems and solutions such as the BSD, GNU, and Linux operating systems, in the process they also invented both a renewed philosophy of code sharing and new collaborative development models based on the concept of open source. From the earliest efforts to develop time-sharing operating systems, the desire to create environments in which programming could take place as a communal activity was an important motivator. The term *time-sharing* itself reflects this desire better than anything, and in short order small hacker communities based on the sharing of code and experiences emerged around the early experimental installations at places such as MIT, Bell Labs, Berkeley, and elsewhere.

The Unix operating system, although developed within the framework of a traditional research institution, was, for all intents and purposes, a hacker creation. Its simple yet flexible and totally open structure appealed to hackers' sense of style and hands-on approach, and during the 1970s and 1980s, it became the OS of choice for most serious hackers. Because the AT&T telephone company in the 1970s was prevented by government order from commercializing Unix, the hackers at Berkeley were able to play with, modify, and add to it as much as they wanted. By the time the AT&T monopoly fell in 1984 and the company began to impose proprietary restrictions on it for commercial gain, the hackers had already appropriated

Unix and made their own version of it: BSD. The cat was out of the bag, and it could not be put back in even though AT&T in the early 1980s went to the courts in an attempt do so.

During the 1980s, as computers in general and the PC in particular helped facilitate an accelerated computerization of society, the hacker ideals of freedom and code sharing came under increasing pressure from commercialization efforts by companies and individuals who saw software as a promising new industry. In a response to these developments, Stallman, once named "the last of the true hackers" (Levy [1984] 1994, 451), founded the Free Software Foundation and embarked on what can only be described as an ambitious collaborative effort to create a free alternative operating system that hackers and others could use, share, modify, and distribute freely. GNU, as the system was called, became an important stepping stone for many hacker activities and projects in the late 1980s and early 1990s, among them one by a young unknown hacker from Finland named Linus Torvalds.

Torvalds started out trying to create a Unix-like operating system for his personal computer. As a bricoleur, he ended up creating the very locomotive for most of the important hacker activities in the 1990s. A major reason for Linux's success was, as I have discussed, the fact that Torvalds was able to build his system mostly from bits and pieces that other hackers had already made. Another equally important reason was that Torvalds, quite unintentionally, was able to harness the collaborative and communicative spirit of the new Internet and thereby capture the imagination of a new generation of hackers.

Bazaar

In 1990, few people outside of the hacker circles had heard of free software and the concept of source sharing. Even fewer thought there would be room for such "radical" ideas in the rapidly evolving commercial world of software engineering. By the turn of the century, however, the hacker ideas of free software and open source were everywhere, and the hacker movement's leading figures and evangelists, such as Richard Stallman, Linus Torvalds, Eric Raymond, and others, had acquired fame and status far outside their home turf. The hackers were no longer the antisocial misfits that the popular media loved to talk about every time there was a computer virus on the loose or a data break-in. Now they were the creative entrepreneurs of the dotcom era, the hybrid creature of Derrida and Lévi-Strauss' imaginations: the engineer/bricoleur.

The widespread adoption of the Internet and the communication technologies associated with it contributed in large part to a further globalization of the hacker movement during this same time period. In the 1960s and 1970s, hackers typically worked in small groups or as individuals in relative isolation from one another. In the 1980s, communication technologies such as email, IRC, Usenet, and later the Web came to facilitate the formation of new and geographically diverse groups of hackers. Linux, which I discussed above, is an example of a technology made possible by three distinct advantages offered by this new environment, collaboration, communication, and distribution.

First, the Internet represented a worldwide communication infrastructure that let people with converging interests connect across geographical barriers and time zones, across age differences and social status. Second, the Internet represented a highly versatile and up-to-date source of information about new developments and interesting projects. It provided the perfect avenue for spreading the "gospel of free software" and recruit new collaborators. The FSF was slow to catch on to the significance of the Internet in this regard. Linus Torvalds, in contrast, may not have completely understood the ramifications of using the Net, but according to Raymond, using it was second nature for him. Third, the Internet represented a hypereffective medium for the distribution of software. It made it possible to share data and software at no, or minimal, cost and at the same time reach a worldwide audience.

As word of the new Linux OS spread rapidly throughout the hacker movement in the early 1990s, it attracted users, testers, and contributors in droves. One of these new Linux converts was Eric Steven Raymond, also known online as ESR. Raymond had first become involved with the hacker movement in the late 1970s, and in the mid-1980s he had been one of the earliest contributors to the FSF's GNU project. Another of his early and important contributions was as editor and maintainer of what was then called the Jargon File (Raymond 2011), an online collection of hacker lore, slang, and jargon. When Raymond first discovered Linux in early 1993, he thought it was something new and big afoot within the hacker movement. Inspired by Linus Torvalds's new and creative development model, he thus began a series of theoretical writings designed, as he says, to "illuminate the social patterns and development methods that culture was already using effectively, in a way that made it possible for other people to understand and emulate them" (Raymond 2001b). The most influential of these writings was an article from 1997 titled "The Cathedral and the Bazaar" (Raymond 2001a).

"The Cathedral and the Bazaar," which incidentally reminds us of Lévi-Strauss' juxtaposition of the engineer/craftsman and the bricoleur (see chapter 2), attempts to describe and understand the Linux approach to software engineering. In traditional software engineering, which Raymond likens to the classic cathedral building of the Middle Ages, a program, he says, is typically crafted by a group of highly skilled craftsmen presided over by a master builder who provides the vision and the grand plans for the project. He explains:

> Linux overturned much of what I thought I knew. I had been preaching the Unix gospel of small tools, rapid prototyping and evolutionary programming for years. But I also believed there was a certain critical complexity above which a more centralized, a priori approach was required. I believed that the most important software (operating systems and really large tools like the Emacs programming editor) needed to be built like cathedrals, carefully crafted by individual wizards or small bands of mages working in splendid isolation, with no beta to be released before its time. (Raymond 2001a, 21)

When he looked at the way in which Linus Torvalds had organized the Linux project, none of these "truisms" was anywhere to be found. On the contrary, to Raymond the Linux engineering model looked most of all like a "great babbling bazaar," in which basically anyone could bring their goods to market. If the project leaders deemed a particular contribution significant and valuable enough, it would then make its way into the code and become part of the bigger mosaic.

> Linus Torvalds' style of development—release early and often, delegate everything you can, be open to the point of promiscuity—came as a surprise. No quiet, reverent cathedral-building here—rather, the Linux community seemed to resemble a great babbling bazaar of differing agendas and approaches (aptly symbolized by the Linux archive sites, who'd take submissions from anyone) out of which a coherent and stable system could seemingly emerge only by a succession of miracles. The fact that this bazaar style seemed to work, and work well, came as a distinct shock. (Raymond 2001a, 21)

To test his theory and to see for himself how the bazaar model would work in a practical setting, Raymond set out to create a new free software project based on Torvalds's Linux model. Raymond had long held the belief that "every good work of software starts by scratching a developer's personal itch" (Raymond 2001a, 23), so consequently he chose an email POP3 client that he had wanted for some time as the test bed for his project. The POP3 client, later named Fetchmail, would only be a by-product of the much more important article that eventually came out of the project. "The Cathedral and the Bazaar" (subtitled "Why Does the Linux Development

Model Work?") was first presented at the 4th International Linux Kongress in Germany in May 1997. It was warmly received by the conference audience and soon made headlines on Linux and free software websites all across the Internet. Raymond had actually succeeded beyond his expectations in his theoretical undertaking. He had managed to dissect the Linux phenomenon and describe its inner workings and benefits in ways that made the hacker community's implicit knowledge of its own practices explicit. Furthermore, he had managed to do this in a way that people outside of the immediate hacker circles could understand. This last point would soon prove to be one of the most crucial upshots of the article.

Code Ideologies

In the late 1990s, in Mountain View, California, a company had a problem. It had once presided over the most successful web browser in the world, but in recent years its hegemony had come under attack from their most ardent competitor. It was looking for ways to remedy the unfortunate predicament in which it found itself, and it believed Eric Raymond's bazaar model presented the salvation. That company was Netscape Communications Corporation (Leonard 1998a). In January 1998, in an unprecedented move that surprised most industry observers, Netscape announced that it would release the source code to its popular but ailing web browser to the free software community. The so-called browser wars that had raged with increasing intensity since Microsoft had first released its Internet Explorer browser in 1995 had left Netscape's market share trailing far behind at this point. It was believed that by opening up the source and letting independent programmers in, Netscape could once again gain the upper hand in the struggle for market dominance. According to their 1998 news release, Netscape hoped that this would enable them to "harness the creative power of thousands of programmers on the Internet" ("Netscape" 1998) and incorporate their best enhancements into future versions of Netscape's software. The decision to "free the source" eventually led to the creation of the Mozilla project. After Linux, this was perhaps the biggest and most influential free software project of the late 1990s and early 2000s.

In the spring of 1998, a new buzzword was beginning to be heard on the Internet grapevine. The term was *open source*. An article in the online *Wired* from May 1998 opens with the following passage: "If you've sent email or browsed a Web site, you've almost certainly come into indirect contact with 'open source' software without even knowing it" (Glave 1998). The author makes only a fleeting reference to the term in this article, but before the end of the year the new phrase "open source" had all but replaced "free soft-ware" in the public discourse. To the uninformed, the distinction between the two may seem semantic at best. In reality, however, while describing more or less the same technical concepts and development processes, the two phrases represent two almost entirely different philosophical views on software development.

When Richard Stallman first coined the term *free software* back in the mid-1980s, he wanted it to say something about personal freedoms to create, use, change, and redistribute software. To him, it was a moral im-perative. "For the free software movement . . . nonfree software is a social problem, and the solution is to stop using it and move to free software" (Stallman 2007). In the English language, the word *free* also commonly refers to something you can get *free of charge*. This double meaning of the word turned out to be somewhat unfortunate, and Stallman later claimed that it was never his intention that free software should also be *gratis*. He explains, "This is a matter of freedom, not price, so think of 'free speech,' not 'free beer'" (Stallman 2007).

In the late 1990s, some people, including Raymond, started to feel that the adoption of Linux and other free software programs, especially within the large and important corporate sector, was hampered by the very label of free software that many, especially outside the hacker movement, fre-quently mistook for free as in *gratis*. Raymond elaborates:

I became aware that our largest problem as a culture was not technology but image. We had created a perception of our work and our goals and our social organization that was hurting us badly and hindering the adoption of our technology and get-ting in the way of our goals. In particular I realized that the term Free Software was a problem. It was not a problem because of what it means inside our community, but because of what it promotes outside. (Raymond 2001b)

When Raymond first learned of Netscape's decision to open the source to their browser software, he realized immediately that a golden opportunity had just opened up for the hacker movement. In an interview with Salon .com shortly after Netscape's announcement, he says:

We knew we had a better way to do things in our software designs and operating systems and the way that we shared work with each other. But we couldn't get any-body to listen. Netscape doing this creates a window of opportunity for us to get our message into corporate boardrooms. The flip side of that is that if Netscape tanks, no one is going to listen to us for another decade. (Leonard 1998a)

There was suddenly a lot at stake, and Raymond wasn't about to let a histor-ical chance go by the wayside. In his own words, "It was time to stop being an accidental revolutionary (a reference to Linus Torvalds's autobiography) and start being a purposeful one" (Raymond 2001b). On February 3, 1998, he met with Todd Anderson and Chris Peterson of the Foresight Institute, John "maddog" Hall and Larry Augustin of Linux International, and Sam Ockman of Silicon Valley Linux User's Group in Palo Alto, California ("History of the OSI" 2011). At this meeting, the group brainstormed various strategies for how best to sell the bazaar-style software engineering models to the corporate world, which, they were convinced, was finally ready to listen now that Netscape had given the all-important imprimatur.

We realized it was time to dump the confrontational attitude that has been associated with "free software" in the past and sell the idea strictly on the same pragmatic, business-case grounds that motivated Netscape. We brainstormed about tactics and a new label. "Open source," contributed by Chris Peterson, was the best thing we came up with. ("History of the OSI" 2011)

Not long after the meeting, Raymond and Bruce Perens cofounded the Open Source Initiative (OSI), a nonprofit organization dedicated to promote the label of open source and a new set of licensing guidelines dubbed the Open Source Definition ("Open Source Definition" 2011). For the purposes of the historical context here, however, I will briefly discuss what it is and how it differs from regular licenses such as the GNU GPL or the BSD license. Perens drafted the original document using the *Debian Free Software Guidelines* (of which he was also the primary author) as a template. Thus, the OSD was not a software license per se; rather, it was a set of guidelines and criteria that an open source software license had to meet.

The founders of the OSI wanted open source to have the broadest possible appeal, especially within the important commercial world; and thus, as opposed to the GNU GPL, there is no reference to the troublesome word *free* anywhere in the OSD document. More important, however, while software licensed under the GNU GPL is largely incompatible with proprietary solutions, the OSD was designed specifically to let companies incorporate open source solutions within their proprietary software and vice versa. In this respect, the OSD takes its cue from the BSD license in which no restrictions are placed on proprietary components. An important stipulation in the OSD is, of course, that programs licensed under an OSD-type license must include source code or the source code must be readily available on request. Also, any work under the OSD guidelines must allow for modification and derivative works as well as redistribution of those works. By 2011, more than seventy different types of software licenses were said to conform to the guidelines set out by the OSD ("Open Source Licenses by Category" 2011). These included licenses from several major corporate actors in the software business such as Apple Computer, Nokia, Microsoft, and many more. The vast majority of free software and open source projects, however, continued to use variations of the GNU GPL or the BSD license.

Not long after the formation of the OSI, a conflict that had been latent within the hacker movement for the better part of the 1990s suddenly came to a head. On one side of the divergence were the proponents of Stallman and his ideology of free software as expressed through the GNU GPL and other writings published by the FSF. On the other side were the proponents of the less restrictive, more pragmatic BSD-style licensing scheme, which the new Open Source Initiative sought to embrace. The conflict was complex and had several different layers to it as Raymond explains from his point of view:

There is an ideological level, there is a practical level, and there is a personal level. On the ideological level, what you are seeing here is a conflict between two ideologies, two value systems that lead to similar behaviors but justify and advocate those behaviors in fundamentally different ways. The difference in ideology is fairly clear. Richard's mode of changing the world is very consciously and explicitly a moral crusade. If you don't buy his abstract moral arguments, you don't sign up. The way that Linus Torvalds and I, and others, have pushed is a pragmatist's way. In effect what we're saying is; "Moral argument? Who needs a moral argument? We like engineering results!" So there is a level at which it is a conflict about what kind of ideology we are going to have. There is a practical level on which it is a conflict about which kinds of tactics work for spreading our message. The argument on that level is; Does it work better to moralize or talk about results? There is also a personal level in that, well, people have egos and they have investments in their ideologies, and if part of what's going on is that you think somebody hijacked your revolution, you kind of resent that. (Raymond 2001b)

Stallman's radical political agenda, coupled with his well-known unwillingness to compromise on the premise of free software, meant that there was, in effect, no room for him in the new open source movement. In their attempts to sell their ideas to the business world, therefore, open source advocates purposefully distanced themselves from Stallman and free software. The last thing they wanted was to alienate potential partners in business and industry by what they saw as Stallman's "infamous" confrontational attitude. Stallman on his side did little to ease the tension. To the contrary, in response, he boldly turned up the rhetoric a few more notches by accusing open source proponents of "neglecting political issues, and jumping on the bandwagon of the day," which, he believed to be, "a common form of shallowness in our society" (Leonard 1998b). To further drive his argument home, Stallman later published an article in which he outlined what he believed to be the fundamental differences between free software and open source. One of the opening passages of his paper reads as follows:

The fundamental difference between the two movements is in their values, their ways of looking at the world. For the Open Source movement, the issue of whether software should be open source is a practical question, not an ethical one. As one person put it, "Open source is a development methodology; free software is a social movement." For the Open Source movement, non-free software is a suboptimal solution. For the Free Software movement, non-free software is a social problem and free software is the solution. (Stallman 1998)

In another position statement titled "Freedom or Power?" Stallman elaborates further on the notion of freedom:

In the Free Software Movement, we stand for freedom for the users of software. We formulated our views by looking at what freedoms are necessary for a good way of life, and permit useful programs to foster a community of goodwill, cooperation, and collaboration. . . . We stand for freedom for programmers as well as for other users. . . . However, one so-called freedom that we do not advocate is the "freedom to choose any license you want for software you write." We reject this because it is really a form of power, not a freedom. . . . If we confuse power with freedom, we will fail to uphold real freedom. (Kuhn and Stallman 2001)

Although the conflict between the ideologists and the pragmatists within the hacker movement eventually quieted down, it had for all practical purposes created two separate wings, a left and a right as it were, within the broader movement. Many, even within the OSI, thought this schism was an unfortunate turn of events. Perens, for instance, had originally envisioned the OSI as a gentle introduction to the deeper philosophy of free software, rather than a separate movement, and for this reason he soon came to be at odds with Raymond's separatist hard line. In an interview with *Linux Magazine* in September 2001, Perens said:

When we founded Open Source, my understanding was that Open Source would be a gentle introduction to Free Software and not a separate movement. I would never have participated in Open Source for the purpose of creating a schism. Especially now, it is important that we stand together. That's more important than it used to be. I harbor some disappointment that Open Source became something that sort of deprecated Richard Stallman's philosophy rather than leading people into Free Software. (McMillan 2001)

The two wings eventually resumed collaboration on practical projects of common interest, but their individual agendas, strategies, and goals would remain different. Unity was not the only casualty from the fallout between open source and free software. On February 18, 1999, Perens resigned from the OSI. In an email distributed on the Net, he said: "It's Time to Talk about Free Software Again" (Perens 1999).

Fueled in part by the media buzz surrounding the open source and free software initiatives, by the end of the 1990s the Linux operating system had grown into a considerably popular server platform and had also started to make some inroads into the desktop market. For many computer users, Linux represented liberation from the perceived firm monopolistic grasp that Microsoft had established in the personal computing market. Thompson, creator of Unix, for instance, believed this more than anything was the reason behind the Linux phenomenon. Like Tanenbaum, Thompson was not particularly impressed by what the hacker bricoleurs led by Torvalds had created either.

I view Linux as something that's not Microsoft—a backlash against Microsoft, no more and no less. I don't think it will be very successful in the long run. I've looked at the source and there are pieces that are good and pieces that are not. A whole bunch of random people have contributed to this source, and the quality varies drastically. (Cooke et al. 1999, 61)

At first glance, it may seem that Thompson was right in at least some of his predictions. Linux is continuing to do reasonably well in the server markets while consumer adoption remains below the 1 percent mark ("OS Market Share News" 2011). Contrary to what Thompson believed in 1999, however, I believe this has more to do with shifting trends in consumer computing toward mobile devices and cloud service solutions than with inherent quality issues in Linux and the collaborative hacker development model. What remains undisputed is that, during the 1990s, the hacker movement morphed from an obscure underground phenomenon into something of a mainstream trend, and the main driving force behind this astonishing development was primarily the success of the Linux operating system and the new Bazaar-style development model that it popularized. Many of the hacker projects of the last two decades owed their success to the "collaborative climate" created by the free software movement. Richard Stallman's tireless efforts to spread the gospel of free software, the GNU GPL, and the free software programs of the FSF were all important preconditions for the developments that followed. The split that occurred when the OSI entered the stage in the late 1990s was perhaps unavoidable and, in the grand scheme of things, something that ultimately, I believe, strengthened the movement as a whole. While the free software wing headed by Stallman continued to be a social movement with a well-defined philosophy on software development, the open source wing was for the first time able to rally the support of the corporate world. Going into the twenty-first century, an increasing number of corporate players such as Apple, IBM, Sun Microsystems, and Google adopted the heuretic open source hacker methodologies as part of their commercial product development strategies.

I opened this chapter with a passage from Ulmer that asks what choral writing can be. He claims that choral writing "must be in the order neither of the sensible nor the intelligible but in the order of making, of generating. And it must be transferable, exchangeable, without generalization conducted from one particular to another" (Ulmer 1994, 67). I believe the concept of choral code, as I have illustrated it through the case studies in this chapter, accomplishes all these conditions. However, there is an even more compelling case when it comes to imagining what choral code might be. That is the case of the multiuser online game, which was a uniquely new technology that didn't exist until hackers invented it. The next two chapters venture into a playful exploration of how choral code morphs and blends virtual and real into a new electrate synthesis that I call *pervasive life*.

4   Venture

"Venture includes flinging into danger. To dare is to risk the game. Heraclitus (Fragment 52) thinks of Being as the aeon, the world's age, and of the aeon in turn as a child's game."

—Martin Heidegger, "What Are Poets For?"

In chapters 2 and 3, the aim has been to trace (and conduct) *a* history of invention, specifically electrate invention with an eye toward hacking electracy in the process. In these next two chapters, I venture into what Stuart Moulthrop calls "intervention" (Moulthrop 2005). Inventing electracy means intervention in invention itself. It means modding what counts as history, as scholarship, as technological development. It means immersing oneself in the choral code, which means avatar. It means skating along the axis of pain/pleasure, of playing the game of life. Ulmer gives us the method of heuretics and challenges us to translate the literate categories that have formed the foundations of schooling into the new apparatus. Ulmer points out the crux of the matter here:

In our case, the translation of the literate categories organizing knowledge into cyberspace makes explicit that these categories or specializations (English, History, Sociology, Physics, Architecture, Engineering) are relative to the social machine (apparatus) of literacy and have no absolute necessity. They correspond, that is, to the requirements of the apparatus, not to the nature of the conditions in the real that cause us so much trouble (which we configure as "problems"). While the entire administrative superstructure of literate specialized knowledge will be translated into cyberspace, once there much of it will evaporate. The practices that will replace specialized knowledge remain to be invented. Who will be the inventors? Why not us? (Ulmer 2003, 4–5).

Stuart Moulthrop asks similar questions in "After the Last Generation: Rethinking Scholarship in the Days of Serious Play" (Moulthrop 2005). He pulls no punches when he opens the article by saying that, "for some of us [in education], it's always the end of the world" (Moulthrop 2005, 208). Citing James Paul Gee's predictions about how video games will bring about educational change, Moulthrop seizes on the opportunity "to posit a new species" of educator (Moulthrop 2005, 209). Furthermore, he calls for a reevaluation of what counts as academic scholarship. It is not enough, he says, for game scholars to play and then write about playing (Moulthrop 2005, 211). It is not enough, in other words, to deconstruct the dichotomy of play and reflect about play in writing. "We must also play on a higher level, which means that we must build" (Moulthrop 2005, 212). Thus, Moulthrop proposes a "new category of cybertextual scholarship called the *intervention* . . . [by which he means] a practical contribution to a media system (e.g., some product, tool, or method) intended to challenge underlying assumptions or reveal new ways of proceeding" (Moulthrop 2005, 212).

But before I discuss invention/intervention in chapter 5, it is necessary to define the problem in education that spawned my specific intervention—the false binary between real and virtual life. This, then, begins the *Venture*, the bridge between real and virtual life that inaugurated the era of *pervasive life*. In 1998, in the introduction to our coedited collection of essays, *High Wired: On the Design, Use, and Theory of Educational MOOs* (Haynes and Holmevik [1998] 2002), Cynthia Haynes and I put it thus:

It is our goal to conceive new metaphors with which to play the *bricoleur*, to design the space with text as the primary metaphor and building blocks. This is what we call *cypher/TEXT*, a word that assembles in one term the notions of cyber, hyper, text, and most important of all, the reader herself. We think of it as a three-dimensional text . . . the effects [of which] generate a different genre, one that breaks the barriers of space and time (not to mention distance), and that produces a unique and seamless fabric of architextures and assemblages, a different genre of writing . . . [inhabited by] discussants [who] engage in real time, by writing text in a space that is *itself* textually assembled, or constructed, and performed by personae that are themselves textually constructed. (Haynes and Holmevik [1998] 2002, 10–11)

Pervasive Life

Over the past 20 years, the proliferation of digital communities, most frequently called virtual communities or worlds, have sparked debates about the effects of new media on notions of the self, community, learning, communication, work, and all aspects of public and private life. Some of the most popular online worlds, social networks, and games (such as *Second Life*, *Quarterlife*, and *Half-Life*) attempt, in their naming, to ground themselves in one common theme—*life*. But they are still distinguished from "real life" by their virtuality or what is commonly perceived as "virtual reality." Jaron Lanier coined this term in the 1980s, basing it in part on earlier ideas from the 1970s, such as Myron Krueger's *Artificial Reality* (Krueger [1983] 1991). Yet it can also be traced back to the late 1930s when the French playwright, Antonin Artaud, described theater as *virtual reality*, "la realite virtuelle" (Artaud 1958, 49). The problem is that we are still drawing a boundary between the "real" and "virtual" world.

The effect of this problem is that the design and management of virtual worlds must continually submit to this conceptual split in ways that deny designers and managers of these worlds the ability to envision life as *pervasive* (i.e., as both real and virtual) no matter what spaces we inhabit, which people we encounter, or in what activities we choose to participate. Our lives are not just increasingly virtual, the notion of virtuality is coming to stand in for what I call "pervasive life."[1] This chapter argues that what we previously believed is a boundary between the real and virtual is an illusion we constructed in order to privilege the material or "real" world over an immaterial or "virtual" world. We have done so for a number of important reasons, among them our penchant for privileging the concrete over the conceptual. This split manifests itself in countless ways, from the split between mind/body, thought/action, and reflection/production to the entrenched (but increasingly blurred) boundary between play and work.

This chapter calls for the integration of first and second life into a concept of *pervasive life*. But it also calls for a rehabilitation of the term *virtual* to henceforth be known as a blended mixed reality. From the beginning of virtual worlds, there has been the compartmentalization of virtual and real life, so to speak, and *pervasive life* counters the notion that these two spheres are separate. In blurring the boundary between virtual and actual life, a new way of thinking about life as pervasive enters into the social consciousness and into academic and commercial approaches to the creation and management of virtual worlds.

The various groups that will benefit from this perspective primarily include virtual world designers, practitioners, teachers, and users. Virtual world designers who may already believe *pervasive life* exists have not, however, had the most productive lines of rhetorical argument and discourse with which to legitimize their projects. I see this approach as empowering these designers to move forward with stronger visions and self-actualization. Other groups will find this useful in terms of learning how the virtual and real worlds have been artificially split and are in truth constituted *as* pervasive life. Such readers will find new motives for inhabiting virtual communities as well as new templates for designing pervasive spaces of the future.

In addition, educators will have a solid context for situating their teaching inside virtual communities, for assigning individual and collaborative work inside such spaces, and for fostering the blurring of boundaries that separate academic from work life, play from work, and play from learning. *Pervasive life* calls for designing virtual communities that draw on open source technologies, software development, and intervention in existing technologies. *Pervasive life* articulates that first life is most important because it argues that second life is not separate from first life. And it resonates with readers for whom second life has become first life to the degree that they no longer see the boundary, yet are pulled by social pressures back into the mindset that second life is secondary (i.e., inferior) to first life.

Other readers for whom this chapter may offer useful insights are computer programmers, computer game developers and game studies researchers, software designers, rhetorical theorists, professional communicators, writers, writing teachers, technical and business communication consultants, distance educators, training and development professionals, and a host of other groups. Of course, research that examines many of these issues began as early as 1984. *The Second Self* by Sherry Turkle is one of the most groundbreaking books on virtual identity and was released in a twentieth anniversary edition in 2005 (Turkle [1984] 2005). Her follow-up book, *Life on the Screen*, was a major influence in academic treatments of virtual community research (Turkle 1995). Because of Turkle's work, Cynthia Haynes and I invited her to contribute a foreword to our coedited collection, *High Wired: On the Design, Use, and Theory of Educational MOOs* (Turkle [1998] 2002; Haynes and Holmevik [1998] 2002), a volume that helped shape the field of virtual community design and research. Howard Rheingold's book *The Virtual Community* (Rheingold [1993] 2000) stands as the first book to cross the academic and trade book line to give a historical and personal account of virtual communities, but its foundation is still tied to the notion of cyberspace as the next "frontier," although Rheingold does question the distinction between "real" and "virtual" communities. *Convergence Culture* by Henry Jenkins is a recent contribution by a major new media theorist, and it offers a cultural perspective that blends criticism and observation into a widely considered seminal work on the new media worlds in general (Jenkins 2006).

In the fields of computers and composition, rhetoric, and professional communication, there are many excellent contributions to this topic. Research in the design and study of online communities for education has significantly enhanced our understandings of how such environments may be used to improve learning and communication. Work by Cynthia Selfe, Gail

Hawisher, Tharon Howard, Lynn Cherney, Beth Kolko, John Barber, Dene Grigar, Anne Wysocki, Johndan Johnson-Eilola, James Porter, and many others has shifted the debates into more nuanced realms of research and more practical methods of implementing new media in education. I should also mention the textbook Cynthia Haynes and I coauthored, *MOOniversity: A Student's Guide to Online Learning Environments* (Holmevik and Haynes 2000), as also contributing to this work.

There are, however, only a few texts that I consider direct precursors to my concept of *pervasive life*: Espen Aarseth's *Cybertext* (Aarseth 1997), Stuart Moulthrop's article "After the Last Generation: Rethinking Scholarship in the Days of Serious Play" (Moulthrop 2005), and Ian Bogost's recent texts *Unit Operations* (Bogost 2006) and *Persuasive Games* (Bogost 2008). Aarseth's work has had a dramatic influence on the new field of computer games studies, but it has also set the context for blurring the boundaries between work and play in relation to both literacy and life. Moulthrop, whose early work in hypertext theory and design is groundbreaking, is a most recent champion of eradicating the line between reflection and production, specifically in terms of the assessment of hybrid academic research that crosses these borders regularly. His notion of scholarship as "intervention" is one of the key linchpins of my argument in this book and has informed my practical research in virtual community design for fifteen years. Like Moulthrop, Bogost's research also straddles the line between reflection and production because he is both a game designer and an academic game researcher. Most important, Bogost's work is informed by rhetorical principles. While these works have common elements to my project, I see this chapter as taking a step both beyond and alongside their work. *Pervasive life* is electrate and life-centric. *Pervasive life* is reflective and productive. *Pervasive life* is rhetorical and design-oriented. In these ways, this chapter marks a new path, and it ventures forth to create the new species of *pervasive life*.

MUD and MOO

Every once in a while, new and uniquely different technologies emerge. The hacker movement has produced many such technologies over the years, but not many have spawned *pervasive* communities, and the historical study in this chapter focuses on the forerunner for all of today's virtual worlds and massively multiplayer online games: the Multiuser Dungeon (MUD). It is not meant to be an exhaustive inquiry into the history of MUDs. Rather, my aim is to explore and highlight the dynamics of user-driven technological development that *evolved pervasively* and *inside* a pervasive community, as seen in the case of MUD. MUD is a good example of a hacker technology through and through. It was developed exclusively by its users and for no other reasons than that it posed fun and interesting challenges. Although commercial motives played a role in early MUD development, almost all the significant developments since have happened through extensive code sharing in the MUD hacker community.

In this chapter, I have chosen to follow a particular branch of the MUD evolution, MOO. It opens with an account of the early days of MUD and goes on to follow the specific branch of MUD technology that produced the MOO system. The main part discusses MOO developments at a specific site named LambdaMOO. One of the most interesting aspects of the LambdaMOO development is that it took place inside the social and cultural setting of a MUD community. Because of this, the story of LambdaMOO serves not only to show the evolution of a unique hacker technology but also shows how technological solutions were forged in a ludic and collaborative effort to meet the social and cultural challenges of the pervasive electrate community in which it was situated. I then go on to show how interventions into MOO technology in the 1990s lead to some of the first educational pervasive multiuser online systems. By appropriating and modifying an existing technology through the power of open source, educators were able to open the doors to a digital learning environment, one inhabited by students sharing electrate experiences and situated on the threshold of a new *pervasive* paradigm.

Birth of a British Legend

The history of MUDs began in 1978 with Richard Allan Bartle and Roy Trubshaw, then undergraduate students at Essex University in the United Kingdom. Like many of their fellow college students at the time, they were both thoroughly fascinated by games and especially adventure games. In these adventure games, players assumed the roles of fantastic mythical characters such as elves, dwarves, paladins, and sorcerers and entered into a Tolkienesque world of adventure and fantasy. Dungeons and Dragons (D&D) is a traditional manual game where players sit down face-to-face with detailed rulebooks, pen and paper, and several fanciful many-sided dice. One of the main attractions of the game is the social experience of the gaming situation. To successfully solve an adventure, the players have to work together as a team, and this creates a collaborative atmosphere that is quite different from the typical competitive nature of most other games. Another important reason for its success is its almost infinite replayability, thanks to a rapidly growing number of commercial add-on stories. In addition, especially creative players can also write their own adventures and invite their friends to play using the standard D&D rules.

Bartle and Trubshaw had also seen the popular computer-based adventure game *Adventure*. This game, generally considered the first of its kind, was created by William Crowther in 1972.[2] Crowther's game soon became very popular and was frequently shared among friends and passed along over computer networks. In 1976, the development of *Adventure* was taken over by Don Woods; much inspired by J. R. R. Tolkien's *Lord of the Rings*, Woods added many of the fantasy features and game elements that became the hallmark of the computer adventure game genre. Also in 1976, Jim Gillogly at the Rand Corporation ported the game's original Fortran code over to C so it could run on Unix systems. As a result, the game soon spread like wildfire across the international computer networks (Montfort 2003).

For Bartle and Trubshaw, a couple of young computer science students fascinated with role-playing games, the idea of combining the role-playing and multiplayer aspects of D&D with the computer-based structure of *Adventure* was not a strange one. In fact, it was precisely the sort of challenge that many young hackers would find highly amusing and entertaining. Between the fall of 1978 and Easter 1980, Thrubshaw wrote two prototypes for an online multiuser game that he named MUD. After he had finished work on the third revision that was later to be known as MUD1 or *British Legends*, Roy Trubshaw graduated and left Essex University. His friend Bartle, who later went on to join the university's graduate program in computer science and eventually became a faculty member there, took over the system and in 1980 set up the first public MUD on the University's DECsystem-10 computer. Essex MUD was open to British players via an experimental packet-switching network called EPPS, which connected six universities in the UK. Players from outside the UK could also connect via the ARPANET. Essex MUD was open only between the hours of 2 a.m. and 6 a.m., when no one at the university used the computer for work. It is very likely that these operating hours contributed a great deal to the popular perception of MUD players as nocturnal creatures who spent long countless hours in the solitude of their dorm rooms, hunkered over their keyboards and hacking their way to the fame and glory of wizardhood. By the time Essex MUD "closed its doors" in 1987, Bartle had already developed a new version of the system, dubbed MUD2. The new system had grown out of Bartle's doctoral work in artificial intelligence and his desire to improve on the earlier version of the game. By this time, the MUD system was enjoying a good deal of popularity among fantasy and role-playing gamers. To capitalize on this interest, in 1985, Bartle and Trubshaw formed the company MUSE to market the system commercially. When Richard Bartle eventually left Essex University in 1987 to work full time on MUSE and MUD2, the MUD phenomenon was on the verge of its golden age, which would soon take it far beyond the imagination of its creators (Bartle 2004, 3–32).[3]

Although Bartle had, in the early days, let a few other people have copies of MUD to run on their own systems, the commercial interests behind the software did not permit a widespread distribution of source code. However, this did not discourage talented young MUD enthusiasts from delving into the breach to design and build their own MUD-type games, and between 1987 and 1991 a host of new MUD systems appeared on the scene. As with the original MUD ten years earlier, most of these second-generation MUD hackers were college students with a passion for adventure gaming and computer programming.

One of the first, and certainly the most influential, of the second-generation MUD systems was AberMUD. It was written in 1987 by Alan Cox (aka Anarchy), who was an avid player on Essex MUD while a student at University College of Wales, Aberystwyth. (Cox later became a central figure in the Linux kernel development.) AberMUD was largely inspired by the original Essex MUD, but it was an independent work done by Cox with the help of a group of other hackers at Aberystwyth. Unlike commercial MUD games such as MUD2, play on AberMUD was free, and it soon attracted a large following among students and hackers in Europe and the United States. The main influence of AberMUD, however, was due primarily to the fact that its source code was freely distributed and shared on the Internet. This allowed all to inspect the inner workings of the system and make changes and new modifications to it as they saw fit. Furthermore, because the AberMUD source code was written in C, it was easily modified and readily portable across Unix systems. As a consequence, AberMUD spawned a flurry of new MUD developments in the late 1980s and early 1990s.

TinyMUD

In the summer of 1989, James Aspnes, a graduate student at Cornell University, developed a new type of MUD that he called TinyMUD. Aspnes knew about AberMUD and similar systems, but he had not studied MUD source code as such. He had, however, studied the source code of another popular game, called *Monster*. Based on this, he set about to write a multiplayer game that would allow players to collaboratively build the game world and the quests and puzzles within (Aspnes 2001). In the typical hacker fashion,

Aspnes had the first version of his system up and running in record time—
just a weekend of fast and furious hacking.[4]

TinyMUD rapidly became a phenomenon that outgrew even its creator's
wildest expectations. People from all over the world began inhabiting the
pervasive/virtual world of TinyMUD, and it gradually took on a life of its
own and evolved into something that its designer had not anticipated. The
computer program became a community.

An important reason for TinyMUD's almost instant popularity was that
many found out about it via highly populated Usenet news groups such as
alt.mud. Another reason that might help explain the TinyMUD phenomenon is that its creation happened to coincide with the popularization
of the synchronous online communication form known as Chat. In the
late 1980s, Internet-based programs such as Internet Relay Chat (IRC) had
created a new digital space in which communication among people from
all corners of the world could take place. The structure of IRC closely re-
sembled its asynchronous counterpart, Usenet, in that communication was
centered on topics or channels to which interested parties could subscribe
or connect. In the early 1990s, IRC was growing quickly, and for millions
of people around the world, the idea of talking to other people, most often
anonymously, by typing on a computer became second nature—akin to
chatting with friends on the phone.

TinyMUD, as well as all other MUD systems, could easily facilitate the
type of chat found in IRC. In fact, this type of informal communication
had been going on in MUDs since the very beginning. What made Tiny-
MUD different, however, was that it had the capacity to create a pervasive
and diverse environment in which to situate the online communication.
In the original MUD, only the game's designers could add to or modify
the game world in significant ways. In MUD1, for example, Richard Bartle
had been the one to design and build most of the spaces and quests in the
game. In later systems, such as Lars Pensjø's LPmud, dedicated players who
achieved wizard status by playing the game were given access to a special
programming language known as LPC, which they could use to build new
areas of the game world and design new quests, monsters, objects, and
so on. In TinyMUD, however, the power to create could be obtained by
anyone. This in itself was a radical departure from previous systems, but
even more groundbreaking was the fact that players performed these building activities directly inside the virtual world itself though the use of special commands like "@dig" and "@create." With these simple but powerful
building tools, users were able to construct digital landscapes for a variety of
purposes. While many of the spaces in TinyMUD remained game-oriented

ones, as Aspnes had envisioned, a growing number of them also served purposes of a purely social nature or no particular purpose at all. Keeping in mind that we are looking to blur the boundaries between work/play, serious/play, and real/virtual, this is a significant development in the history of pervasive worlds. And it shares an affinity with rhetoric and the mixture of motive balancing called for by Richard Lanham in *The Electronic Word* (Lanham 1993, 188).

In TinyMUD, someone interested in, for example, twentieth-century science fiction literature could easily create a discussion forum that consisted of several thematic spaces in which to conduct these discussions. Anyone with telnet and an Internet connection anywhere in the world could easily connect to this space inside TinyMUD and participate in the synchronous discussions or just hang out and visit, meet new people, and make friends in distant places. The attraction of TinyMUD was the social interaction that took place in the virtual spaces created by its users. Text-based pervasive life had established a toehold in the dominant dimension of "real" life.

Although TinyMUD represents a milestone in the history of online multiuser systems, its lifespan remains remarkably short. After only seven months, TinyMUD began to crumble under the weight of its own popularity. Like a frontier town that had grown too quickly without any plan or regulation, the TinyMUD world had, as Aspnes later put it, become "a bloated and poorly-managed slum overshadowed by its more youthful cousins. It was time to put the sorry bold beast out of its misery" (Aspnes 2001).

MOO

Although the original TinyMUD was gone, numerous TinyMUD clones continued to draw in more and more people, and the MUD phenomenon was just starting to gain momentum. One hacker who was totally fascinated by Aspnes's TinyMUD was Stephen White (aka Ghondahrl), who in 1990 wrote, "I've been bitten by the MUD programming bug, a most heinous disease" (White 1991). His interest in MUDs related, among other things, to ways in which they could be used for "writing multi-user interactive fiction and creating a virtual reality." White's first attempt at modifying TinyMUD to his own specifications he called TinyMUCK. In typical hacker fashion, he wrote the new system in "one sleepless weekend" using Aspnes's TinyMUD source code and building his own extensions on top of it. Although he thought of it as a "neat hack" at the time, he eventually concluded that there were several problems with it. "I started thinking

about what TinyMUD is. Okay, so it's like a virtual-reality, whose neat at-
tribute is that you can modify the VR from _inside the database itself_. No
need to have separate compilation or external control; you're actually 'in
there,' modifying the way things work. This seemed to be the antithesis of
edit-compile-run programming, whose natural interface is 'batch mode,'
rather than interactive" (White 1991). One of the ideas that White had
started thinking about was the addition of a programming language to the
MUD system. The existence of a powerful tool such as a programming language could, he surmised, make objects much more interesting and interactive and make the game world as a whole much more immersive. "Okay, so
here's a dilemma: my experiments with TinyMUCK seemed to indicate that
a programming language was needed, but this seems to violate the nature
of the VR. Hmm. Well, I talked with James Aspnes about it, and he seemed
to be in favour of a programming language. After talking with him, he convinced me that it was the way to go" (White 1991). White's second attempt
at creating a TinyMUD-type system was dubbed MOO (Multiuser Dungeon,
Object-Oriented). Around 1990, object-oriented programming was quickly
becoming the new program design paradigm in computer science, and it is
not surprising that White would tack on to this new wave spearheaded by
widely used programming languages like, for example, C++. With MOO,
White says, he "opted out of the 'one crazy weekend' approach, for the
better of the code and my own mental health" (White 1991). He spent two
months on the design and actively solicited comments and feedback in
both Usenet discussion groups and in MUDs that he frequented. MOO was
his big project, and he wanted to get it right.

   In the summer of 1990, Pavel Curtis, a research scientist at Xerox PARC
and a graduate of Cornell University, first stumbled upon MUDs. Curtis had
found out about MUDs through MUD-related news groups on Usenet and
had looked at some of the systems he could access online. He eventually
came across White's MOO system running on a machine at the University
of California at Berkeley. The MUD was called AlphaMOO, and when he
logged in, he met a person there by the name of Frand who told him about
the system and provided him with some documentation. Curtis studied the
information carefully and concluded that the MOO system showed promise and was worth a closer look. Because of his background in programming language design and implementation, he found the MOO language
that White had designed of particular interest. He says, "Stephen had actually done a reasonably tasteful language and I think that's remarkably rare
among amateurs" (Curtis 2001). He approached White and suggested that
they collaborate on further developments of the MOO system. The idea of

collaborating on programming projects was not novel to Curtis. He was at the time familiar with the Free Software Foundation and their GNU project and had even contributed some to that project in the form of bug reports and bug fixes. Also, Xerox PARC had a large code base that was freely shared among its programmers, and he had frequently made contributions to that. White, who had been working on MOO on and off for some time, readily agreed and sent Curtis a copy of the MOO source code. Curtis recalls that "it was his [White's] first large C program so it had some of the attributes you can imagine, but overall he had done a pretty good job. He had done a good job of taking code that others had written, the TinyMUD, or a variant of the TinyMUD network module, and he had brought that in" (Curtis 2001).

Curtis was different from most other MUD hackers in the sense that not only was he was a professional programmer with a PhD in Computer Science, but he also happened to work for one of the most respected research institutions in the United States, Xerox PARC. To be sure, his interest in MUD technology was driven by much of the same curiosity and fascination for clever coding so characteristic of hackers. However, because of his more extensive experience and training, he was able to look at the MOO project from a systems point of view and apply his knowledge of large complex systems to the MOO project. White had built a promising foundation on which Curtis could refine and enhance the system. As Curtis poured over his copy of the MOO code during the early fall of 1990, he would occasionally send bug reports and bug fixes back to White. "I started sending him bug reports. I had fixed my copy [MOO server], and I sent him a disk; but at some point he declared that he wasn't really doing much with it. He said something like, I am not actually preparing a release right now so you go ahead, and that's when I started sort of owning it" (Curtis 2001).

LambdaMOO

Curtis now began working on the MOO system in earnest. He had numerous ideas for enhancements and new features that he wanted to incorporate.[5] He was not only concerned with purely technical aspects of the MOO, however; he had also started to think about developing a MOO virtual world that would complete the system. Being new to MUDs, Curtis had assumed that because AlphaMOO was running on a machine at Berkeley, the people he met there were also from Berkeley. When he eventually learned that they all came from totally different places, as far flung as Australia and Israel, it came as a total surprise, and it opened his eyes to the community capabilities of MOOs (Curtis [1998] 2002). The MOO system consists of two main components. The server, which Curtis inherited from White and on which his initial work focused, is what we may call the MOO's "operating system." It handles all the low-level system tasks, such as networking, communication management within the system, and more. The other component is the MOO world itself. This is a database with information about objects in the system, how they relate to one another, how they look, who owns them, and so forth. Whereas the server is mostly transparent and invisible to the users, the database is tangible and concrete. It *is* the virtual world that people experience when they go to a MOO.

On his first explorations into the world of MUDs, Curtis had used the handle Lambda, so for his own system, the name LambdaMOO was a natural choice (Curtis [1998] 2002). By the end of October 1990, Curtis felt that LambdaMOO had progressed to a point where he could start sharing it with other people, so on Halloween he invited two of the people he had met in AlphaMOO to visit the newly established LambdaMOO. These two people were Tim Allen, aka Gemba, and Gary_Severn. They would both play significant roles in the early collaborative developments of LambdaMOO. In Curtis's own words, that particular evening in 1990 came to represent the "first drops of water in what later became the rushing river of LambdaMOO" (Curtis [1998] 2002, 30).

In the weeks and months that followed, the three of them spent most of their free time working on LambdaMOO. Curtis fondly recalls:

During the earliest days of LambdaMOO, through the beginning of 1991, everything was fascinating every day. The technical work was especially so as Gary, Gemba, and I tried to build the core libraries of MOO programming, as I furiously wrote new functionality into the MOO server and then furiously wrote new MOO commands that took advantage of it. I pounded the keyboard for hours at a stretch trying to write a comprehensive reference manual for this language and system. (Curtis [1998] 2002, 30)

The core libraries of MOO programming that Curtis refers to above were the Application Program Interface (API), a new addition that he had brought into the MOO system. In White's original MOO server, functions and procedures used by the programming language were hard coded directly into the server software as built-in functions. The downside of this was that only people with access to the server code could add new programming functionality to the system. Curtis wanted LambdaMOO to promote programming collaboration and code sharing, so he came up with a system of APIs located inside the database itself. These APIs were called Utility Packages, and they functioned as repositories for often-used utility-type MOO programs. With the new API system, programmers could now do all their coding inside the virtual world of LambdaMOO. Curtis says, "The collaborative feel of it was fascinating as we worked closely together from our separate offices thousands of miles apart" (Curtis [1998] 2002, 30).

During the early days of LambdaMOO, those who visited came mostly on invitation from Curtis himself. As it happened, the AlphaMOO at Berkeley had by this time been shut down, and soon people from there, among them Frand, the programmer who had given Curtis his first introduction to MOO, began migrating over to LambdaMOO. A few of Curtis's coworkers at PARC also became interested in the new system, and little by little LambdaMOO began to grow into a small community.

Judy Anderson, aka Yduj, a legendary LambdaMOO hacker and wizard, recalls her first visit to LambdaMOO: "This was in early November of 1990. So, I signed on to this thing and started wandering around in it and I said; 'Oh, it's a MUD!' He [Curtis] was all disappointed because I had seen one before. I was walking around but he hadn't told me it was the house yet, so it was kind of fun because there I was sitting in the house on some computer walking around in the LambdaMOO house, and eventually I said, 'Wait! This is his house'" (Anderson 2001). Curtis had built the LambdaMOO world around the physical layout of his own house. In keeping with the informal tradition of MUDs, visitors to LambdaMOO would enter the virtual world though a dark coat closet and suddenly find themselves in the middle of Curtis's living room. Doorways led off to other parts of the mansion and the surrounding grounds. The textual descriptions of the various locations were descriptive and true to life, and visitors really felt that they were present in Curtis's house without actually being there physically. In "fact," they were pervasively real *and* present.

The Living Room
It is very bright, open, and airy here, with large plate-glass windows looking southward over the pool to the gardens beyond. On the north wall, there is a rough stonework fireplace. The east and west walls are almost completely covered with large, well-stocked bookcases. An exit in the northwest corner leads to the kitchen and, in a more northerly direction, to the entrance hall. The door into the coat closet is at the north end of the east wall, and at the south end is a sliding glass door leading out onto a wooden deck. There are two sets of couches, one clustered around the fireplace and one with a view out the windows.

You see Welcome Poster, a fireplace, the living room couch, Cockatoo, Helpful Person Finder, lag meter, a map of LambdaHouse, and The Birthday Machine here. Dott (dozing), Jethromeo, Mack-the-Knife (out on his feet), Loki (passed out on the floor), Bear(tm) (distracted), Neeners (out on her feet), GumNut (dozing), Goat, habibi (navel-gazing), Pink_Guest, Subwoofer (dozing), Ultraviolet_Guest, and Beige_Guest are here. (LambdaMOO 2011)

Whether it was the welcoming atmosphere or the exciting technical developments that went on there, LambdaMOO soon became a regular hangout for a growing number of outsiders, and with them came new challenges. Curtis recalls, "I used to personally welcome each and every new user for the first few months. . . . It was neat, all these people from around the country and, as time went on, from around the world, coming to this program, this server, this place that I had created; they came, many of them stayed, and many of those helped make the place even better. It was magical" (Curtis [1998] 2002, 31).

Whereas TinyMUD had been an experimental sprawl where pretty much anything would pass muster, LambdaMOO was from the very beginning set on a different path. Curtis had realized that he would need help from other people, not only in regard to the technical programming projects but, as would become abundantly clear later, also with the day-to-day operation of the MOO. To aid him, he therefore invited a few of his most trusted online friends to join in a "wizard team." MOO administrators are called wizards because they are the most powerful players in the virtual world. In MUDs, the title wizard was used to denote the highest attainable player class and was usually only bestowed upon the most dedicated and experienced players. In a MOO, however, a wizard is typically someone who has more in common with a computer systems administrator. Yudj, who had been a close friend and housemate of Curtis in the 1980s and who had been invited to join the wizard team right from the beginning, explains:

Mostly I was there to get people out of trouble and to help Pavel build up the infrastructure. There was a lot of stuff that we didn't have yet that we have now, stuff that needs wizard permissions in order to run. But there weren't really any duties, I was just logged on a lot and I was spending a lot of time logged on to the MUD rather than working which was a personal problem for me, but LambdaMOO benefited from it. So I just hung out at the MUD a lot and when there was some trouble I tried to help out. I guess back then we had the "Wizards Grant Quota" system, so if people wanted more quota, I helped evaluate whether they should get it and that kind of stuff. (Anderson 2001)

Unlike many other MUD operators at the time, the LambdaMOO wizards were mostly adults. Most of them were also professional programmers rather than amateur hackers, and this gave the MOO a distinct flavor that set it apart from other MUDs. LambdaMOO and its wizards would soon enough experience its share of the social and technical problems that had plagued TinyMUD and other early online communities, but in those early days the MOO was a blissful environment where, as Curtis later put it, "everything was fascinating every day" (Curtis [1998] 2002, 30).

Throughout 1991, Curtis and his collaborators built most of the core technology that LambdaMOO has been based on ever since. All the technical development, except work on the server, which was mainly done by Curtis himself, took place inside the LambdaMOO world. It did not follow any set plan or specification. Mostly people would code things that they needed to accomplish some larger project or things that they just thought would be fun or interesting to do. Programming had been perhaps the most powerful new feature that White had conceived of, and in LambdaMOO it was used to its fullest. Yduj says, "The beauty of LambdaMOO is that the extensions, the building, the richness comes from the programming, so we wanted to encourage people to program. So, pretty much if you wanted a programmer bit you could have it" (Anderson 2001). Because of this rich and creative programming activity, LambdaMOO could soon boast a wide variety of interesting objects, puzzles, and components.

LambdaMOO's first puzzle, for instance, was written by Yduj herself. She had designed the master bedroom and adjoining rooms of the LambdaMOO mansion; to make it more interesting, she programmed a burglar alarm that would be triggered whenever someone entered. The puzzle would challenge the player to find out how to turn the alarm off. Another of Yduj's puzzles, one that I came to experience firsthand on one of my early adventures into LambdaMOO, was a paper bag that, once you entered it, would not let you out until you had written a little program that could disable the bag's locking mechanism. Inside the paper bag, there were clues as to how this escape program might work, but it took several attempts to actually get it to open the bag so you could get back out.

Paper Bag
Welcome to the Paper Bag puzzle! Hope you're up to it!

A rumpled brown paper bag with the words "Can you program your way out of a paper bag?" neatly typeset on the side.

Hyperpelosity (asleep) is here. (LambdaMOO Object #6231 2011)

The Paper Bag puzzle (Object #6231) was not only fun and challenging, but it required you to learn some MOO programming in the process. When asked how she came up with the idea of the infamous paper bag, Yduj says:

When I make an error [in programming], I often say, "I can't program my way out of a paper bag" as some sort of a self-deprecation way of saying that I made a boo-boo. So, I had this sort of vision that "Look! I have a paper bag that you can program your way out of." So that phrase was the impetus for the creation of that. People are always trying to make little traps and stuff for others, especially to trap guests or their enemies or whatever, anyway, so I made this trap, right, but it had hints and clues as to how to get out. When you try to exit, a verb gets called on your object and it drags you back, that's the mechanism that it uses. It evaluates how it was called and if it was called by a verb that you wrote then it lets you out, if it was called by a verb that you didn't write, like @move for example, then it drags you back. It gives you ten tries or something so if you keep trying it will let you out. (Anderson 2001)

Another example of early creative programming projects in LambdaMOO was the role-playing system. Unlike most MUDs, MOO did not have any role-playing capabilities, so it was not a game in the traditional sense. A typical MUD command such as *kill*, or fantasy player classes such as elves, dwarves, and orcs, for instance, did not even exist in MOO. Although one might play a role-playing game without these features, the lack of a score system as well as a good nonplayer character (NPC) control system did not really allow for proper role-playing. Gemba and Gary_Severn, who were both dedicated role players, made it, therefore, their first project in LambdaMOO to design and implement a proper role-playing system (Anderson 2001). The fact that they could even accomplish a task of such magnitude by using only the MOO language and the programming tools inside the LambdaMOO environment attests to the strengths and versatility of LambdaMOO as a development environment.

In time, many other components would be built by either the wizards or other programmers in the MOO. The in-MOO mail and programming editors, for example, nicely illustrate the collaborative and user-driven evolution of MOO development. Early on, Curtis had written a simple mail editor that people could use to send electronic mail to one another inside LambdaMOO. There was at the time, however, no programming or "verb" editor, and this made programming quite difficult for people using client programs such as telnet without cut-and-paste capabilities. If they wanted to write a MOO program, they basically had to type in each and every line of their code, and if the compiler produced an error, they had to fix it and retype the program again and again until their code compiled. Needless to say, this was an arduous process that could dishearten all but the most dedicated hacker. Yduj decided to do something about this, so she set about to write a verb editor. She says, "I felt so bad for them because they had to enter their whole verb again each time they wanted to make a little change, and I was like, 'Oh my God I can't stand this!' so I wrote simpler version of the mail editor" (Anderson 2001).

Yduj's editor was line-based, meaning it would accept input one line at a time just like the default UNIX text editor, vi. Programmers could now open and edit code in the MOO directly. Shortly after she finished the verb editor, another player, Roger, told her he had some ideas for improvements. He

had observed that the mail editor and the verb editor performed basically
the same function—namely, to allow people to enter and edit text. The fact
that one had to do with mail and the other with programming was irrel-
evant. In an object-oriented system like MOO, abstraction is fundamental.
Because both editors performed almost, but not quite, the same function,
he surmised, one should be able to combine them. In short, Roger's idea
was to build a generic editor that would contain all the code for general
editing and then build subclasses with code specific to mailing and verb
programming. Roger was at the time in the middle of doing his dissertation,
but the MOO programming project must have been much more appealing
because over the next few weeks he designed and implemented a new generic editor system that replaced both the mail and verb editors. "It seems
that the voices of work avoidance tend to get LambdaMOO having richer
stuff. I sort of feel bad that we're kind of a parasites site in that way, but
oh well! Anyway, so he wrote the generic editor improving the verb editor
that I had written . . . replaced it and the mail editor that Pavel had written
with his new generic editor stuff. That was, I would say in the summer of
91" (Anderson 2001).

Another project that Yduj and Roger worked on illustrates what real-time
collaboration on programming in the MOO was like. The project was the
MOO's player name database. She explains:

We had two windows open, we had our non-wizard characters and they were somewhere together talking and we had our wizard characters and they were in private
rooms editing. I would say, "I wanna do this to this verb, and he'd say "Okay, it's
yours," and would work on it, because there is no locking, right, and if we are both
editing the same verb, whoever writes it second wins so we had to actually say "I'm
going to edit this verb," "Okay I'm done now" so we would not step on each other's
toes. That was kind of fun. (Anderson 2001)

This type of close real-time collaboration didn't happen as often as one
might think, though. Most of the time, collaborative projects tended to
follow the hacker tradition where someone would write a piece of code
and then later someone else would pick it up and improve or extend it in
some way.

One reason for this must be attributed to the MOO's permission system,
which only allows the owner of an object to edit it. In any multiuser system, an access control mechanism needs to be in place to ensure that only
those with the proper permissions can read or modify files. In MOO, only
the owner of an object has permission to edit it, so if two or more people
wanted to collaborate on a programming project, they could not easily edit
verbs and properties on the same object without juggling ownership of the

object between them. The MOO permission system had a *write-flag*, which, when set, allowed anyone to edit an object, but the potential security risks involved in this made it impractical and more or less useless for collaborative purposes. The permission control system in MOO does not apply to wizards, which explains how Yduj and Roger were able to collaborate in real time on the LambdaMOO player database.

Code Community

As LambdaMOO's code base grew, so did its user community. After a particularly clever April Fools' Day hack in 1992, in which the wizard team had pulled a prank on Curtis by simulating a system-wide fire and furthermore appeared to be handing out wizard privileges to everyone so they could help clean up the place, the popular press became interested in LambdaMOO. From that point on, the influx of new users would soon number in the thousands, and with them came new challenges of a sociotechnical nature that Curtis and his hackers had not foreseen. One such problem arose from the way the character request system was set up. In the early days, character accounts could be created automatically by anyone, and there was no limit on how many accounts a person could have. The problem with this was that troublemakers could not really be banished or shut out from the MOO because they could easily create another character for themselves and continue making trouble. To deal with this problem, the wizards implemented a character application and registration system where users would be identified by their email address. The development of the player registration database mentioned above was part of this effort. Another issue that became more and more of a problem was intentional or unintentional "theft." A MOO object that is not locked can be picked up by anyone, and more often than not, the person who picked it up would not return the object to its original location. After Frand complained to him about this, Curtis wrote a brief statement called "Help Manners," in which he outlined what he considered to be appropriate behavior in LambdaMOO. This document was for a long time "the only written 'law' that LambdaMOO had" (Curtis [1998] 2002, 33). For the wizards, the law turned out to be a double-edged sword because, once it existed, someone had to sit in judgment, apply the law, and settle conflicts that arose when players broke the law. That someone could only come from the wizards' own ranks, and even if they shared the responsibility, it soon added a considerable amount of work to their burdens. After some time with growing tensions within the wizard team, Curtis decided that the wizards, who in his opinion were hackers and not social arbiters, should no longer perform these duties. In a position statement named "LambdaMOO Takes Another Direction" (LTAND), he outlined a new policy where the wizards would no longer interfere with social life of the LambdaMOO community. He says, "It was so simple in my mind: there was a clear distinction between social and technical, between policy and maintenance, between politics and engineering. We wizards would become technicians and leave the moral, political and social rudder to 'the people.'. . . In hindsight, I forced a transition in LambdaMOO government, from wizardocracy to anarchy" (Curtis [1998] 2002, 38). What Curtis failed to recognize, of course, was that there is no clear distinction between the social and the technical, the real and virtual, that they are in fact tightly interwoven in a *pervasive* complex mesh that cannot be cleanly disentangled. LambdaMOO would pay for this oversight. Once central control of the community had been disbanded, social conflicts soon reached new heights that culminated with the infamous "Rape in Cyberspace" affair chronicled by Julian Dibble in the *Village Voice* in 1993 (Dibbell 1993).

The whole affair started when a character named Mr. Bungle created a remote-controlled puppet and used it to verbally abuse other players. The abuse, which had clear sexual overtones, hence the reference to rape, caused a public outcry in the LambdaMOO community, and people started calling for the removal of the Mr. Bungle character. Curtis was away on a business trip when all this happened, and in order to contain the situation, another wizard took it upon himself to disable Mr. Bungle's account. This reaction, however, fueled another public outcry of even bigger proportions; the wizards had promised to stay out of social conflicts, and now they had broken that promise. The incident has been described and analyzed many places (Vitanza [1998] 2002), so I won't go into further details here; but it had a profound bearing on the sociotechnical developments that followed. The state of anarchy in which the cyber rape incident occurred had to be brought to an end. Curtis's problem was how to do it without resorting to what he called the "wizardocracy" of the past. The solution that he chose was a form of direct democracy using a petitions and ballots system. Curtis explains, "Once again . . . I forced a governmental transition on the MOO; we would, I declared, move from anarchy to democracy. . . . It was simple in outline: any LambdaMOO citizen could create a petition proposing that the wizards take some action; if it got enough signatures, it became a public ballot measure that passed on a two-thirds majority vote" (Curtis [1998] 2002, 39). The technical infrastructure for the new democratic system that the wizards eventually developed is a striking example of the way technological solutions arise out of nontechnical challenges and how they in turn are used to support social and political decisions and processes.[6] Through the experiment with direct democracy, the LambdaMOO community was able to pass several successful measures, but, according to Curtis, overall it failed to live up to expectations. He says, "It seems to me now that the voting population could never agree on any measures of real substance. . . . On LambdaMOO, this incapacity engendered a profound stagnation; true progress is impossible to achieve in the petition system" (Curtis [1998] 2002, 40).

By 1996, social tensions and conflicts again reached the breaking point. Curtis explains, "The wizards have been at every turn forced to make social decisions. Every time we made one, it seemed, someone took offense, someone believed that we had done wrong, someone accused us of ulterior motives. . . . The result was a constant stream of messages to the wizards full of anger, suspicion, and of stress" (Curtis [1998] 2002, 41). Once again, Curtis was compelled to step forward and change the course of events, and together with the other wizards, he drafted a third pivotal policy statement that was made public to the LambdaMOO community on May 16, 1996. In it, he says, "We formally reputed my earlier theory of a social/technical dichotomy; we explained how impossible that fiction was and declared our intent to cease apologizing for our failures to make it reality. It was, in a way, a wizardly coup d'etat; out with the old order, in with the new" (Curtis [1998] 2002, 41). Throughout the entire affair of social tumults in LambdaMOO, the hackers had learned an important lesson—technology is inherently a social affair.

Sharing the Code

From the time Curtis first started hacking on the MOO server, it had been his intention to give it back to the MUD community. The source code had originally come from White, so his employer, Xerox PARC, he says, was not able to place any intellectual property restrictions on it even if it had wanted to. This enabled Curtis to distribute his modifications freely. The first release of the LambdaMOO server, as Curtis now called it, coincided with the public opening of LambdaMOO itself in 1990.

From the beginning my intent was to give it back. In fact, as soon as Stephen sort of bowed out I started hacking on the code in earnest, to fix bugs and improve the quality of things and write documentation. LambdaMOO the server and LambdaMOO the community were announced publicly on the same day and that had been the plan the whole way along. I set certain goals for cleaning up the server and its language early on, and one of the goals was that I wanted a complete manual for the language and its libraries and that there were no built-in commands unless it was absolutely necessary. (Curtis 2001)

Along with the server, Curtis also distributed what he called a Minimal MOO database that people could use to build their own MOOs. The Minimal database was an extraction of the AlphaMOO core by Gemba and Gary_ Severn. It defined the first ten or fifteen objects in the database and was in fact what Curtis himself had used when he built the original LambdaMOO database. The Minimal database had most of the core functionality necessary to run a MOO, but it did not have any of the added libraries and features that were being built in LambdaMOO proper. When the decision eventually was made to include the more feature-rich core of LambdaMOO with the server distribution, it did not come at anyone's request. "It was the natural thing to do," says Curtis (Curtis 2001). With a powerful, streamlined server and a rich user-programmable core, MOO was now among the most potent development environments in the MUD world. Many of the more technically savvy users of LambdaMOO soon began to look with interest on the Lambda distribution as a jumping-off point for building their own MOO systems, and in time so would many others. The LambdaMOO server development was almost exclusively handled by Curtis. He did have a few summer interns at PARC who helped him out on certain things, but mostly he wanted to be in control of the development. LambdaMOO had become quite a prestigious project. It had from the very beginning been his pet project, so of course he cared a great deal about it for that reason. However, as MOO started to become popular and more and more people downloaded and looked at the code, it became increasingly important that the code met more rigorous standards for pedagogical clarity, efficiency, and elegance. Curtis says, "I was certainly writing code for an audience both in the sense that I knew there were lots of people who were downloading the server and compiling it and running it, but also in the sense that, and I made a very strong point of this to the summer interns that I got, that the code we were writing was going to be read by other people and needed to be of pedagogical quality" (Curtis 2001). The fact that other people would be reading his code and not just using the binary server program led to a heightened sense of self-awareness that ultimately produced a better and more durable product. Being a professional programmer, Curtis tended to be quite strict in matters of quality of code in general, but, he says, "I would not have been quite as strict if I had not been going through an audience. There was also a strong sense that these programs were hard to understand. I knew that they were not that complicated and I wanted them to be understandable, so I had almost a pedagogical purpose in mind" (Curtis 2001).

By 1993, his work on the LambdaMOO server had led to a new in-house project at PARC named Jupiter. The Jupiter project was based on the LambdaMOO server and had a graphical user interface and live audio and video capabilities. It had grown out of the experiences with LambdaMOO and was targeted at professional online collaboration. Work on the Jupiter project had revealed a number of shortcomings in the LambdaMOO system. One of them was the lack of a proper system for error handling. As he worked on Jupiter, Curtis would make notes of the fixes and new features that he implemented, and in time he would roll many of them back into the LambdaMOO server. Almost none of these new changes came about as a result of pressure from the MOO programmer community. Curtis says, "Nobody outside of PARC was knocking down my door saying we need error handling and we need it more structured than the d-bit" (Curtis 2001).

Early on, Curtis had set up a mailing list for developers called MOO Cows. The list was intended to function as channel of communication between Curtis, the developer, and the growing community of MOO programmers and administrators. According to Curtis, the list failed to generate any substantial contributions of code to the server development effort, but this, he admits, may partly have been his own doing. He explains, "I would occasionally get server patches, or people pointing out a bug and maybe not necessarily giving me the patch. I may very well have projected a 'this is my server, I'm the one who is qualified to do this' etc. etc.', which may have encouraged people to just tell me about problems and not give me solutions" (Curtis 2001).

By 1996, Curtis was looking to end his involvement with LambdaMOO. The social tumults in the LambdaMOO community had taken its toll, but, more than that, after six years of dedicated MOO development, he felt it was time for him to move on. The development of the LambdaCore database distribution took a different and more collaborative direction. Although Curtis was the arch-wizard of LambdaMOO, his influence did not have nearly the same effect as it had on the server development. To be sure, the wizards did develop many of the core tools and features, but other programmers in the LambdaMOO community also contributed to it. Curtis explains:

On the database side people brought it [code] in themselves, and the key people who were innovating were the Jay's House MOO folks, and Judy [Yduj] was one of those. She was a wizard at LambdaMOO so when something was developed over there it got brought in directly, but by and large people were doing it themselves inside the MOO. There would occasionally be a single verb wizzified and we would go and look at it and try to understand what it was trying to do. Then people did things like inter-MOO portals and all sorts of things once open network connections were available and mostly they were just doing those things inside the MOO and sometimes asked us to take them over. So I think it was really quite different from the usual open source thing. (Curtis 2001)

Over time, the LambdaMOO core became a bricolage of code collaboratively authored by a large number of programmers. Some contributed large system components such as the editors mentioned above, whereas others contributed smaller programs or improvements on existing code. Sometimes the programmers would team up to implement new ideas, but most of the time they would work alone. Communication between them occurred in either real time in the MOO or via the MOO mailing list system. Yduj says, "It was a very subtle kind of collaboration because there wasn't a hierarchy of people who decided what to do. The project was always sort of free-floating" (Anderson 2001). There was no set release schedule for when new versions of the LambdaCore would come out. It would simply happen whenever one of the wizards decided that it was time. Yduj, for example, didn't have any plans one Christmas, so she decided it would be a good time to work on a core release. She says, "I would make the announcement and then there would be a frenzy of work for the next month while people added stuff that they wanted to go in the core" (Anderson 2001). Whenever a piece of code was put in the core, ownership of it was transferred to one of two special characters, Hacker or Wizard, and there would typically be no trace left of who was the original programmer. Occasionally a programmer would include her name in a comment in the code, but in most cases programmers who contributed code to the LambdaCore remained anonymous to the outside world. For people who used LambdaCore to build new MOOs, the core appeared to be one large collectively owned code base.

One important legacy of LambdaMOO is the academic and educational MOO. In 1992, Amy Bruckman, a graduate student at MIT, started MediaMOO as an online meeting place for media researchers. MediaMOO became in effect the birthplace for a whole new direction in the evolution and use of MUD technology. By 1995, the utilization of MOO technology for professional and educational purposes was taken up by academics in many different fields. In the next chapter, I will look at how this intervention played out as it pertained to educational MOOs, LinguaMOO, and the enCore Open Source Project that followed from it.

5   Intervention

So how does this maneuver address our primary problem, the dissociation of experience and reflection? Most obviously, by expanding the ambit of writing to include
not just the secondary creativity of play, but also the primary production tasks of
programming, and by extension, media design. In fact, by situating the letter within
the cybernetic process or feedback loop, this extended literacy directly connects
writing with play. I mean not simply that it reveals the control structures that gov-
ern our experience of play, but that those structures *themselves become objects of play*.
—Stuart Moulthrop, "After the Last Generation"

The MUD was a unique hacker technology, one that did not exist prior to
being invented by Richard Bartle and Roy Trubshaw in 1979, and one that
could not have existed if it were not for the evolutionary hacker development model. Clearly, a *venture* (ad/venture) had become an *invention*, and
my contributions became an *intervention*. It all began because Bartle and
Trubshaw decided they wanted to play fantasy games in a multiuser online environment. No one had told them that MUD would be a neat idea.
They simply invented the concept because it was an interesting challenge
that could produce something that would be fun to play with. When the
MUD phenomenon caught on, others such as Alan Cox became interested
in how it could be modified and expanded, and because the MUD source
code was not available due to commercial restrictions, he and his hacker
friends developed their own version of MUD. When the AberMUD source
code was eventually released, anyone who was interested could look at it
and see for themselves how a MUD worked. This spurred a flurry of activity in the MUD community, and new versions of MUD sporting funny and
imaginative names, such as TinyMUD, LPmud, TinyMUCK, FurryMUCK,
DikuMUD, MUSH, MUSE, and MOO, appeared in numbers. Many of these
systems had the basic gaming functionality of the original MUD, but they
were also individually different. In the late 1980s and early 1990s, new

MUD installations such as the ones mentioned here were one-of-a-kind systems. They were unique because of the extensive system-level modifications made by the hackers who established them. With LambdaMOO and the LambdaCore distribution in the 1990s, that uniqueness gave way to a more uniform evolution. The LambdaCore distribution provided a feature-rich platform that made system-level hacking less compelling; with the addition of a simple but powerful programming language, the focus of MOO development shifted toward community building. Other branches of the MUD technology tree evolved in a similar fashion. The LPmud system, for example, also had a programming language named LPC (after its inventor Lars Pensjø) and a core database called "mudlib" that ensured consistency and compatibility among the many LPmuds built during the 1990s.

The hacker development model depends on new programmers stepping up to take over when the old programmers move on. Thus, while some branches of the MUD technology sprawl eventually withered and died because no one took an interest in furthering them, others, such as MOO, blossomed and advanced the technology. There was no single owner or entity that determined its history. MUD technology was owned collectively and developed collaboratively by the community of people who used it.

Intervention: The Educational Use of MOO

The collaborative software development methodologies that I am tracing formed the framework for the enCore Open Source project that is the focus of this chapter. As I have shown in previous case studies of BSD and GNU/Linux, the open source model has yielded some remarkable results for hackers and programmers in what we might call the traditional areas of software engineering. Through the enCore project, I wanted to see whether this model could also be successfully applied to programming and development efforts situated in the humanities.

The next few sections of this chapter focus on the academization of MOO technology in the early 1990s and go on to discuss the notion of the educational MOO as it materialized from the mid-1990s onward. As an example of one such educational MOO, I will focus on the LinguaMOO project, which was begun by Cynthia Haynes and myself in January 1995. Based on experiences from the LinguaMOO project, in 1997 we began the new project called High Wired enCore. The rationale for this project was to spread the use of MOO technology in education through traditional book publishing efforts as well as the distribution of a MOO software package called enCore. The main portion of this section is devoted to a discussion of enCore and the Xpress Graphical User Interface that I later developed under the umbrella of an open source project. The chapter concludes with some thoughts on results from this project and the open source development methodologies that I used.

LambdaMOO's growing popularity in the early 1990s attracted all sorts of people to the online community. Some came because they wanted a change of pace from the typical adventure role-playing world of MUDs. Others came and stayed because they enjoyed socializing with folks online. Yet others stopped by simply because they were curious to see what synchronous online communities were all about. While most users were content simply to avail themselves of the services provided by Pavel Curtis and the LambdaMOO staff, others discovered that MOO was a powerful community-building technology waiting to be explored. One of those who saw a potential in MOO technology was Amy Bruckman, a graduate student of MIT's Media Lab, who in October 1992 founded the online community MediaMOO. At the time, Bruckman noted that "most MUDs are populated by undergraduates who should be doing their homework. I thought it would be interesting instead to bring together a group of people with a shared intellectual interest: the study of media. Ideally, MediaMOO should be like an endless reception for a conference on media studies" (Bruckman [1998] 2002, 17).

The virtual place that Bruckman created became, in effect, the birthplace for much of the academic research and professional activities related to MOO technology in the 1990s. At its most popular (1995), MediaMOO had more than one thousand members from thirty-nine countries, with several academic groups such as the Techno-Rhetoricians, the Netoric Project, and Tuesday Café, all of which utilized MediaMOO for online meetings and other professionals.

In 1993, not long after Bruckman founded MediaMOO, Gustavo Glusman, a student of the Weizmann Institute of Science in Israel, founded another early academic MOO called BioMOO. Just as MediaMOO was designed as an online meeting place for media researchers, BioMOO was designed as a virtual meeting place for biologists. According to BioMOO's purpose statement, which echoed the one Bruckman had written for MediaMOO, "BioMOO is a *professional community* of Biology researchers. It is a place to come meet colleagues in Biology studies and related fields and brainstorm, to hold colloquia and conferences, to explore the serious side of this new medium" (Glusman 1996). Over the years, BioMOO played host to a number of academic groups within biology and bioinformatics. The Ecology and

Evolution Journal Club, the Neuroscience Journal Club, and other groups used the space for online meetings in the mid-1990s.

Although MediaMOO and BioMOO were not the only academic MOOs in the early 1990s, they are both good examples of the professionally oriented spaces that people sought to create at the time. In the minds of most people, MOOs and MUDs in general were games and not something suited for serious academic purposes. The creators of these first-generation academic MOO spaces, therefore, sought to legitimize the use of the technology by focusing strictly on traditional professional activities such as conferencing and networking. Another early MOO, AstroVR, was designed for astrophysicists. Such was the nature of the discipline-oriented first generation of academic MOOs. Special purpose statements were drawn up to emphasize the professional nature of the systems, and anonymity, a fundamental feature of role-playing games and social-interaction-oriented MUDs, was abolished in favor of responsibility, accountability, collaboration, and networking among the members.

While LambdaMOO had always had an open-door policy, where anyone could become a member, the early academic MOOs adopted more stringent entry requirements. Only those who in some way could claim a connection to the mission and purpose of the MOO were eligible to join. In the case of MediaMOO, Bruckman explains that she was "loose on the definition of media—writing teachers, computer network administrators, and librarians are all working with forms of media—but strict on the definition of research" (Bruckman [1998] 2002, 19). Michael Day, one of the MediaMOO veterans, explains, "MediaMOO always has had a strict character application policy. When you do @request name for email, you have to answer a series of questions about your research interests, and at its peak, a team of 5 reviewers would review the applications to let Amy, former head janitor (as wizards on MediaMOO have always been called) know whether to accept someone or not" (Day 2003).

Strict admission policies notwithstanding, MediaMOO was a popular place in the years between 1993 and 1997. Some of the people who found their way to Bruckman's digital world were not content just using the technology for themselves. They wanted to share it with their students to see how such online spaces could help enhance teaching and learning. In MediaMOO, however, there was little or no room for this type of activity. One reason might have been that MediaMOO was so popular and attracted so many users that there was simply no additional bandwidth to accommodate large classes of students. Another reason, which seems to resonate well with MediaMOO's emphasis on professionalism, might have been that large groups of potentially unruly undergraduate students would not be conducive to the serious academic community that Bruckman wished to foster. Starting around 1994, therefore, a few members of MediaMOO began setting up their own academic MOOs specifically for educational use. The LambdaMOO source code was readily available online, and with some knowledge of MOO and Unix systems, it was not too difficult to get started. One of the first new educational MOOs was CollegeTown, built by Professor Ken Schweller of Buena Vista University in Storm Lake, Iowa. Schweller had been a LambdaMOO regular since the early days and also one of MediaMOO's first and most active members. CollegeTown MOO was modeled after a traditional college campus with academic buildings, lecture halls, and office spaces for faculty situated around the virtual commons. In the small but growing world of educational MOOs, CollegeTown MOO was known for its consistent use of detailed ASCII graphics to represent the spatial organization of the digital space. For many students, and especially teachers in the mid-1990s, the text-based virtual reality of MUDs was something quite foreign and unsettling. A simple two-dimensional ASCII representation of spatial layouts, therefore, went a long way toward visualizing the geography of the textual world. A more detailed discussion of various aspects of spatial representation and layout in MOO design will follow later in this chapter. CollegeTown was only one of many new academic MOOs that sprang up during the mid-1990s. MediaMOO had inspired most of them, but they also had another thing in common. Most of them were designed for educational use. In the next section, I discuss the creation of one of the new generation of educational MOOs.

LinguaMOO

LinguaMOO was started by me and Cynthia Haynes at the University of Texas at Dallas (UTD) in January 1995. At the time, Haynes was an assistant professor there, while I was working for a science policy research institute in Oslo, Norway. When we first started the LinguaMOO project, we had two main research objectives in mind. First, we wanted to see whether a technology that had been developed primarily for the purposes of gaming and social interaction could also prove to be a viable and interesting environment for teaching online. Second, we wanted to explore the potential of MOO as a collaborative online research environment. As we set out to design and build LinguaMOO, therefore, we had a set of key design objectives in mind. Specifically, we wanted to create a new type of learning environment that would facilitate collaboration, encourage communication, stimulate student interest in reading and writing, transcend geographical and cultural barriers, be a fun and creative place to work and socialize, and, last, provide a space in which to conduct as well as present collaborative research and writing.

Collaboration in real time in a virtual world was something of a novelty at the time, and every day it seemed to provide new opportunities for electrate learning and heuretic invention. Working out of her home in Fort Worth, Texas, Haynes drew up plans for the various facilities we wanted the MOO to accommodate, and she secured a space for the project on one of UTD's Internet servers. From my office in Oslo, I downloaded and installed the LambdaMOO distribution on the UTD server. Once everything was up and running, we could both log in from our different locations and begin the task of designing the first few public spaces in the new MOO. Nowadays this kind of online real-time collaboration is becoming more commonplace, but back then we were both amazed at how well MOO technology facilitated both invention and development. It appeared that LinguaMOO was yielding some interesting and productive results even as it was being built.

Before we started building the MOO, we went out to see what other people were doing. Besides MediaMOO, BioMOO, CollegeTown, and a few others, there weren't many educational MOOs in existence at that time; so we gathered what inspiration we found and added our own ideas about what we thought an online learning space should look like. In our original design of LinguaMOO, we wanted to situate the learning environment within the ancient abbey of Umberto Eco's novel *The Name of the Rose* (Eco [1980] 1983). We thought the ancient pastoral setting of a medieval abbey would provide an interesting juxtaposition to the modern-day technology used to implement it. Also, by situating the MOO within the framework of a novel, we hoped to foster the notion of writing as building blocks of community. Third, the dark, brooding, almost gothic atmosphere of Eco's novel provided the kind of thrill and excitement that we hoped would stimulate our users to be creative in the design of their own spaces within the MOO. Choosing the ancient abbey as our architectural metaphor allowed for a star-shaped layout with a central hub. "The Courtyard" and the various main areas of the MOO, such as the teaching and research areas (The Library), the administrative offices (Lingua House), and the player quarters (The ComMOOnity), were directly connected to it. The spatial orientation provided by such concepts as rooms and locations, exits and entrances, objects and players reinforces the sense of space, place, and time in which we wanted to situate the online learning experience. Because these are concepts that we all know well from the outside world, we hoped they would ease the transition from the physical to the digital learning environment by giving students known concepts and cues with which to navigate, negotiate, and domesticate the space.

During the late winter of 1995, we spent a great deal of time online designing and redesigning the public spaces of LinguaMOO. This included creative work such as building and writing descriptions and ASCII maps for rooms and other objects, but also technical work such as bringing in objects and features from other MOOs and making various modifications and additions to the MOO core database. One of the first tasks we tackled in this respect was to remove as much evidence of the system's gaming roots as we possibly could. For example, we replaced the keywords *player* and *wizard* with *user* and *administrator*. The original words were later reinstated, but in the beginning we felt that it was important to create a professional-looking system that would garner the support of faculty members and university administrators.

Although we did most of the early design work ourselves, we did have outside help on special projects, the most important of which included a simple World Wide Web interface originally written for CollegeTownMOO by Mark Blanchard, as well as an inter-MOO communications network by Gustavo Glusman of BioMOO. By late March, we felt that the Lingua system was ready to receive its first users. The grand opening ceremony was April 4, 1995, and we celebrated the big day with virtual champagne and fireworks. Because neither of us had much prior experience with software development and user support, the first couple of months after the opening brought new lessons every day. Among the first things we learned was that, in a creative environment such as the MOO, it is almost impossible to steer and control the evolutionary direction of the space. Enterprising users soon added their own areas to the MOO, which had totally different themes than the one we had envisioned. Hence, over time, the evolution of the LinguaMOO environment came to resemble a typical urban sprawl rather than the planned, linear design of a software program.

We also learned early on that the users were in fact our most important assets. Not only were they instrumental in helping us find and fix bugs and other malfunctions, but also many of them became important sources of inspiration with regard to ideas for enhancements and new features. A case in point is Brian Clements (also at that time with UTD), who, besides Haynes, was one of the first teachers to bring students into LinguaMOO. After he had used the system for a couple of weeks, he came to us one day and asked whether there was a way to simultaneously monitor and record student activity in multiple rooms. He had already attempted to use the basic recorder object that we had brought in from another MOO but had found it lacking in several respects. We asked him to give us a specification of the features that he wanted, and with this in hand we were able to develop a new system that became known as the LinguaMOO Recording and Intercom System. Another example of user-driven MOO development is the Moderated Room that we developed for Dene Grigar's doctoral defense, the online portion of which was held in LinguaMOO on July 25, 1995 (Grigar and Barber 2002). When Grigar first asked us whether she could hold her doctoral defense in LinguaMOO, it was evident that the basic MOO room would not be able to accommodate a serious academic event such as a PhD defense. The main problem was that the basic room had no mechanisms for controlling speech; anyone can say and do whatever they wanted at any time; and this, we surmised, could create problems and reflect poorly not only on the candidate but also on us and MOO technology in general. We began searching for alternatives and found that Ken Schweller had developed a moderated room for CollegeTown that he called the Classroom. This room had a limited set of moderation features in that the owner (typically a teacher) could set up a series of tables at which students could communicate privately without disturbing the rest of the room. With Schweller's permission, we ported the Classroom to Lingua and did some testing to see how it would work for a conference-type event. After a few weeks, it became clear, however, that the classroom's moderation features were not rigorous enough for what we needed. In the process of porting and installing the code for the CollegeTown classroom, we had learned how the room's speech control system worked; so we decided to build a new moderated room with our own features based on that code. The new room, which became known as the Moderated Room, was based on the notion of an auditorium where the speakers and the audience occupy two different and clearly defined areas of the room. Speakers are often seated on a stage or a panel, whereas the audience members are seated in the audience. This concept allowed us to implement a system where speakers could address the whole room, but audience members could only talk among themselves. If they wanted to ask a question of a speaker, they had to send it first to a moderator who in turn could field it to a speaker at the appropriate time. To make the room more versatile, we also built in a feature that allowed the moderator to open it up for free discussion much like a basic room. Grigar's PhD defense in LinguaMOO became quite a success, with more than fifty people in attendance from all over the world (Grigar and Barber 2002).

The online dissertation defense, as well as many of the other early Lingua events, demonstrated that MOO technology held a greater potential than many of us had realized. From a technical point of view, what might have taken several professional programmers to write in a traditional proprietary environment, all the technology needed to produce the online defense was accomplished with free software and less than one hundred lines of specialized MOO code by two humanities scholars. From a pedagogical point of view, we could see that students and others were able to make the MOO space their own by constructing personal spaces within the virtual world. The MOO system provides simple but effective tools that allow users to extend and decorate new spaces; by doing this, we found, users domesticated their learning environment by investing in it. Instead of being simply a tool for learning, like most traditional instructional software, the MOO became a place where they could also engage in extracurricular activities, such as meeting old and new friends from all over the world or just hanging out after school. The importance of the very reasonable technical requirements for accessing and using the MOO system also became increasingly clear. Basically all that was needed to use a MOO was a simple telnet connection, and this made it possible for anyone with an Internet connection, regardless of computer platform (i.e., Mac, Windows, Unix, etc.) or network speed, to be able to access the system and use it productively. No student was left behind because of the lack of state-of-the-art technology. In academic settings, where schools often have older computer technology in their labs, this made a strong case for MOO technology in education.

LinguaMOO was primarily designed as a learning environment. In addition to being used extensively by freshman writing classes from UTD, we also supported classes from other schools across the world. Many of the outside institutions that availed themselves of the services provided by LinguaMOO would later set up their own educational MOOs, but others continued to take their students to our MOO.[1]

Over the next few years, LinguaMOO also played host to a number of academic conferences and meetings. The organization Teaching Online in Higher Education (TOHE) held its annual conferences in Lingua several years in a row, and other groups such as Electronic Literature Organization (ELO), the e-journal *Kairos*, and the *trAce* online writing community also used the space on a regular basis. All of these groups helped make the MOO a vibrant and creative community where you never knew whom you might run into. By 1996, we started to see a growing interest in MOO technology coming from a number of new academic areas. Whenever we presented the LinguaMOO project at conferences such as the Modern Language Association (MLA), Conference on College Composition and Communication (CCCC), and Computers and Writing (CW), there was always significant interest from people who wanted to learn more about the technology and how it might be used for learning purposes.

From the very start of the LinguaMOO project, we had offered educators from other institutions space in the MOO for their own projects and classes. However, as their proficiency and experience with the digital learning environment grew, many of them began to think about setting up their own educational MOOs. Also, during this time, we heard from several educators outside the LinguaMOO community who wanted our advice and assistance in starting educational MOOs of their own. It was clear that we could not possibly help everyone who wanted to set up a MOO, but what we could do was to create a resource that would teach interested parties how to establish and teach with MOO. Thus was born the High Wired project.

High Wired

Although the philosophy of free software was fairly well known in most technical areas of academia, in the humanities it was still largely an unknown phenomenon. Thus, it didn't occur to us at first to create a complete software package as part of the effort to get more educators involved with MOO. Instead, we went the traditional humanities route of publishing a book. The ideas for the book had begun to materialize as early as the summer of 1995, and the basic purpose was to create a resource that would teach prospective MOO administrators and teachers not only how to set up and run a MOO, but also instruct them on how to teach with it, as well as provide a theoretical framework for educational MOO activity. To this end, we invited a number of scholars and researchers with an interest in MOO technology to each write a chapter on their respective areas of expertise. The University of Michigan Press picked up the book early on, and for the next year and a half we were busy writing and editing the manuscript for *High Wired: On the Design, Use, and Theory of Educational MOOs* (Haynes and Holmevik [1998] 2002). The first edition of *High Wired* was published in 1998, and a second edition with updated information on how to set up enCore MOOs with a new graphical user interface named Xpress was published in 2002.

Our original idea had been to base the technical references in the book on the popular LambdaCore distribution, but in the late spring of 1997, as we were putting the final touches on the *High Wired* manuscript, we came to realize that it might be helpful to have a special education-oriented version of LambdaCore to go with the book. We knew from experience that the first task that faced a new MOO administrator was to port and install popular educational tools such as Ken Schweller's Classroom object, our own Moderated room, recording systems, and more. It seemed to us that to provide a special MOO core with all these tools preinstalled would save new MOO administrators a lot of time and trouble and allow them to focus more on the pedagogical aspects of their new site. Thus, as part of the High Wired project, we also wanted to provide a MOO software package specifically designed for educational use. This software package was eventually named the High Wired enCore, or simply enCore.

As I have mentioned above, when we built LinguaMOO, we used the LambdaCore software. This MUD software was designed with a built-in programming language that allowed us to expand and adapt the system to a new set of specifications for academic use. The fact that the technology placed this powerful programming tool at our disposal was one of its major advantages. The other major advantage that MOO offered was that its code was openly available to anyone who wanted to modify or change it. So while keeping the core functions and compatibility with other MOOs based on LambdaCore, we could easily expand and build in new functionality and remove functions that we deemed unsuited in an academic setting. For these reasons, as well as from a technical point of view, it was clear to us that MOO offered the best and most flexible starting point for building the academic online environment that we wanted.

enCore

In 1997, there were basically two MOO software packages that could be used as foundations for building new MOOs. The first one, LambdaCore, was discussed in the previous chapter. The other core package, JHCore, was developed by Jay Carlson, Ken Fox, and others at Jay's House MOO. Both of these packages can be described as generic and to some extent bare-bones; yet it was clear to us that if we wanted to encourage the adoption and use of MOOs in educational settings, we had to provide a core package that was not only more rich in the kind of features that educators wanted but that also made it easy for nontechnical people to get started.

The primary design objective of the enCore project, as formulated in the summer of 1997, was therefore to create a MOO software package that : (1) was designed specifically for educational use; (2) was easy to set up and administer for "nontechie" educators; (3) had a built-in suite of popular educational MOO tools; (4) used an open source model of development to ensure that users have the freedom to modify and adapt the software; and (5) was available to anyone free of charge. By this time,

LinguaMOO was already a mature, educational MOO system with many new tools and enhancements, so we deemed it a good foundation for a new core distribution. As it turned out, however, instead of extracting the new core from the Lingua database, we ended up using the then-latest LambdaCore distribution, which was from February 2, 1997. During the summer of 1997, we ported over most of the tools and features that we had added to LinguaMOO, and we also begun soliciting contributions from other MOOs. Back in 1997, the MOO world was still dominated by the traditional text-based interface, but with the rapid rise of the World Wide Web (WWW) and all the possibilities for multimedia content that it opened up, we felt that it would be very useful to have an interface to the WWW in addition to the traditional text-based interface. At the time, one of the most advanced MOO web interfaces was a system called BioGate, originally developed for BioMOO by Gustavo Glusman, Eric Mercer, and others. The BioGate system was much more advanced than the simple browse-only web interface that we had obtained from CollegeTown, in that it enabled users to browse and interact in the same session. By this time, the new Java programming language, with its client-side applet, was beginning to take off, and a number of people were experimenting with ways to build telnet applets that could be used in an integrated MOO web interface. When the BioGate system was ported to Diversity University MOO (DU) sometime in 1995–1996, Eric Mercer and Alex Stewart, aka Richelieu, expanded it into a fully integrated MOO web interface, using HTML to deliver persistent MOO content while delivering dynamic real-time content through the Java telnet applet Cup-O MUD. We wanted our new educational MOO core to have as many state-of-the-art tools as possible, so we contacted the BioGate Partners (the group of people behind the design and development of the system) and asked whether we could incorporate their web interface into our MOO core. Their answer was affirmative, but there was one problem. Their license stipulated that while the system was free for educational and noncommercial use, there was a $1,000 license fee for commercial users. On one hand, this might not have been such an obstacle because our target audience would be educational users. On the other hand, pairing our MOO Core distribution with the BioGate system would in effect tie us to their noncommercial use license because if we wanted to provide both systems as an integrated package, we could not have separate licenses for each part. We had not really paid any attention to licensing before the BioGate issue came up, but it demonstrated to us that we needed to decide on a license before we went ahead with the release.

Ask any software developer, and he or she will tell you that licensing issues are some of the least enjoyable aspects of software engineering. Nevertheless, a license of some sort is a necessary component of any software release to protect the developers' intellectual property rights and liabilities. So we began looking around at the types of licenses other people used. Because we did not have the money or the desire to hire a lawyer to draw up a specialized license for the MOO Core distribution, we looked with particular interest at the Free Software Foundation's GNU General Purpose License (GPL) and at the BSD license. Both of these seemed to offer the legal framework that we sought (i.e., protection from warranty claims resulting from the use of our software). Our initial idea was to ensure that any not-for-profit entity could use our software in any way they wanted, including the right to modify and redistribute their own versions of it. As mentioned previously, the nature of MOO is such that each installation will take on its own unique characteristics as users and administrators make changes and additions to it. In this regard free and open source software licenses aptly express the core philosophy of MOO development: collaboration and sharing. As we studied the GNU GPL and the BSD license, it became clear to us that both of them followed closely the tradition established by the original LambdaCore releases in which no restrictions were placed on usage and redistribution. If someone took our work and made a profit from selling it, that would be ok. While the BSD license was certainly the more open-ended of the two, we felt that it failed to protect one of the key things that we wanted our software to promote—collaboration. Both licenses protect the users' right to obtain, modify, and redistribute software; but only the GPL also protects the developers themselves. Robert Chassell, formerly of the Free Software Foundation, explains that in the GPL you "have the freedom to do things, but also the freedom from other people taking things away from you. It's the freedom from that ensures that you reward the good guys and not the bad guys" (Chassell 2001). By using the GPL, we could prevent users from taking our code and adding their own proprietary elements to it. Any works derived from our software would have to be licensed under the same terms as the original software, which meant that changes and modifications in one enCore MOO could freely be shared with other MOOs. In other words, the GPL protected us from people who might otherwise want to take advantage of our work without being willing to channel their own contributions back to the community. Although we didn't grasp the full significance of it at the time, the choice of the GNU GPL license was a major milestone for the whole project. It provided a legal framework for our work and also a philosophical foundation for the kind of community we wanted to foster.

Beta

The first beta version of enCore was released on the Internet on August 10, 1997. Because the software was provided free of charge, we could not, for obvious reasons, provide the kind of technical support that a commercial company could. However, it was clear that, despite our efforts to make the enCore system as intuitive and easy to use as possible, users would inevitably encounter problems and bugs. Among the first things we did following the release, therefore, was to set up an email discussion list with the purpose of creating a virtual "help desk" where users could help one another.

Like so many other software projects, enCore evolved in a cyclical fashion. As I have just mentioned, we started with an initial design and brainstorming phase where the foundations of the system were laid out, and because we decided to build on the core of Lingua, we had most of the features we wanted already in place. Because of this, we had the great advantage of being able to ship the first version very quickly. The second and most important phase, however, was the circular design, implement/redesign, reimplement phase. With the advent of the Internet, software products could be sent to market with a single keystroke. Because you can reach your users easily, this means that they can also reach you. The advantages of this are substantial. Not only can your product be spread and tested among a wide group of users very quickly (public beta testing), you can also get unsolicited comments, feedback, and feature requests at a stage when the software is still in development and at a time when it is still possible to incorporate them into the design and implementation of the product. Thus, during the whole enCore project, we adopted an active beta-release program that allowed us to continually fix bugs and add new features while giving our users frequent and timely updates of the software. The enCore mailing list has been instrumental in providing us with valuable user feedback, and many of the feature requests that came across the list were subsequently included in the enCore distribution.

The open source model of development means that anyone has the right to see a program's source code and the freedom to change and modify it as they wish. Because the enCore MOO database is essentially a source code structure with no compiled binaries, giving users access to the source is a natural thing. In fact, the MOO system was set up to allow users to read source code by default. If you wished to prevent them from doing so, you had to disable the read-flag for each of the more than 2,400 verbs (MOO programs) in the distribution. We knew that once people started to download enCore and use it to set up their own MOOs, they would want to start making modifications and additions to it. Some of these modifications might be bug fixes that could benefit the whole user community. Additions might include new features that MOO users elsewhere would also want to use. Through postings on the enCore mailing list, we encouraged sharing as much as possible; to facilitate this, we created a special section of the enCore website called the enCore exChange, which was intended to be an archive of MOO code that anyone could download and install on their own sites. As a special incentive for sharing, we also let it be known that the best contributions to the enCore exChange would be included in the enCore distribution whenever we released new versions. We had great hopes for the new code archive. This was during the heyday of text-based educational MOOs, and new installations sprang up almost every week. As time went on, however, we came to realize that it was much harder to get contributions from the outside than we had anticipated. One reason for this was that whatever collaboration there had been in the past increasingly became a victim of what seemed like a beginning rivalry between installations and competition for users. Although there was little or no monetary gain in operating a successful MOO with a large user base, it did give its administrators and host institution a certain reputation within the academic world. Another, more significant reason for the seemingly lax attitude toward inter-MOO collaboration, however, was that most of the new enCore MOO operators were not programmers or even technical specialists. Most of them were graduate students or faculty members from the humanities and the social sciences. Most of them ran vanilla installations with few or no core changes at all; and the few who had actually made modifications often felt that what they had done was not significant enough to contribute it back to the community. Although we did receive a handful of unsolicited contributions, many of which made their way into the enCore distribution, most of the code in the exChange archive was either written or solicited by us. One example of code that we actively solicited during this time was Amy Bruckman's MacMOOSE utilities, which was a set of MOO verbs and modifications that enabled users to take advantage of the advanced editing features in her MacMOOSE MOO client program (Bruckman 1997). In retrospect, the enCore exChange was an interesting experiment because of what it told us about the differences between trying to run an open source–type project in a humanities setting as opposed to doing it in the traditional computer science world.

Xpress

After the final release of enCore version 1.0 in April 1998, we turned our attention to the predominant users of the MOO, the students, to see what we could do to make the system easier to use and more appealing to them. Because we had both been using LinguaMOO in our own teaching since 1995, we had a pretty good idea about its shortcomings; to put it simply, the text-based command line of the 1980s and early 1990s did not seem particularly appealing or user-friendly to the web-savvy students of the late 1990s. It seemed clear to us that something had to be done to "modernize" the MOO interface. The other thing we found was that there were no textbooks that would do for students what *High Wired* had done for MOO administrators and educators—namely, teach them how to use and make the most out of the MOO as a learning environment. The textbook problem subsequently led to a book we named *MOOniversity* (Holmevik and Haynes 2000). It was the first of its kind, and it was designed to give a comprehensive overview of educational MOOs as well as being a combination text, tutorial, and reference book that could guide students through the world of MOO. We wanted to show students how to use the dynamics of real situations to evoke authentic writing in which collaborative and individual learning are enhanced through conversation, research, real-time events, multimedia presentations, and other interactive situations. The book was conceived of as a complement to standard writing texts with clear, useful instructions for writing online, as well as productive assignments and discussion questions to involve students with the technology by writing in real time with real people. To coincide with the publication of *MOOniversity*, we set about also to modernize the MOO interface, which turned into the graphical user interface project *Xpress* (figure 5.1).

From the beginning, enCore had had a simple web interface that allowed for the incorporation of multimedia content such as images, movies, and sound into the MOO experience. This system was very limited, however, because you could only experience the value-added content while browsing the MOO in a noninteractive mode. We wanted to preserve this multimedia capability in the new Xpress interface, but we also wanted it to do much more. In outline, our design goals for Xpress were to create a system that would bring the many hidden power features of the MOO system, such as mailing, creating, and editing objects, extending the environment through building, and programming, right to the surface and make them as simple and intuitive to use as possible. Furthermore, we wanted to preserve and extend the ability to incorporate multimedia content directly into the

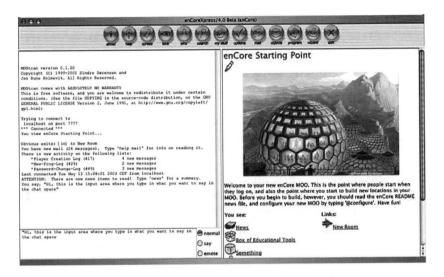

Figure 5.1
enCore Xpress web application 2001.
Source: Courtesy of the author.

MOO experience and enhance it by making it accessible directly from in-side the real-time MOO experience. Finally, we wanted to create a platform-independent system based on WWW technologies such as HTML, Java, and Javascript, with the web browser as the primary software for accessing and using the system. In short, with Xpress we invented a distributed web application, but at the time we didn't know yet what to call it.

In enCore 1.0, we had used a telnet applet by Ken Schweller called "Surf and Turf." This applet allowed users to connect to the MOO and view graphical content in their web browser, but our experience with it had taught us that students and other novice users often found it confusing and frustrating to have to navigate through many open windows on their screen. In the BioGate system, the telnet applet Cup-O MUD was integrated right into the main client screen, and this made for a much more streamlined and less confusing experience. We contacted Schweller to ask for permission to design a new applet based on his code, but he politely declined and told us that he was still in the process of working on it and that he would release the source code at a later time. Once again we found ourselves looking at the BioGate system. As I have already explained, it was clear that we could not incorporate it into enCore due to licensing issues, so instead we began to study the source code to see whether we could reverse engineer a new system with the same basic functionality. One of the main strengths of free and open source software is that you can read and learn from other people's code, and the BioGate code taught us a lot about how to implement an http-type web server via MOO code. After a couple of hectic weeks of coding in October 1998, we had what amounted to a BioGate clone up and running on our development site. It was very basic at that point because the synchronous telnet aspect of it was not yet implemented. We could not go forward with Ken Schweller's Surf and Turf client because we did not have access to the source, but we had learned about a new MOO telnet applet written by Sindre Sørensen of the University of Bergen, Norway (UiB). The applet was called MOOtcan and seemed to be the perfect fit for the new enCore web interface. Sørensen was at the time affiliated with what was then called the CALLMOO project (later named Lingo.uib), headed by Espen Aarseth and Carsten Jopp, also of UiB. Aarseth's project was one of the first to adopt enCore 1.0, and its aim was to use MOO technology in foreign language learning. Specifically, the goal was to create an online learning environment called "Dreistadt" for the German Department at UiB. The project was funded by the Norwegian Research Council and became one of the most vibrant and creative MOO development projects in the world. After only a brief discussion with Aarseth, it was clear that enCore and the CALLMOO project would both stand to benefit from a closer collaboration. Hence, while Sørensen continued to improve his MOOtcan applet, we set about to expand the capabilities of the new enCore web interface, which later became known as Xpress.

While the BioGate system provided an elegant solution to the integration of MOO and the web, we realized that it had only tapped into a tiny part of what was possible. Our design objectives involved bringing out and simplifying the creative aspects of MOO, thus making it as easy as possible for users not only to create new rooms and other objects but also to access the built-in help, mail systems, editors, and more. Another significant benefit of building a web-based client was that it would be platform-independent by running inside a web browser. With the appropriate browser plug-ins, users would be able to broaden the application of MOO to any available web-based multimedia technology. In other words, we could offer a totally new and rich MOO experience while still maintaining compatibility with the traditional text-based system. As educators teaching with MOO in labs, we also knew firsthand about the problems of downloading and installing traditional MOO clients on a large number of machines, not to mention the problems stemming from students trying to download and install said clients on their home or office computers. By using the web browser as the platform for our new MOO client, we could avoid most of these problems because nearly every computer shipped since 1995 had some sort of web browser already installed.

Work on the new Xpress client commenced in earnest in October 1998, and by January of the following year we had the first working prototype ready. During this time, we worked closely with the CALLMOO project, and although it was not a formalized collaboration, both projects had fairly well-defined areas of responsibility. The first beta version of Xpress was a very simple system that only had a few features completed, but it allowed us to test the overall design on a select group of users in LinguaMOO and solicit their feedback. By April 1999, we had a usable system with most of the features we wanted included, and on April 15 (the date was chosen to coincide with my birthday), we released the first beta version of enCore 2.0 with Xpress.

In keeping with the open source model of development, which says to "release early and often," we shipped several beta versions of the enCore that spring, fixing bugs and adding new features. The first complete version of the system to include the Xpress interface was released as version 2.0 on June 1, 1999. By this time, we had already noticed a considerable increase in traffic on the enCore list due to new subscriptions and also correspondence from new MOO administrators who wanted to try out the new enCore. Although the enCore exChange project had failed to generate the kind of sharing and collaboration that we had hoped for, we had not given up on the basic premise. By then, the ideas of free software and open source were everywhere, thanks in large part to the success of Linux and the other free software technologies that I have discussed previously. Also the renewed interest in MOO that the Xpress system generated encouraged us to try and achieve our goals via a different route—namely, the enCore Open Source Project, which was formally launched in the fall of 1999. For the purpose of that project, we totally redesigned the enCore website and wrote a new set of instructions for how to contribute, in addition to a "manifesto" that outlined the basic ideas and goals on which the project was founded. The site was modeled after other similar open source sites, with specific sections for information, downloads, and updates.

Reflections

Our final release of enCore Xpress was version 4.0, on January 4, 2004 (coinciding with my doctoral defense at the University of Bergen, Norway). When we launched the enCore Open Source project in the fall of 1998, we had great hopes that MOO users in academia and elsewhere would want to become involved and contribute to the project. Looking back today, I am proud to say that even now, almost fourteen years later, MOOs are still in use. Because we adopted an active beta release program right from the start, many of our users have been able to help find and fix bugs and other problems along the way. The enCore community email list was instrumental in this regard. Following a release, users would discover problems that we were not able to catch during beta testing, and they would report them to us so we could fix them. In quite a few instances, we also received new and improved versions of code from other MOOs long after the original release date. Another aspect in which the user community played an important role was as a supplier of ideas for how to improve existing features. The enCore Documentation project, co-coordinated by Lennie Irvin of San Antonio College and Erin Karper of Purdue University, was another example of concrete, nontechnical contributions from the community. This was an independent project in which we had no involvement, but one that greatly benefited the enCore project as a whole. Another very important outgrowth was the nonprofit organization enCore Consortium (enCore Consortium 2004) founded by Lennie Irvin, Daniel Jung, Barbara McManus, Jeff Schneider, Cynthia Haynes, and myself in 2004 as a site for further development in order for external funding to be applied to enCore projects. With the help of the Consortium, enCore 4.0 was significantly enhanced by Daniel Jung (University of Bergen), who took over the technical development work from me and eventually released enCore 5.0 a few years later. Barbara McManus received a series of grants for VRoma MOO, and the Consortium continues to actively seek open source code and funding contributions to the enCore project. Kevin Jepson maintains a major source of MOO code on the Consortium site called "The Barn" (Jepson 2004). I am grateful to all those contributors and Consortium charter members for perpetuating the work and carrying our vision forward. LinguaMOO was resurrected in the summer of 2011, and it is now available at http:// electracy.net (LinguaMOO [1995] 2011). It is one of the world's oldest MOOs still in existence, and in addition to its historic value, it will continue to serve as a site for interaction and invention of electrate practices in textual digital space. Guests are welcome to visit the more than 4000 avatars, who from 1995 to the present have made this multimodal world their home.

With all the media attention surrounding open source and the hacker bazaar-style collaborative development models in the late 1990s and early 2000s, the enCore project was perfectly situated to tap into the zeitgeist of the time. The project clearly demonstrated that open source methodologies afford some truly remarkable opportunities for learning and heuristic invention. By building on open source and existing technology, we were able to learn from those who came before us. We did not have to "reinvent the wheel" to create a more suitable program for our needs. Complete access to the MOO source code gave us the opportunity to study how things were done so we could improve and change what we wanted and also add new features as we went along—in other words, to intervene. MOO technology was truly *free* in both senses of that word, and it afforded us a virtual sandbox of *free play*. First, it cost nothing to acquire and very little to operate; thus, it was ideally suited to the needs of often cash-strapped educational institutions. Second, and even more important, users were free to change and modify it to suit their own needs and specifications. They were free to make it their own site for electrate invention.

Another important lesson has been the significance of actual user experiences and input on the design and implementation process. With most software products, users typically have no influence over the design, so they just have to make the best use they can of the software as handed to them. In the open source hacker model that we used for enCore, not only was the design of the system informed by our own teacher/user experiences, we also actively solicited comments and feedback from other users in an attempt to make our software even more useful and empowering.

More than anything, the enCore project showed us that we do not have to settle for commercial products that either force us to work in certain ways or that take away our ability and freedom to be creative and bend the technology to our own needs. Through the open source model of development, we, as educators in the humanities, can intervene in existing platforms and forge our own technologies to make them work the way we want and need. As players, we can monumentalize our own memorials by following the signifiers of a ludic postliterate transversal that Ulmer challenges us to invent. It is when we intervene in technologies as a means of reimagining education and/as ludic pervasive life in this way that we become egents of the EmerAgency. It is my next task to examine the ludic in terms of ethics.

6   Ludic Ethics

To recognize untruth as a condition of life: that, to be sure, means to resist custom-
ary value-sentiments in a dangerous fashion; and a philosophy which ventures to do
so places itself, by that act alone, beyond good and evil.
—Friedrich Nietzsche, *Beyond Good and Evil*

No doubt the pairing of ludology and ethics can be examined along the
lines of violence, morality, and problematic virtual social interactions, as
scholars such as Miguel Sicart have done in his book, *The Ethics of Computer Games* (Sicart 2009). Such studies are necessary and significant. But
before I engage Sicart, it is also necessary to situate the context in which
play and morality have long been injuriously paired. This context has an
ancient history and is born of the conflicts that arise when human anxiety
is unable to cope with its own mortality. Into this context, Nietzsche in-
jects the pre-Socratic philosopher Heraclitus, who understood the struggle
of *all* life as a game. Nietzsche explains in *Philosophy in the Tragic Age of
the Greeks*:

Do guilt, injustice, contradiction and suffering exist in this world? They do, pro-
claims Heraclitus, but only for the limited human mind which sees things apart
but not connected, not for the con-tuitive god. For him all contradictions run into
harmony, invisible to the common human eye, yet understandable to one who, like
Heraclitus, is related to the contemplative god. Before his fire-gaze not a drop of
injustice remains in the world poured all around him; even that cardinal impulse
that allows pure fire to inhabit such impure forms is mastered by him with a sublime
metaphor. In this world only play, play as artists and children engage in it, exhibits
coming-to-be and passing away, structuring and destroying, without any moral additive, in forever equal innocence. And as children and artists play, so plays the ever-
living fire. It constructs and destroys, all in innocence. Such is the game that the aeon
plays with itself. Transforming itself into water and earth, it builds towers of sand like
a child at the seashore, piles them up and tramples them down. From time to time it

starts the game anew. An instant of satiety—and again it is seized by its need, as the artist is seized by his need to create. Not hubris but the ever self-renewing impulse to play calls new worlds into being. (Nietzsche [1873] 2006, 111)

If the "impulse to play calls new worlds into being," then this chapter argues that such new worlds are both ludic and ethical insofar as they are innocent of human-centered morality. If the "limited human mind which sees things apart but not connected" begins (anew) to think associatively, conductively, then this chapter aims to play with ethics "without any moral additive." Derrida famously formulated the dilemma in terms of "the tension between play and presence" in his essay, "Structure, Sign, and Play in the Discourse of the Human Sciences" (Derrida [1966] 1978, 292). For Derrida, play is "always the play of absence and presence, but if it is to be thought radically, play must be conceived of before the alternative of presence and absence" (Derrida [1966] 1978, 292). And, I (with Nietzsche) would add, beyond good and evil.

What Derrida suggests is a return to a "Nietzschean affirmation" of play,

the joyous affirmation of the play of the world and the innocence of becoming, the affirmation of a world of signs without fault, without truth, and without origin which is offered to an active interpretation. This affirmation then determines the noncenter otherwise than as loss of the center. And it plays without security. For there is a sure play . . . [that] dreams of deciphering a truth or an origin which escapes play. . . . The other, which is no longer turned toward the origin, affirms play and tries to pass beyond man and humanism, the name of man being the name of that being who, throughout the history of metaphysics or of ontotheology—in other words, throughout his entire history—has dreamed of full presence, the reassuring foundation, the origin and the end of play. (Derrida [1966] 1978, 292)

What this chapter explores is the problem of *negative* ethics that, in its desire for a moral center, seeks the "end of play." The irony is that the history of play reveals the birth of the unethical impulse, and the literate drive to diminish and end play ultimately becomes the unethical position. Borrowing a term from Derrida, therefore, with this chapter I seek to *decenter* the debate on ethics by forging a new understanding, one that is informed by electracy more so than morality.

The question of ethics for game studies, it seems to me, must circle back to the question of being and mastery that spawned a highly questionable link between ethics and morality. It must also circle back to the rhetorical dimension of being and play—namely, language. Sicart's research, while invaluable in injecting ethics as a primary concern for game studies, sustains the link that has not been conductively forged but deductively determined. Following his logic, "ethics can be defined as a system or set of moral values, and the tools for analyzing these values" (Sicart 2009, 4). So far, so good. Next, he defines morals "as the right or wrong of actions or objects" (Sicart 2009, 4). Where I think he makes a wrong turn is in connecting the two *inextricably* and making the move to lodge the link firmly between games and players by applying this logic. Sicart argues that the "application of ethics is the rational, philosophical approach to the questions of good, evil, harm, duties, and values. [*The Ethics of Computer Games*] is then an exploration of the moral nature of computer games and computer game players" (Sicart 2009, 4). Yet, much later, Sicart relies on phenomenology (specifically Gadamer) and the "hermeneutic circle" (Sicart 2009, 86) to claim that a circular process of interpretation and understanding of ethical experience is "where the ethical being of the player-subject takes place and finds meaning" (Sicart 2009, 88). Granted, early on Sicart asks of his reader "a certain degree of openness to the rhetoric of ethics" (Sicart 2009, 3), but we are not treated to a rhetorical perspective of ethics. It is a thoroughly logical, and by that I mean philosophical, treatment of ethics. And yet the logic is contradictory. It attempts to be both linear and circular. It calls on Aristotelian ethics and Gadamerian hermeneutics, which focus on virtue and self-understanding (respectively) as constitutive of being a player-subject. If we recall both Nietzsche's and Derrida's reminders of the role of "play" in being, it is difficult to understand Sicart's rhetorically restricted argument wherein virtue, phronesis, and praxis overrule play, sandcastles, and the ever-living fire. With electracy, in the context of play, we do not overrule fire; it is the burning chrome that plays with us and shapes us as we shape it.

Natural Born Killers

On the morning of March 11, 2009, seventeen-year-old Tim Kretschmer of Winnenden, Germany, shot and killed fifteen people. Later that day, he died from a self-inflicted gunshot to the head, bringing the death toll to sixteen. According to the news media afterward, Tim had played the video game *Far Cry 2* for two hours the night before. In other news, it was also reported that he liked to play *Counterstrike*. The tragic event caused much outrage in Germany. Chancellor Angela Merkel called it "incomprehensible" (BBC News 2009). In June 2009, Germany's sixteen interior ministers proposed a ban on the production and distribution of violent video games within the country's borders. "Incomprehensible" events always raise the question why; the public and the media demand immediate explanations, and politicians come under pressure to do something—anything.

Ten years earlier and half a world away in an affluent suburb of Denver, Colorado, two other high school students, eighteen-year-olds Eric David Harris and Dylan Bennet Klebold, massacred twelve of their fellow students and one teacher before committing suicide in the school's library on April 20, 1999. Adam Foss, himself a senior at Columbine High School that fateful day Tuesday, described the horrific scene in an interview on CNN: "All I saw was the barrels of the guns just going off blazing . . . saw a couple of teachers . . . with a bunch of blood . . . saw a couple of kids just get shot and after that I just turned around and had a bunch of my buddies help get a bunch of people get in the room and barricade ourselves in there" (CNN 1999). The question on everyone's lips in the weeks and months, and even years, that followed was *why*. Why had these two kids committed such horrific acts of violence? How could this have happened in a safe, affluent neighborhood such as Littleton, Colorado? In a special report about the event, *Newsweek* magazine wrote, "How did brainy kids from seemingly stable, affluent homes become killing machines without a hint of remorse? The murders fascinated and appalled the country, not least because the mayhem unfolded in an archetypal place (a suburban high school) and touched on cultural forces (the Internet, violent movies and videogames) familiar to all Americans. Still, there is one overarching question: why?" ("Anatomy of a Massacre" 1999). In its search for answers as to why Harris and Klebold did what they did, the article goes on to say that "the two became 'obsessed' with the violent videogame Doom—an interactive game in which the players try to rack up the most kills—and played it every afternoon" ("Anatomy" 1999). Police records later published by *Denver Post* and the *Rocky Mountain News* also contain a plethora of evidence that points to the fact that they were more than just casual players.

In a drawing by Harris contained in the Columbine case files (Columbine Documents 2000), we can clearly see the familiar logo of iD Software's blockbuster game *DOOM*, which was published in several sequels between 1993 and 2004. The iconic double-barreled shotgun that was used by the game's protagonist is also prominently featured below the logo. In the same drawing, we can further make out the phrases "AOL: WHeRe KEWLz HaX0Rz ArE," "AoleeT d00d," "The true HaX0R," and "Mamma" (Columbine Documents 2000, 69) scrawled across the page.

In another note contained in the police documents dated August 24, 1998, eight months before the killings, Harris writes about "25 things that make me different" (Columbine Documents 2000, 270). The first entry reads : "1 My love for a computer game called DOOM. DOOM is such a big part of my life and no one I know can recreate environments in DOOM as good as me. I know almost anything there is to know about that game, so I believe that separates me from the rest of the world" (Columbine Documents 2000, 270). Harris had first started playing DOOM in November 1994 (which, incidentally, is about six months after I first started playing it), so by the time he writes this, he had been playing the game for four years (Columbine Documents 2000, 931). He continues:

DOOM is so burned into my head my thoughts usually have something to do with the game. Whether it be a level or environment or whatever. In fact a dream I had yesterday was about a "Deathmatch" level that I have never even been to. It was so vivid and detailed I will probably try to recreate it using map editor. It had 3 ledges and a very high tree house like area also, but describing it would take forever. What I can't do in real life, I try to do in doom, like if I walk by a small building I would recreate it as good as I could and then explore it. go on the roof, under it, or even shoot at it. The fact is, I love that game and if others tell me "hey its just a game" I say "I don't care." (Columbine Documents 2000, 272)

For the casual observer who perhaps has not played digital games and who is not familiar with the first-person shooter genre that *DOOM* popularized in the 1990s, Harris's thoughts as they are expressed here might seem frightening and be cause for alarm. Did he commit such atrocious acts because the game taught him to do it? Was it all just a rehearsal for the real-world carnage that he and Klebold subsequently carried out? In the rush to find explanations for disasters such as this, we are often guilty of sacrificing the complexities of the whole rhetorical situation for the sake of clarity and expediency. *World of Warcraft* statistics tells me that at the time of this writing, my current character, the Blood Elf paladin Raik, has killed more than thirty thousand alliance characters in player versus player (PvP) combat. If I take into account how many game characters I have "killed" across all my avatars in various role-playing and first-person shooter games over the past twenty years, the "death toll" would be nothing short of staggering. Should I be concerned that I may one day snap and take my twenty years of experience with virtual killing in digital games into the physical world? Am I another Harris, Klebold, or Kretschmer waiting to happen? Of course not. The kind of deductive inference logic—which says gamers learn how to kill by playing digital games, and you are a gamer, therefore you know how to kill and can become a killer yourself—represents a reductionist and behavioral cognitive position that is completely inadequate to explain why people in extreme circumstances do the things they do. Neuroscientists Steven Quartz and Terrence Sejnowski, in *Liars, Lovers, and Heroes: What the New Brain Science Reveals about How We Become Who We Are*, provide support for this:

It is no coincidence that the marines have customized a version of Doom, an immersive shoot-em-up computer game, for their own combat simulations. This does not mean that the path from video game to violence is simple and straightforward. Searching for *the* cause of violence is as misguided as searching for *the* cause of a tornado. Both are the product of a web of forces that accumulate in subtle and complex ways until they reach some critical point. The forces that cause a tempest in the brain that leads to violence are complex, sometimes interacting with one another, sometimes multiplying their joint effects, sometimes canceling each other out. Indeed, it is likely that children like Eric Harris are drawn to these violent games. Once Harris was exposed, obsessive game playing interacted with other risk factors present in his life to nudge him closer to acting on his fantasies. It is chilling to consider that Harris customized the rooms in Doom to simulate the physical layout of Columbine and that he played it over and over again in that mode. (Quartz and Sejnowski 2002, 213)

Why *some* gamers snap and kill people while the vast majority does not, however, is a bigger question that shall have to remain outside the scope of this book. However, if we are to look for more telling clues as to why Harris did what he did, a couple of other entries on his list of things that made him different seem to offer more promising leads: "14 My anger management problems" and "15 My attitude towards people around me" (Columbine Documents 2000, 270).

In Ian Bogost's *Persuasive Games* (2008), the case is made for understanding all discourse as ideological, but, unlike Sicart, Bogost makes no claims to link ethics and morality. What Bogost does is situate the problem of language and morality in games into the context of procedural rhetorics. Drawing on George Lakoff's theories of metaphor and morality in *Moral Politics*, Bogost aims to shift the tone by reminding us that such a shift will take time. With Lakoff, Bogost understands that a "restructuring is necessary because citizens tend to assume that language and its carriers—from politicians to news media—are neutral. The public has little purchase on the 'moral conceptual systems' that underwrite verbal and written political utterances themselves" (Bogost 2008, 119). He agrees that this is the challenge facing video games in terms of their political and moral roles in society. The problem, as Bogost sees it, is that "this situation underscores both a promise and a threat. On the one hand, the medium of the videogame has not (yet) become attached to a particular worldview, thus welcoming all varieties of ideological frames. On the other hand, lessons from other media suggest that the political groups with stronger media strategies effectively lock out other voices" (Bogost 2008, 120). Thus, the question of ethics in video games is, for Bogost, a rhetorical one. He does not go so far as Sicart to link ethics and morality inextricably, although Bogost does acknowledge that time and context will ultimately affect the power of video games to shift the discourse on politics and morality. Whereas Sicart and Bogost both offer powerful and compelling discussions of ethics, politics, and rhetoric, Ulmer's model returns us to the Nietzschean affirmation of play that is beyond good, evil, right, and wrong. It is helpful to situate a vital industry such as video games within an ancient framework of our basic human condition and in the process perhaps help us understand the complexities inherent in the Columbine shootings and other tragedies that have been linked to video games.

In *Electronic Monuments* (2005) and *Avatar Emergency* (forthcoming), the second and third volumes in his electracy trilogy, Ulmer is concerned with, among other things, the same question that people were asking after Columbine: *why*. In this chapter, I explore Ulmer's electrate *Axis* pain/pleasure as a radically different ethics from the oral apparatus binary right/wrong and the literate apparatus binary true/false.

That the *Challenger* wrote a Y in the sky when it exploded gives us a clue to the changes that choragraphy brings to consulting on public policy problems. Nearly every description of a disaster or a foolishness (ATH), whether coming from victims, witnesses or commentators, poses the question *"why?"* But as the context of Auschwitz for Celan's poetry would indicate, the kinds of problems engaged by choragraphy falls into the category of being "without why." (Ulmer 2005, 156)

When I read the Harris file, the image that materializes before me is that of a troubled young man caught in a downward, although not inevitable and irrevocable, spiral toward destruction, but also someone with whom I can identify as a gamer. He thinks of himself as a "HaX0Rz," leet speak for hacker noir. He fashions himself an "AoleeT d00d" (AOL leet dood), someone who is connected to the Internet and all the cool things that are going on outside of his suburban life in Littleton, Colorado. The fact that he even refers to AOL as "leet" says a lot about his provincial outlook and limited exposure to the Internet as a whole. AOL may well have been "leet" in the late 1980s, but ten years later it most certainly was not the place where the "kewl haX0Rz" hung out. Harris's dream about designing new cool levels to play is something that most hardcore gamers have had at one point or another. It was one of the first things I did when I got my first computer, and it is what professional game designers get paid a hefty salary to do for a living. There is nothing nefarious or abnormal in this. Harris was not just a player of digital games, however; he was also an aspiring designer of content for *DOOM* user-created maps or levels commonly known as WADs. Some of these so-called *Harris levels*, such as the two-level single player *U.A.C. Labs* for *DOOM 2* plus a few more multiplayer deathmatch-style maps, are still in circulation on the Internet today. Contrary to rumors at the time, which were repeated in Quartz and Sejnowski, there is no evidence of any WADs based on the Columbine High School in the files that the police investigators collected from Harris's home.

The Readme file that accompanies *U.A.C. Labs* describes a first-person shooter scenario that is not really that remarkable or unique in any way.[1] There are myriads of fan-created content just like it all over the Internet. Even the strong, profanity-laden, and self-glorifying language that he uses is fairly common within many gaming communities. Viewed against the horrific acts of cold-blooded murder that Harris and Klebold later committed, however, it becomes a chilling and gut-wrenching reminder of what humans are capable of doing to one another. To me, as a life-long gamer, playing Harris' *U.A.C. Labs* scenario that is described in the text document makes me feel very uneasy and uncomfortable. It represents what Roland Barthes called a *punctum*, "that which stings or pricks one emotionally" (Barthes 1981, 43; quoted in Ulmer 2003, 44) when viewing a photograph or an image. Ulmer explains that "the punctum, whether or not it is triggered, it is an addition: it is what I add to the photograph [or in Harris' *DOOM* level in our case] and what is nonetheless already there. The punctum then," he continues, "occurs when there is a match between the signifier in the scene (in the photograph), and a scene in memory" (Ulmer 2003, 45). The punctum serves to reveal what Barthes called the *obtuse*, or indirect significance of an image, something that electracy attempts to account for, and which will vary from observer to observer.

Had I not known who the author of *U.A.C. Labs* was, I might have played it once and quickly forgotten about it like so many other unremarkable game mods. However, knowing what I know and seeing what I see, this evokes an inexorable *punctum* that reveals to me a third meaning that was already always there, and that mercilessly hurls me into an abject subject position that I cannot escape. Harris, himself the ultimate abject, victim of his own self-destruction, a killer who murdered thirteen people in cold blood, has created in *U.A.C. Labs* an *electronic monument* to the abject that exists within us as players of violent digital games. Borrowing a term from Ulmer, I want to call it a *MEmorial*. In *Electronic Monuments*, he explains, "What memorials are to ideals, MEmorials are to abjects" (Ulmer 2005, 43). He continues, "Perhaps this is what Virilio had in mind when he said that accidents [and indeed man-made tragedies such as Columbine] could serve as revelations" (Ulmer 2005, 43). For Ulmer, the MEmorial "treats the disaster as a source for understanding contemporary values, specifically as a mode of self-knowledge, rather than attempting to impose on the disaster a predetermined meaning" (Ulmer 2005, 109).

The Columbine memorial, which was completed and dedicated in September 2007, serves as a remembrance of the ideal, all those young people whose dreams and aspirations, and life itself, were denied. The interior of the memorial is an oval stone outer wall (the Wall of Healing), which is softened by a grove of trees in the center and low native plantings around the edges. Steep landforms of the existing hills gently fold back from the top of the outer retaining wall. These hills surround a majority of the memorial, embracing, comforting, and protecting the visitor and the community. As the memorial elements are revealed, the visitor notices the inner Ring of Remembrance and the outer Wall of Healing.

The MEmorial to the abject exists only in the virtual ludic space and can be seen only by those who seek for it in the deepest, darkest recesses of the Internet. Yet it stands there as a grotesque totem signifying all digital games that turn violence into entertainment. It is a rhetorical argument that signifies what Ulmer calls the *peripheral*. "Peripheral monuments, like their computer counterparts add functionality to an established memorial. The peripheral is a transitional device relating literal monumentality to its electrate counterpart" (Ulmer 2005, 46). This chapter constructs a peripheral to the abject subject position into which violent digital games interpellate us and out of which the axis of pain and pleasure flings us, perpetually, against the edifice of right/wrong.

Epideictic Rhetoric

Game enthusiasts, players, and industry representatives, in an effort to distance and protect themselves from the enormity of the disaster, will often take the alternative position to that which the *punctum* reveals—namely, that which Ulmer calls *disavowal* or defense (Ulmer 2005, 87). Some argue that "Guns don't kill people, people kill people," that violent behavior is not caused or influenced by the games themselves, but is rather a symptom of deeper problem-solving strategies in our culture. Games, movies, and literature embody and express the discursive formations from which they arise. Game enthusiasts are not overly concerned with the ethical implications of violent video games. They don't generally ask why. Instead, they are concerned with far more mundane issues such as "innovative game play," photo-realistic appearance of the game "worlds," and the accuracy of the game's physics engine and whether it can realistically paint blood splatter on a wall. In 2008, IGN.com reviewed Rockstar Games' *Grand Theft Auto IV*: "GTA IV gives us characters and a world with a level of depth previously unseen in gaming and elevates its story from a mere shoot-em-up to an Oscar-caliber drama. Every facet of Rockstar's new masterpiece is worthy of applause" (Goldstein 2008).

Epideictic rhetoric, and the topoi of blame and praise, is the dominant discursive form when it comes to video games, and this creates a barrier that all too often prevents us from seeing past moral questions of right and wrong. If we wish to understand how video games affect our experience of ethics, we must move beyond the epideictic discourse based on traditional deductive and inductive reasoning that says violent video games lead to violent behaviors.

As discussed earlier, Sicart examines "computer games as moral objects and players as ethical subjects" (Sicart 2009, 4–5). While I agree with the basic premise, the past forty years of postmodern thinking have also taught us that these objects are socially constructed by subjects. A technology that may be *charged* with a certain ethics from its creator may have that charge reinforced or reversed by its users. The metaphor of electrical *charge* is helpful here when seen in the context of what Ulmer terms conductive logic (Ulmer 2003, 9). Video games, I believe, do not necessarily impose an encoded ethics on players. Players, to a large extent, charge the game with their own ethics through the act of playing. Ludic activities, therefore, construct ethical dilemmas and considerations. In order to understand the whole picture, we need to understand how the technology is being charged by the players' own ethics.

As an example, I want to introduce you to an acquaintance of mine, John Marston. John is the main protagonist in Rockstar Games' newest game, *Red Dead Redemption*. The game is set in 1910, at a time when romanticism gave way to modernism, and the myth of the frontier where anything was possible was rapidly collapsing on itself. This time period has been me/morialized by movie directors such as John Ford and Sergio Leone and iconic actors such as John Wayne and Clint Eastwood. When federal agents kidnap John's wife and son, it is up to the player to guide him on an epic journey through the Old West to bring former members of his gang of outlaws to justice. Game designer Sid Meier has defined a *good* game as "a series of interesting choices" (Rollings and Morris 2000, 38). If that is so, then *Red Dead Redemption* is a series of ethical choices. Everything the player does has consequences in the game world. The game utilizes Rockstar's well-known "sandbox" technology to allow the player to roam free anywhere within the game world and solve any of the game's many quests in any number of creative ways.

In his book *Avatar Emergency*, Ulmer uses the concept of avatar as the "site of a new dimension of identity formation, supplementing spirit (oral) and literate (self) formations" (Ulmer forthcoming, 3). With Ulmer's help, we can finally start to move past the current epideictic rhetoric on video games. It is through the study of this new dimension of "identity forma- tion," facilitated by a conductive logic that assembles personal associations and ethical considerations differently, that we can observe that which has been obscured by current rhetorical practices. Similar to Charles Babbage's "difference engine," a machine designed to tabulate complex polynomial functions, the video game is an *experience engine* that can help us experience ethics and its implications in new and persuasive ways.

As with all cultural and industrial innovations, especially those that dra- matically transform human experience, the gap between use and design is filled by the rattle and hum of *epideictic* rhetoric. As I have suggested, the move to assign blame to, or to take credit for, video game *effects* is too of- ten a game of underestimating or overplaying the *epideictic* card. The ques- tion to consider is whether the *epideictic* dilemma actually, and ironically, works in our favor. Gerard Hauser's research parses the various ethical and pedagogical implications of the epideictic genre of rhetoric by recasting it as inventional rather than purely ceremonial (Hauser 1999, 5). According to Hauser, there is a sound "relationship between epideictic and *phronesis*" in Aristotle's discussion of epideictic rhetoric (Hauser 1999, 6): "In Books II and VI of the *Nichomachean Ethics*, Aristotle is intent on distinguishing the philosopher's wisdom, *sophia*, from the practical wisdom that he considers our best guide amidst the contingencies of prudential conduct. Whereas *sophia* offers insight into truth, the preserve of *phronesis* is insight into what to think and do when confronted by conflicting alternatives" (Hauser 1999, 12).

The upshot of this insight is that this "relationship between epideictic and *phronesis*" allowed citizens to "experience" public issues in such a way that they helped invent their own understanding of their social and politi- cal lives (Hauser 1999, 6). Hauser concludes that "Aristotle also enhances the role of epideictic by assigning its practitioners the responsibility for tell- ing the story of lived virtue" (Hauser 1999, 14). In essence, by telling stories of praise and blame, citizens take on the role of narrating ethical ways of life. Furthermore, the audiences of epideictic speeches or tales "experience the story of the golden mean as it is lived in their community" (Hauser 1999, 16). If the stories of lived virtue help invent how we confront ethical dilemmas, Hauser's exploration of "an alternative tendency in Aristotle's remarks" (Hauser 1999, 17) offers the first step in moving beyond the more didactic version of epideictic rhetoric that dominates the praise and blame game of video games.

The next step is to adopt the invention of ethics as the experience of lived virtue for games studies. For this, I aim to problematize the cause/effect topos—namely, that the technology and design of games is unavoidably "charged" in one direction and thus causes unethical (or violent) conduct by users. Ulmer points us to Heidegger and Nietzsche, each of whom (in distinct ways) deconstruct the right/wrong and true/false dichotomies with which Western metaphysics has hamstrung the rhetorical play of pain/pleasure. The linchpin that unhinges these well-oiled constructs turns out to be "Moment." According to Ulmer, "the Moment, in other words, makes room for the 'step back,' allowing the 'decider' to take an attitude, and create a second-order relationship to the now-circumstance. The Moment is Heidegger's version of the withdrawing opening (chora) required to keep life in play" (Ulmer forthcoming, 119). Next, Ulmer recounts Nietzsche's "insight, his changed attitude" about the tradition in Western metaphysics that rejects "'life' as it is, including its pain and suffering, the 'spirit of revenge' against the passage of time" (Ulmer forthcoming, 120). The following passage from Nietzsche's *Zarathustra* is, according to Ulmer, a prime example of "how to communicate a new thought (how to change the hegemonic system of values), since Zarathustra is shown trying out most of the available approaches" (Ulmer forthcoming, 120).

"Stop, dwarf!" I said. "I! Or you! But I am the stronger of us two— you do not know my abysmal thought! That thought—you could not endure!"

Then something occurred which lightened me: for the dwarf jumped from my shoulder, the inquisitive dwarf! And he squatted down upon a stone in front of me. But a gateway stood just where we had halted.

"Behold this gateway, dwarf!" I went on: "it has two aspects. Two paths come together here: no one has ever reached their end.

"This long lane behind us: it goes on for an eternity. And that long lane ahead of us—that is another eternity.

"They are in opposition to one another, these paths; they abut on one another; and it is here at this gateway that they come together. The name of the gateway is written above it: 'Moment.'" (Nietzsche [1883] 1961, 178; quoted in Ulmer forthcoming, 120).

Moment is an emblem of a gateway where three, not only two, axes intersect. Ulmer suggests that in Heidegger and Nietzsche, Moment "is where ethics begins to take place" (Ulmer forthcoming, 120). Nietzsche's "value of the preservation of life as that which is 'beyond good and evil'," and Heidegger's "unpacking of the thought of eternal return" is "necessary to make explicit the formal procedures by which flash reason produces the experience of Moment against the dromospheric Now" (Ulmer forthcoming,

121). For Ulmer, "Avatar is this *eidos*," the saying yes to "life as a whole" in Moment (Ulmer forthcoming, 121). And yet Ulmer is quick to acknowledge that "Avatar is not everything of course. We cannot forget how we got here or the skills and habits accumulated thus far in history" (Ulmer forthcoming, 20). This is precisely why we examined hacker and computing history in chapters 2 and 3 in light of the electrate apparatus. Yet the question of why still looms over our decisions, and the decisions of gamers, not to mention of policymakers who keep repeating the mantra of "good and evil" in the epideictic game of engineering the end of play (Derrida [1966] 1978).

Ulmer's Avatar moves us out of such engineered and straightjacketed notions of ethics in the age of ubiquitous computing. "Something is happening to us and through us that goes by the name 'avatar' these days," he writes (Ulmer forthcoming, 20). And yet Ulmer predicts:

We have not yet begun to avatar, although there are futuristic scenarios and scholarly histories, looking forward and back in time, to consider the possibilities. You need to meet avatar, that part of you inhabiting cyberspace (for lack of a better term). You and I need to meet the avatar that we already have, that we already are, now that it may be augmented within the digital apparatus (electracy) as a prosthesis of decision. Avatar knows more than you or I do, or rather, it knows better than you or I do about what to do now, or what you or I truly know and understand and value and wish in our various respective situations. This claim must be not only understood, but undergone. It is not only an idea, a theory, but an experience. (Ulmer forthcoming, 20)

Games, I am arguing, are experience engines. Avatar, Ulmer claims, must be "undergone." Life, Nietzsche warns, is "beyond good and evil." We are beginning to hack electracy using serious play in order to invent a new image of ludic ethics.

Unnatural Experience

In *My Life as a Night Elf Priest* (2010), Bonnie Nardi explores play as "aesthetic experience" (Nardi 2010, 45), drawing on the work of John Dewey and others to situate her ethnographic study of *World of Warcraft* in the diverse realms of human experience. As I have also argued in chapter 1, ludic activity (play) is a conductive bridge that allows us to participate in the invention of the institutional practices of electracy. Nardi's work highlights the aesthetic nature of play and, through Dewey, connects such experiences to "everyday life" (Nardi 2010, 50). According to Nardi, "modernity sequesters the aesthetic in regulated institutions outside normal processes of living. Dewey suggests how deeply *peculiar* this is. He argued that active aesthetic activity must be reconceptualized and reintegrated into everyday life to infuse normal processes of living with the 'delighted care' and 'genuine affection' that move collective life toward excellence of experience" (Nardi 2010, 50–51). Clearly Nardi considers *World of Warcraft* as "a work of art" (Nardi 2010, 198), and yet she understands (via Dewey) that aesthetic human experience *as* art should never be cordoned into "cultural fortresses" (Nardi 2010, 198). Her disposition about game play in *World of Warcraft* strikes a balance between the complexity of human motivations for play and the sheer delight that comes not from seeking "categorical purity" (Nardi 2010, 199) but from experience of play in everyday life.

As a correlative, we are inventing a new ethics through the *act* of ethics, through playing, where experiencing outcomes and consequences is the key element. This is not about establishing a universal ethics but micro ethics applied individually. When you join a pick-up group in *World of Warcraft* and experience someone's virtual bad behavior, you learn from it in order to become a better person or to handle others' bad conduct. As an experience engine, the game makes possible the move beyond epideictic rhetoric and the topoi of praise and blame toward a new understanding of ethics in an electrate time. Through play we can experience the consequences of the ethical choices we make.

But judging such behavior is not the point. It isn't the point of a ludic ethics. Jean-François Lyotard claims that "the ability to judge does not hang upon the observance of criteria" (Lyotard and Thébaud 1985, 17). In fact, "that which ought to be cannot be concluded from that which is," by which he means that we are always "without criteria, yet one must decide" (Lyotard and Thébaud 1985, 17). Justice (ethical judgment) does not hinge upon moral law. Lyotard points to Kant's *Critique of Judgment* (on aesthetic and teleological judgment) and concludes that the "form that [judgment] will take in the last *Critique* is that of the imagination. An imagination that is constitutive. It is not only an ability to judge; it is a power to invent criteria" (Lyotard and Thébaud 1985, 17). The upshot of Lyotard's analysis means that without criteria we are nevertheless obligated to act in the face of violence and unethical behavior. But injustice itself only occurs "if the pragmatics of obligation, that is, the possibility of continuing to play the game of the just, were excluded. That is what is unjust. Not the opposite of the just, but that which prohibits that the question of the just and the unjust be, and remain, raised. Thus, obviously, all terror, annihilation, massacre, etc., or their threat, are, by definition, unjust. The people whom one massacres will no longer be able to play the game of the just and the unjust" (Lyotard and Thébaud 1985, 66–67).

In the context of virtual play, in which real death, real threats, and real injustice are played out as fantasy, the question of justice (ethical judgment) remains an issue of what Lyotard claims would be any obstacle to "contuining to play the game of the just" (Lyotard and Thébaud 1985, 66). In *World of Warcraft* and other social multiplayer game environments, in which player behavior is woven among nonplayer actions and game rules, the burden of inventing ludic ethics could be said to rest with some intricate interplay of these elements (both human and technological). But Sicart has argued, in *The Ethics of Computer Games* (2009), that "*World of Warcraft* is an unethical game" (Sicart 2009, 187).

The basis for Sicart's claim is his analysis of the player-versus-player system, implemented by the game developers, and which he contends is inherently unethical. Because imbalances exist between how players engage in PvP play and the degree to which players can intervene in the system if other players are unethical (efforts, he claims, that are unsuccessful), this constitutes an "essential design mistake" (Sicart 2009, 187), and therefore the game is unethical. Sicart's book contains highly nuanced and balanced discussions of ethics, but there is, at the outset, a major premise that runs counter to an Ulmerian take on ludic ethics. From the beginning, Sicart defines ethics "as a system or set of moral values, and the tools for analyzing these values. Morals can be defined as the right or wrong of actions or objects. The application of ethics is the rational, philosophical approach to the questions of good, evil, harm, duties, and values. [Sicart's] book is then an exploration of the moral nature of computer games and computer game players" (Sicart 2009, 4). As I have shown, through Ulmer, Derrida, Heidegger, Nietzsche, and Lyotard, the *Axis* of orality (right/wrong) and literacy (true/false) are elements of an apparatus at one with the history of reason as morality, not of life and Moment. To be sure, ethics and play seem to be strange bedfellows, but it is my view that they need not be mutually exclusive, and they are always already in the process of being invented—via play itself.

This may seem unnatural. But can we say that experience is unnatural? Or that play is unnatural? Or that invention is inherently unethical? These questions should be held open as we shift now to my final chapter on the ludic transversal.

7   Burning Chrome

The paradox of modern knowledge circulates around the incompleteness theorem postulating the paradox that no system is able rigorously to account for itself. There is a blindspot at the very core of clarity.
—Gregory Ulmer, *Electronic Monuments*

Why do some people choose not to play games? In *A Casual Revolution*, Jesper Juul explores this question. He says, "Many video games ask for a lot in order to be played, so it is not surprising that some people do not play video games. Video games ask for a lot more than other art forms. They ask for more time and they more concretely require the player to understand the conventions on which they build. A game may not fit into a player's life" (Juul 2010, 10). While Juul's book is primarily concerned with the concept of time and what the player's investment thereof means for the renewed interest in casual games, *Inter/vention* has explored the question, and its inverted counterpart, as it pertains to the conventions on which digital games build. If it is correct that video games do ask for more than other art forms, which is a supposition that hearkens back to Espen Aarseth's groundbreaking work on cybertext and ergodic literature from the mid-1990s, then we need to account for that in some meaningful way. I have wrestled with this question in many forms and through many games for the better part of a decade. Yet it was not until I started reading Ulmer's work that it suddenly dawned on me that digital games are uniquely different phenomena that cannot be adequately explained or understood through the conventions and genres we all know from the literate apparatus. So, with this in mind, I would like to respectfully hack Juul's statement above a little bit and say that one reason that people choose not to play digital games is perhaps because we don't yet know exactly what they are or what they do for and to us. With this book, I aim to resituate games as *electrate expressions*, that is to say, artifacts of a new apparatus that is different from that which came before them. Because the digital game can only be as old as the universal digital computer itself, less than seventy years if we mark it from the introduction of the Von Neumann architecture at the end of World War II, then it should not come as a big surprise that the digital game is a mystery/ mystory that still eludes us. As Ulmer so poignantly reminds us, it has taken more than 2,000 years to develop the literate apparatus and even longer to develop the oral apparatus that came before it, so we are only at the very beginning of an understanding of what electracy and its multitude of expressive forms might be. "Electracy does not already exist as such," he says, "but names an apparatus that is emerging 'as we speak,' rising in many different spheres and areas, and converging in some unforeseeable, yet malleable way" (Ulmer 2003, 7).

People who *do play* digital games, from the hardcore *World of Warcraft* raider to the casual *Farmville* player, often tell me that they do it for the entertainment value. They play to relieve stress, to take a break from "work," to escape the "real-world" problems and complexities of their "first lives," or for any number of other personal reasons. Interestingly, there is one distinction they all seem to share in common—namely, the distinction that people draw between work and play, between productivity and consumption (entertainment). Rarely have I heard anyone explicitly state that they play to improve the world. Yet if we try to find some larger purpose in why we play, as I believe we must, then improving the world is precisely what we should aim to do. In this book, I have made a case for the hacker as ludic egent. I purposefully chose to expand the notion of what constitutes a player in order to show how electracy functions as the charge being conducted and invented by people whose ambition it is to effect change, for good or bad. For the hacker, the code itself is a game, the *chora*, described by Derrida as

irreducible to the two positions, the sensible and the intelligible, which have dominated the entire tradition of Western thought, it is irreducible to all the values to which we are accustomed—values of origin, anthropomorphism, and so on. . . . *Chora* receives everything or gives place to everything. . . . It remains foreign to the imprint that it receives; so in a sense, it does not receive anything—it does not receive what it receives nor does it give what it gives. Everything inscribed in it erases itself immediately, while remaining in it. Thus it is an impossible surface—it is not even a surface, because it has no depth. (Derrida and Eisenman 1997, 10; quoted in Ulmer 1994, 65)

The choral code, what it *receives* from the hacker/player (playing hack) and what it *gives* to the player/hacker (hacking play) who realizes the impossible possibilities of its program, assembled at the moment of run time, constitutes the new ontology that Ulmer proposes for the electrate apparatus. The choral code remains foreign to the meaning of its program. It has no conception of how players play that which it gives, nor does it care because it cannot possibly know. What it inscribes can only be experienced through the act of play and then is immediately erased, leaving only a memory behind in the player's mind. The choral code has no depth because it has no surface, yet it inspires in the player deep and profound experiences that are situated along the *ludic electrate transversal*. In Ulmer's terminology, the transversal is that which assembles, a concept that he draws from Félix Guattari who put it thus:

> When we speak of abstract machines, by "abstract" we can also understand "extract" in the sense of extracting. They are montages capable of relating all the heterogeneous levels that they traverse and that we have just enumerated. The abstract machine is transversal to them, and it is this abstract machine that will or will not give these levels an existence, and efficiency, a power of ontological auto-affirmation. The different components are swept up and reshaped by a sort of dynamism. Such a functional ensemble will hereafter be described as a machinic assemblage. The term "assemblage" does not imply any notion of bond, passage, or anastomosis between its components. It is an assemblage of possible fields, of virtual as much as constituted elements, without any notion of generic or species' relation. (Guattari 1995, 35; quoted in Ulmer 2005, 84)

Assemblage plays a crucial role in our mission to invent electracy. "There is a blind spot at the very core of clarity" Ulmer (2005, 85) says that we can only get at by following the assemblage of components, fragments, or repeating signifiers, revealed to us through the sting of memory, of the *punctum*, as the assemblage traverses the heterogeneous levels of meaning or discourses that we relate to. The electrate assemblage does not confront this task in the direct, perpendicular way that we are accustomed to in literacy; rather, it approaches it transversely through the conductive inference logic of the elements themselves (repeating signifiers) that it encounters along the way. The ultimate goal of the assemblage is to invent new meaning, skills, and practices that may help us see, then, the "blindspot at the very core of clarity" (Ulmer 2005, 85). Play assembles the conditions of possibility for electrate invention that is transversal to the dichotomies and ontologies with which ludology, as a field of academic inquiry, has concerned itself; of writer and reader, game and narrative, producer and consumer, developer and player. It *plays through* all of these in a rhetorical inter/vention that conflates them into a new *ludic emblem*, that of the hacker, which is not reductionist in any way but is a morphism that contains within itself the full scale of the *anthropos* ranging from the ideal to the abject, the hacker noir, and the HaX0R turned mass-murderer.

Ludic Egency

If we aim to effect change through the ludic transversal, then we as hackers and players must become egents for that change. For Ulmer this is a fundamental condition that gives direction and meaning to our playful activities. In *Internet Invention*, he relates the my/story of how he himself came to this realization when trying to convince his father and his father's friend Mr. Richards why he had changed his major from economics and political science to English during his sophomore year in college. I am including his/story here because it resonates so well with the kind of arguments that players must also face when trying to explain or justify why we play.

These adults explained to me that real work added value to the world by taking something and making it useful to society, the way Mr. Richards turned his cattle into beef, or the way my father in his business took sand and gravel out of the hills . . . and turned them into building materials. What about poetry, didn't poetry add value to life? No, was the unequivocal answer. Poets and people who taught poetry were parasites living off the labor of others—those who turned the stuff of nature into (commodities.) "You are wrong," I insisted, "and I can prove it." My proof at the time didn't go much beyond the fable of the ants and the grasshopper. I never won the argument with the patriarchs of my parents' generation, but I am still trying to prove something. (Ulmer 2003, 2)

In his earlier works, especially *Internet Invention* and *Electronic Monuments*, Ulmer's continued efforts to prove that a humanities education is also a worthwhile way to improve the world is situated within a framework he calls the EmerAgency, a "distributed virtual online consulting agency without portfolio" (Ulmer 2003, xiii). His latest book, *Avatar Emergency*, advances the concept of "flash reason, a practice for deliberative reason, for public policy formation, making democratically informed decisions in a moment, at light speed, against the threat of a General Accident that happens everywhere simultaneously" (Ulmer forthcoming, 3). Ulmer is responding to "Paul Virilio's challenge to our information society: every technology brings with it its own disaster" (Ulmer forthcoming, 11; Virilio and Lotringer 1983, 31–32). The invention of the automobile, for instance, also invented the automobile accident, which is the leading cause of death "among those age 5–34 in the U.S." (CDC 2010).

Online ludic space generated by computers is situated squarely within this *dromospheric* time warp that Virilio says "reduces to nothing, or next to nothing, the expanse of a constricted planet hanging in the vacuum of space" (Virilio 1997, 40). "How can we live if there is no more here, and everything is now?" he asks rhetorically (Virilio 1997, 37). For the urbanist

Virilio, the loss of space as measured in physical distances means the loss of the modern city's prominence and importance in society. Born, as he was, in the city of lights in the year 1932, we might understand where he is coming from and why he bemoans the city's perceived demise. Essayist and literary critic Sven Birkerts did the same thing in *The Gutenberg Elegies* (1994), where he mourned what he perceived to be the impending "fate of reading in an electronic age" (Birkerts 1994). As we now know, Birkerts was really lamenting the fate of the print culture, which is indeed in a slow process of decline. The concept of reading itself, however, is not. It is morphing out of the old literate apparatus and into a new electrate one. Similarly, the city is also being reinvented. Virilio explains, "While the topical City was once constructed around the 'gate' and the 'port,' the teletopical metacity is now reconstructed around the 'window' and the teleport, that is to say, around the screen and the time slot" (Virilio 1997, 26). To invoke William Gibson, the Sprawl is a metaphor for the topical city, while the teletopical metacity exists in the Matrix. As ludic egents, we are invited to join Ulmer's EmerAgency and help invent the new teletopical metacity with its flash reason and its myriad of electrate practices. To do so, we need only follow the ludic transversal where it may take us.

Punctum

At the heart of darkness, the still center, the glitch systems shred the dark with whirlwinds of light, translucent razors spinning away from us; we hang in the center of a silent slow-motion explosion, ice fragments falling away forever, and Bobby's voice comes in across light-years of electronic void illusion—"Burn the bitch down. I can't hold the thing back—" The Russian program, rising through towers of data, blotting out the playroom colors. And I plug Bobby's homemade command package into the center of Chrome's cold heart. The squirt transmission cuts in, a pulse of condensed information that shoots straight up, past the thickening tower of darkness, the Russian program, while Bobby struggles to control that crucial second. An unformed arm of shadow twitches from the towering dark, too late. We've done it. The matrix folds itself around me like an origami trick. And the loft smells of sweat and burning circuitry. I thought I heard Chrome scream, a raw metal sound, but I couldn't have. (Gibson 1986a, 200)

This passage from Gibson's short story *Burning Chrome* is a *punctum* that connects with a pleasant memory for me. Between 2005 and 2008, I ran a virtual community of several hundred people in *World of Warcraft*. As the guild master for this community, Equinox, I organized role-playing events, raids, and dungeon crawls, and I dealt with the day-to-day conflicts and problems that invariably occur when a large and diverse group of people come together like this. In some ways, my "job" was not unlike that of a director of a midsized company, and I freely admit that it sometimes felt more like drudgery than play. But such is the nature of play that situates itself along the electrate axis of pleasure and pain. In *World of Warcraft*, as in most other massively multiplayer online games, there comes a point at which players cannot progress any further on their own. They need to collaborate with others to achieve the goals they set for themselves, and this was the mission of the Equinox guild: to provide a ludic collective that would help players achieve goals that sometimes required upward of forty people to work together in unison. The punctum that the passage from Gibson's story represents for me connects with an image in my memory from 2006. Our guild had been working diligently for months to defeat the raid boss Ragnaros in the classic forty-man instance Molten Core. Anyone who has tried to organize forty people to collaboratively accomplish such a task will know that it is not nearly as trivial as it may sound, but I digress. When we finally made our way to Ragnaros's inner sanctum and took him on in an epic battle that lasted almost thirty minutes, I felt exactly like Jack in Gibson's story. By my side that night, fighting Ragnaros, the Lord of Fire, was my Texan wife, the English professor, the Swedish nurse whose cancer prevented her from leaving home in case her liver transplant came in, and her British boyfriend, whom she had never met face to face. There was the German cinema operator, and his friend the automobile mechanic, the Norwegian high school kid who was in love with a Finnish girl playing a druid healer who didn't love him. There was a young British boy who we didn't know was lame from the neck down and frequently had to go AFK (away from keyboard) in the middle of raids to take his medications. There was the Danish single mother of two who rushed home from work as a secretary in the city each day to play her night elf hunter. There were many others whose occupations and geographical locations I never knew. We were Equinox, and together we defeated the Lord of Fire (see figure7.1). When we had done it, "the matrix [folded] itself around me like an origami trick. And the loft [smelled] of sweat and burning circuitry. I thought I heard [Ragnaros] scream, a raw metal sound, but I couldn't have" (Gibson 1986a, 200). I experienced real community that night and yet "when the extreme spatial distancing suddenly gives way to the extreme proximity of real time of exchange *there still remains an irreducible gap*" (Virilio 1997, 38).

I was joking one day with a colleague and fellow member of my new academic guild, Venture (U.S. *World of Warcraft* server Argent Dawn) (see figure 7.2), that we should publish our achievements in the game as scholarship, teaching, and service toward tenure. We both laughed because we know

Figure 7.1
Equinox rocks! September 26, 2006. Equinox Guild on Argent Dawn, EU defeats Ragnaros the Fire Lord in Molten Core.
Source: Courtesy of Blizzard Entertainment.

Figure 7.2
For the horde! Venture Guild outside Orgrimmar, Argent Dawn US, January 24, 2011. Guild members standing from left: Hessie, Norandor, Raik, Saurastus, Imir, Innocenzo. Seated from left: Nyssara, Anaxagora, Myntiepwny, Zynlessa, Senormuerto, Fiammifera, Gawbo, and Maripel.
Source: Courtesy of Blizzard Entertainment.

that this is not going to happen in 2011. Like Ulmer, we still need to prove to our "patriarchs" and peers that what we do is a worthwhile pursuit that has a place within humanities learning. I have a great many achievements in the ludic space, but the greatest achievement of all in my/story is that since 1995 I have brought people together and helped facilitate communities of electrate learning that, while virtual in form, were no simulacrum, no less real than other communities with which I engage. It was the ludic transversal that led me here; all I did was play along.

Afterword: The Frog Critic

Ian Bogost

I never know what to say when people ask me, "What's your favorite game?" I'm bad with favorites. But it's an easy half-personal, half-business question that interviewers and auditorium audiences like to throw as a softball. It gives them a sense of their interlocutor. It's polite conversation.

In response, I usually hedge, talking about the games I've been playing recently, or the ones that have interested me over time, or the ones that I've found the most influential in my own work as a critic and a creator. It's an unsatisfying answer, and it probably seems disingenuous. Really, my audiences must think, shouldn't this guy be more excited about the object in support of which he purportedly advocates?

I'm sure I'll tug at no heartstrings for saying this, but for me, video games are *work*. They're what I do for a living—as both a researcher and a developer. That's not to say that I dislike them or that I'm bitter for having the ridiculously good fortune of being able to make and play and write about this wild, magic medium for a living. It just means that I hold it at arm's length, inquisitive, suspicious even. What can games do? What have they done? How do we make them do it? These questions require a certain distance. As scholars, we should be somewhat disinterested—not entirely disinterested, of course, but somewhat detached.

Such an idea runs counter to the notion of the *aca-fan*, an idea advanced by media scholar Henry Jenkins and embraced heavily within media studies. This somewhat awkward portmanteau signifies the academic-cum-fanatic, a critic who allows the love of a work, genre, or form to inspire and guide his or her scholarly pursuit. For the aca-fan, fanaticism opens the door to deep engagement rather than risking its oversight.

When Espen Aarseth joked some years ago that game studies risked becoming *World of Warcraft* studies, he meant it as a provocational warning. But there really are corners of media studies content to call themselves

Buffy Studies, Lost Studies, or what have you. They wear their fandom as a badge of commitment and honor.

Aca-fandom is most frequently associated with scholars of popular culture like television and the Internet. But it doesn't take too much squinting to see that just about every form of scholarship is a kind of weird fandom.

This is perhaps more easily seen in the humanities, where scholars of Shakespeare or Homer are no less susceptible to eccentric, absent-minded, blinkered commitment to a single object, one that goes well beyond reason and normalcy. But arguably, aca-fandom extends just as easily to science and engineering, fields in which dorkship and obsession drive insular, laser-focused infatuation with protein structures, algorithm optimization, polymer synthesis, aeronautical logistics, or any number of other specialties.

In truth, all academics are aca-fans first. All are driven by freakish overcommitment to a particular object or idea. The PhD is a credential that skews the world like a funhouse mirror, stretching one subject to comical proportions while shrinking everything else into insignificance.

It's this threat of madness, perhaps, that makes me withdraw when people ask about my personal video game obsessions. I fear such obsessions. They dot the landscape like countless rabbit holes, all threatening to slurp me into so many video game wonderlands.

Yet the alternative is likewise stark. If Lewis Carroll's Alice best analogizes the lurid, carnal indulgence of favoritism and fanaticism, then T. S. Eliot's J. Alfred Prufrock characterizes its opposite, the prim, formal, timorous cerebralism that worries so much at the consequences of doing anything that it dooms itself to doing nothing. If Alice is a Pollyanna, Prufrock is a cynic. If Alice asks what could possibly go wrong, Alfred asks what could possibly go right. If Alice surrenders to curiosity, Alfred yields to ennui.

This book offers a compelling alternative to this dichotomy. It shows us an alternative to both Alice and Alfred, to both groupie and skeptic. This is how I understand Jan Holmevik when he calls himself an *amphibian*: capable of breathing when immersed but likewise content when dried out on the rocks. The one does not long for the other. Neither takes priority. Despite the implications of their visages, the frog and the newt are not apathetic but merely content.

Both Holmevik and Jenkins advocate for immersion. But when the latter's species comes up for air, they explode with critical exclamation, dumping the fruit of their passion at our feet. They are not amphibians but whales, mammals who can't breathe under water but who nevertheless can hold their breath for a very long time until they surface explosively.

It's a glorious sight, the sensuousness and passion of the heaving, deep breath, the thrill and eagerness as blog posts erupt after the latest episode of *The Wire* or the latest raid in *World of Warcraft*. Brace yourselves and keep your distance for I erupt with *insight!* There's a reason tourism industries are built around whale watching rather than frog watching.

You've read this far, so let's admit it: There's a heavy dose of jargon in this book. Some of it is the jargon of philosopher Jacques Derrida, but much of it is borrowed from Derridean rhetorician Gregory Ulmer, whose foreword bookends these pages. We've got electracy, mystory, emerAgency, heuretics—some of the neologisms that make Ulmer's style characteristic. It's a risk that chances equal extravagance as that of the aca-fan or of Alice.

Yet in the preceding pages, Holmevik manages to tame these elephants, swatting his frog's tongue at the flies they draw. Highfalutin concepts are roosts for pigeons as much as they are billboards for highway travelers. Rather than relying on the implications of juxtaposition, Holmevik extends wordplay to play itself, reflecting on his own experiences making, playing, discussing, critiquing, and contextualizing games over the course of many years. There's a kind of normalcy in this practice. It's no big deal. Whales don't surface and girls don't shrink to enter magical doors. Holmevik just does the work, weaving his experiences with other historical and rhetorical threads.

The amphibian is an allegory for modern criticism, for what it might be if we let it.

Everyone knows the classic fairy tale "The Frog Prince," the story of a princess who befriends a frog, who then transforms into a prince. There are two generally recognized forms of it. In the more well-known version, the princess must kiss the frog to unleash its magic. But in the Brothers Grimm version of the story, the princess grows weary of the frog's truculence and throws it against the wall in disgust. It is this act of violence that undoes the spell and releases the prince.

These two ways of relating to the secret amphibian prince correspond roughly to the optimist and the cynic, the Alice and the Alfred. Either the frog must be lovingly excited into celebratory liberation or the thick skin of misinterpretation must be annihilated. One act is naive and saccharin, the other is cynical and ferocious.

Playing the role of the amphibian, Holmevik offers an alternative: The frog can also just be a frog. The games and technical apparatuses that comprise his subject can be both inspiration and curiosity, and the critic can be both fanatic and skeptic, dousing itself in the water when the mood strikes and then relaxing calmly on the rocks for reflection.

If only we could all be so enchanted, to be able to become the frog in the pond. So humble, so unassuming, so stately. Perhaps we will learn to do this, replacing favorites with subjects, obsessions with experiences, conclusions with observations. The frog is a humble role-model for the critic precisely because he does not become a prince but merely remains a frog.

Notes

Chapter 1

1. Nietzsche's maxim is articulated a bit differently in *Philosophy in the Tragic Age of the Greeks*, although Gilles Deleuze cast it in this way: "Nietzsche says that three anecdotes are sufficient to define the life of a thinker (PTG)—one for the place, one for the time and one for the element. The anecdote is to life what the aphorism is to thought: something to interpret" (Deleuze 1983, 110).

2. In 2004, MIT Press published *First Person: New Media as Story, Performance, and Game* (edited by Noah Wardrip-Fruin and Pat Harrigan), which also saw two sequels, *Second Person: Role-Playing and Story in Games and Playable Media* (2007) and *Third Person: Authoring and Exploring Vast Narratives* (2009). Three titles of great interest to the exploding game studies curriculum were published in 2005: (1) *The Game Design Reader: A Rules of Play Anthology* (edited by Katie Salen and Eric Zimmerman), (2) *Handbook of Computer Game Studies* (edited by Joost Raessens and Jeffrey Goldstein), and (3) Jesper Juul's *Half-Real: Video Games between Real Rules and Fictional Worlds*. In 2006, MIT Press published both Ian Bogost's *Unit Operations: An Approach to Videogame Criticism* and T. L. Taylor's *Play Between Worlds: Exploring Online Game Culture*. Bogost's ambitious (and highly influential) *Persuasive Games: The Expressive Power of Videogames* came out in 2008. Also, the first *World of Warcraft* reader was among their listings that year, *Digital Culture, Play, and Identity: A World of Warcraft® Reader* (edited by my good friends and one-time fellow PhD students Hilde G. Corneliussen and Jill Walker Rettberg). Along those lines, they also released Michael Nitsche's *Video Game Spaces: Image, Play, and Structure in 3D Game Worlds* in 2008. But 2009 surpassed previous years with MIT Press's publication of six key books in this field: (1) Miguel Sicart's *The Ethics of Computer Games*; (2) Celia Pearce's *Communities of Play: Emergent Cultures in Multiplayer Games and Virtual Worlds*; (3) Mary Flanagan's *Critical Play: Radical Game Design*; (4) Jesper Juul's *A Casual Revolution: Reinventing Video Games and Their Players*; (5) Nick Montfort and Ian Bogost's *Racing the Beam: The Atari Video Computer System*; and (6) Noah Wardrip-Fruin's *Expressive Processing: Digital Fictions, Computer Games, and Software Studies*. Finally, in 2010, we have seen from MIT Press William

Bainbridge's *The Warcraft Civilization: Social Science in a Virtual World* and Ian Bogost, Simon Ferrari, and Bobby Schweizer's *Newsgames: Journalism at Play.*

Chapter 4

1. Markus Montola defines a pervasive game "as a game that has one or more salient features that expand the contractual magic circle of play spatially, temporally, or socially" (Montola 2009, 12). In the collection *Pervasive Games*, however, the focus is on designing game worlds as pervasive spaces, although he does acknowledge that the boundary between the "real and the artificial" is largely blurred in such a way that Huizinga's notion of the "magic circle" "loses its meaning as a ritualistic separator of ordinary and playful, becoming only a representation of a code of conduct within the game" (Montola 2009, 19).

2. In addition to being a computer programmer, Crowther was also an avid cave surveyor. When he decided to write a computer-based adventure game for his children, setting it in a world of caverns and dungeons was perhaps an obvious choice, especially because Crowther was also a fan of role-playing games such as D&D.

3. In addition to the Essex MUD, there was also one other official MUD1 system in operation in the 1980s. This was the now famous "British Legends," which ran on CompuServe from 1987 to 1999 when the company's DECsystem-10 machine on which it ran was finally decommissioned as part of Y2K cleanup efforts (Toth). Thanks to Viktor Toth (aka MrSpock), in 2000, British Legends is still available online and can still be enjoyed by fantasy players with a flair for history.

4. TinyMUD is now available via telnet.

do "telnet LANCELOT.AVALON.CS.CMU.EDU 4201" to connect. The game should be reasonable self-explanatory.

If you have trouble, use the "gripe" command inside TinyMUD to complain (or if you don't, use it to let me know what you think). Don't expect too much out of the parser.

Note: It's ok to build things, the database will (mostly) survive crashes and new program versions.

—Jim (Aspnes 1989)

5. One of the things he was particularly concerned about was a security issue known as "Buffer overrun." Only a few years before, in November 1988, Robert T. Morris, a young graduate student at Cornell University, had written a program later known as the Internet Worm, which caused serious havoc at Internet installations all across the world due to its ability to propagate by exploiting security holes such as buffer overruns.

6. Twenty years later, Blizzard Entertainment is experiencing similar problems arising out of attempts to regulate community challenges through technology. In

Blizzard's case, the problem relates among other things to the "Looking For Dungeon tool" and the vastly negative impact that it is having on the player communities.

Chapter 5

1. The following list includes some of the institutions that actively used LinguaMOO during this time: University of Bergen (Norway), Old Dominion University, Hanyang University (South Korea), University of Wisconsin, Shlzuoka University (Japan), Colorado State University–Boulder, Colorado University–Denver, Institute for Media Communication (Germany), Nottingham University (England), George Mason University, University of Southampton (England), University of North Carolina–Greensboro, University of Illinois–Chicago, University of Louisiana–Lafayette, University of Sioux Falls, South Dakota, University of Texas at Austin, University of Texas at Arlington, University of Rochester, New York, Texas Tech University, California State Polytechnic University, Southern Methodist University, Ohio University, Purdue University, and Vassar College.

Chapter 6

1. The ReadMe file of Eric Harris's *DOOM* level:

Title: U.A.C. LABS
Filename: uaclabs.zip
Author: Eric Harris
Email address: REBDOOMER@aol.com
Misc. Author Info: Whatsup all you doomers out there! REB here, bringin you another kick-ass doom2 wad! This one took a damn long time to do, so send me some bloody credit man! Sorry the file is so damn big, but you know how it is when you change sprites . . . well, you should know if you've every made wads like this. Enjoy the new death frames, made em all myself!
=DO NOT GO TO ANY OTHER LEVEL BESIDES THE 2 IN=
=THIS WAD, MANY SPRITES WHERE DELETED IN THE =
=WAD TO MAKE IT AS SMALL AS I COULD. SO SOME =
=MAPS MAY HAVE DELETED SPRITES IN THEM AND IT =
=WILL CRASH DOOM2. so dont do it, man. =
Description\Story: OK, here goes: After defeating the demons on Earth, you learn of a new terror. Phobos, where this hellish battle all began, has been taken over again! When you were fighting hell on Earth, the demon back-up crew decided to pay a visit to Phobos again. No problem, right? All the installations were already destroyed by you and the first attack, right? Yeah, that part's right, but half the surviving humans from earth took refuge there! We just redid the structures to fit our needs and moved in again. Bad idea. Those gates were still active. Sooo aah, chalk up another kill for the demons. After the 2nd attack on phobos, only 99% of the human population is left. Once you emerged from hell, you took the first ship you could to phobos. Once

again, there were no survivors. Now it's PAYBACK TIME! Those goddamned alien bastards are gonna get one helluva BFG blast up their FREAKIN ASS! You land on the other side of phobos. Where the humans landed for the 2nd time. Your mission is to destroy the 2 main gates and destroy the platoon of demons at the main teleporter from phobos to Earth. Use the maps, you'll need them to find all the hidden secrets and doors. Beware of the 2 gates, they ARE still active, and more demons might come through any second. The platoon guarding the teleporter out is VERY large, so beware. Good luck marine, and don't forget, KILL 'EM AAAAALLLL!!!!!

Authors may NOT use this level as a base to build additional levels.

You may NOT change a damn thing with this WAD, if you do, i will blow you up. And it will be cool. (Harris 2011)

References

Aarseth, Espen. 1997. *Cybertext: Perspectives on Ergodic Literature.* Baltimore, Md.: The Johns Hopkins University Press.

Anatomy of a Massacre. 1999. *Newsweek.* May 3. http://www.newsweek.com/1999/05/02/anatomy-of-a-massacre.html.

Anderson, Judy. 2001. Personal communication with the author. January 28.

Appeal, Morris. 1991. http://morrisworm.larrymcelhiney.com/morris_appeal.txt.

Artaud, Antonin. 1958. *The Theatre and Its Double.* Trans. M. C. Richard. New York: Grove Press.

Aspnes, James. 1989. TinyMUD Now Available Via Telnet. Email. http://www.linnaean.org/~lpb/muddex/a-o.html.

Aspnes, James. 2001. Personal communication with the author. February 27.

Aspray, William. 1990. *John Von Neumann and the Origins of Modern Computing.* Cambridge, Mass.: MIT Press.

Atanasoff, John V. 1972. Interviewed by H. Tropp, June 7. Smithsonian, National Museum of American History. http://invention.smithsonian.org/downloads/fa_cohc_tr_atan720607.pdf.

Babbage, Charles. 1864. *Passages from the Life of a Philosopher.* London: Longman, Green, Longman, Roberts, & Green.

Bainbridge, William Sims. 2010. *The Warcraft Civilization: Social Science in a Virtual World.* Cambridge, Mass.: MIT Press.

Barthes, Roland. 1981. *Camera Lucida: Reflections on Photography.* Trans. R. Howard. New York: Hill and Wang.

Bartle, Richard. 2004. *Designing Virtual Worlds.* Indianapolis, Ind.: New Riders Publishing.

Baudelaire, Charles. [1863] 1986. The Painter of Modern Life. In *The Painter of Modern Life and Other Essays*, ed. Jonathan Mayne. New York: Da Capo Press.

Baudrillard, Jean. [1983] 2008. *Fatal Strategies*. Trans. Philippe Beitchman and W. G. J. Niesluchowski. Los Angeles: Semiotext(e).

BBC News. 2009. http://news.bbc.co.uk/2/hi/in_depth/7938000.stm.

Benjamin, Walter. [1972] 1999. *The Arcades Project*. Trans. Howard Eiland and Kevin McLaughlin. Cambridge, Mass: Belknap Press.

Bijker, Wiebe E., Thomas Hughes, and Trevor Pinch, eds. 1989. *The Social Construction of Technological Systems: New Directions in the Sociology and History of Technology*. Cambridge, Mass.: MIT Press.

Birkerts, Sven. 1994. *The Gutenberg Elegies: The Fate of Reading in an Electronic Age*. Boston, Mass.: Faber and Faber.

Bizzell, Patricia. 1986. Foundationalism and Anti-Foundationalism in Composition Studies. *Pre/Text* 7 (1–2):37–56.

Bogost, Ian. 2006. *Unit Operations: An Approach to Videogame Criticism*. Cambridge, Mass.: MIT Press.

Bogost, Ian. 2008. *Persuasive Games: The Expressive Power of Videogames*. Cambridge, Mass.: MIT Press.

Bogost, Ian, Simon Ferrari, and Bobby Schweizer. 2010. *Newsgames: Journalism at Play*. Cambridge, Mass.: MIT Press.

Brand, Stewart. 1988. *The Media Lab:Inventing the Future at M.I.T.* New York: Penguin Books.

British Legends (MUD1). 2011. Accessed February 20. http://www.british-legends.com.

Bruckman, Amy. 1997. MacMOOSE. http://web.archive.org/web/20050216070546/http://www.cc.gatech.edu/~asb/MacMOOSE.

Bruckman, Amy. [1998] 2002. Finding One's Own in Cyberspace. In *High Wired: On the Design, Use, and Theory of Educational MOOs*. Eds. Cynthia Haynes and Jan Rune Holmevik, 15–24. Ann Arbor: University of Michigan Press.

Caillois, Roger. [1961] 2001. *Man, Play, and Games*. Trans. Meyer Barash. Urbana, Ill: University of Illinois Press.

CDC. 2010. Motor Vehicle Safety. Centers for Disease Control and Prevention. http://www.cdc.gov/motorvehiclesafety/index.html.

Ceruzzi, Paul E. [1998] 2003. *A History of Modern Computing*. Cambridge, Mass.: MIT Press.

Cha, Theresa Hak Kyung, ed. 1980. *Cinematographic Apparatus: Selected Writings.* New York: Tanam Press.

Chalmers, Rachel. 2000. The Unknown Hackers. *Salon.com.* May 17. http://dir.salon .com/tech/feature/2000/05/17/386bsd/index.html.

Chassell, Robert. 2001. Personal communication with the author. February 7.

Christensen, Ward, and Randy Suess. 1989. Birth of the BBS. http://chinet.com/html/ cbbs.html.

CNN. 1999. Interview with Adam Foss. April 20. http://www.youtube.com/watch ?v=qMOKucUrRmY.

Columbine Documents. 2000. http://denver.rockymountainnews.com/pdf/900 columbinedocs.pdf.

Cooke, Daniel, Joseph Urban, and Scott Hamilton. 1999. Unix and Beyond: An Interview with Ken Thompson. *Computer* 32 (5):58–64.

Corbató, F. J., and V. A. Vyssotsky. 1965. Introduction and Overview of the Multics System. *Multicians.org.* http://www.multicians.org/fjcc1.html.

Corneliussen, Hilde G., and Jill Walker Rettberg, eds. 2008. *Digital Culture, Play, and Identity: A World of Warcraft Reader.* Cambridge, Mass.: MIT Press.

Curtis, Pavel. 2001. Personal communication with the author. January 25.

Curtis, Pavel. [1998] 2002. Not Just a Game: How LambdaMOO Came to Exist and What It Did to Get Back at Me. In *High Wired: On the Design, Use, and Theory of Educational MOOs.* Eds. Cynthia Haynes and Jan Rune Holmevik, 25–42. Ann Arbor: University of Michigan Press.

Day, Michael. 2003. Personal communication with the author. March 11.

Deleuze, Gilles. 1983. *Nietzsche and Philosophy.* Trans. H. Tomlinson. New York: Columbia University Press.

Deleuze, Gilles, and Félix Guattari. [1972] 1983. *Anti-Oedipus: Capitalism and Schizophrenia. Trans. Robert Hurley, Mark Seem, and Helen R. Lane.* Minneapolis: University of Minnesota Press.

Derrida, Jacques. 1974. *Of Grammatology.* Trans. G. C. Spivak. Baltimore, Md.: Johns Hopkins University Press.

Derrida, Jacques. [1966] 1978. Structure, Sign, and Play in the Discourse of the Human Sciences. In *Writing and Difference.* Trans. A. Bass, 278–293. Chicago: University of Chicago Press.

Derrida, Jacques, and Peter Eisenman. 1997. *Chora L Works.* Eds. Jeffrey Kipnis and Thomas Leeser. New York: The Monicelli Press.

Dibbell, Julian. 1993. A Rape in Cyberspace: How an Evil Clown, a Haitian Trickster Spirit, Two Wizards, and a Cast of Dozens Turned a Database Into a Society. *Village Voice* (December 23). http://www.juliandibbell.com/texts/bungle_vv.html.

DiBona, Chris, Sam Ockman, and Mark Stone, eds. 1999. *Open Sources: Voices from the Open Source Revolution.* Sebastopol, Calif.: O'Reilly Media.

Diderot, Denis. [1772] 1987. *Rameau's Nephew and D'Alembert's Dream.* Trans. Leonard Tancock. Middlesex, UK: Penguin Books.

Dreyfus, Suelette, and Julian Assange. 1997. *Underground.* Kew, Australia: Random House. Available from Project Gutenberg at http://www.gutenberg.org/catalog/world/readfile?fk_files=1456705.

Duvall, Robert. 1997. *The Apostle.* USA Films.

Eco, Umberto. [1980] 1983. *The Name of the Rose.* Trans. W. Weaver. New York: Warner Books.

enCore Consortium. 2004. http://encore-consortium.org.

Eskelinen, Markku. 2009. *Travels in Cybertextuality: The Challenge of Ergodic Literature and Ludology to Literary Theory.* PhD Dissertation. University of Jyväskylä, Finland.

Festa, Paul. 2001. Present at the 'e'-Creation. *Cnet.com.* October 10. http://news.cnet .com/2008-1082-274161.html?legacy=cnet.

Flanagan, Mary. 2009. *Critical Play: Radical Game Design.* Cambridge, Mass.: MIT Press.

Frasca, Gonzalo. 2003. Ludologists Love Stories, Too: Notes From a Debate That Never Took Place. In *Level-up: Digital Games Research Conference Proceedings.* Eds. Marinka Copier and Joost Raessens. DIGRA and Utrecht: Utrecht University. http://www.digra.org/dl/db/05163.01125.

Fusoco, Coco. [1999] 2001. Performance Art in a Digital Age: A Conversation with Ricardo Dominguez. *The Hacktivist Magazine* (1.0 January). http://www.iwar.org.uk/hackers/resources/the-hacktivist/issue-1/vol1.html#04.

Galloway, Alexander R. 2004. *Protocol: How Control Exists after Decentralization.* Cambridge, Mass.: MIT Press.

GCC Releases. 2011. *GNU.org.* Accessed February 20. http://gcc.gnu.org/releases .html.

Gibson, William. 1984. *Neuromancer.* New York: Ace Books.

Gibson, William. 1986a. *Burning Chrome.* New York: Arbor House.

Gibson, William. 1986b. *Count Zero.* London: Victor Gollancz, Ltd.

Gibson, William. 1988. *Mona Lisa Overdrive.* London: Victor Gollancz, Ltd.

Giloi, Wolfgang K. 1997. Konrad Zuse's Plankalkül: The First High-Level, "non von Neumann" Programming Language. *Annals of the History of Computing* 10 (2):17–24.

Glave, James. 1998. Putting a Price on Free Source. *Wired.com*. May 12. http://www .wired.com/science/discoveries/news/1998/05/12262.

Glusman, Gustavo. 1996. BioMOO's Purpose Statement. http://tecfa.unige.ch/moo/ VMDL/VMDL-26.html.

GNU Emacs FAQ. 2011. *GNU.org*. Accessed February 20. http://www.gnu.org/ software/emacs/emacs-faq.text.

GNU General Purpose License. [1989] 2007. *GNU.org*. http://www.gnu.org/licenses/ gpl.html.

Goldstein, Hilary. 2008. Grand Theft Auto IV Review: This Is the American Dream. *IGN.com*. April 25. http://ps3.ign.com/articles/869/869541p1.html.

Goldstine, Herman. 1972. *The Computer from Pascal to von Neumann*. Princeton, N.J.: Princeton University Press.

Greenberg, Andy. 2010. An Interview with WikiLeaks' Julian Assange. *Forbes.com*. November 29. http://blogs.forbes.com/andygreenberg/2010/11/29/an-interview-with -wikileaks-julian-assange/6.

Grigar, Dene, and John F. Barber. [1998] 2002. Defending Your Life in MOOspace: A Report from the Electronic Edge. In *High Wired: On the Design, Use, and Theory of Educational MOOs*. Eds. Cynthia Haynes and Jan Rune Holmevik, 192–232. Ann Arbor: University of Michigan Press.

Guattari, Félix. 1995. *Chaosmosis: An Ethico-Aesthetic Paradigm*. Trans. P. Bains and J. Pefanis. Sydney: Power Publications.

Hacktivismo. 2001. A Special Message of Hope. Cultdeadcow.com. July 4. http:// www.cultdeadcow.com/cDc_files/declaration.html.

Hafner, Katie, and John Markoff. [1991] 1995. *Cyberpunk: Outlaws and Hackers on the Computer Frontier*. New York: Touchstone.

Hafner, Katie, and Matthew Lyon. [1996] 2006. *Where Wizards Stay Up Late: The Origins of the Internet*. New York: Simon & Schuster.

Harpold, Terry. 2009. *Ex-foliations: Reading Machines and the Upgrade Path*. Minneapolis: University of Minnesota Press.

Harrigan, Pat, and Noah Wardrip-Fruin, eds. 2007. *Second Person: Role-Playing and Story in Games and Playable Media*. Cambridge, Mass.: MIT Press.

Harrigan, Pat, and Noah Wardrip-Fruin, eds. 2009. *Third Person: Authoring and Exploring Vast Narratives*. Cambridge, Mass.: MIT Press.

Harris, Eric. 2011. UACLABS.TXT. Accessed February 20. http://www.doomworld .com/10years/bestwads/infamous.php.

Hauben, Michael, and Ronda Hauben. 1997. *Netizens: On the History and Impact of Usenet and the Internet.* Los Alamitos, Calif.: Wiley-IEEE Computer Society Press.

Hauser, Gerard A. 1999. Aristotle on Epideictic: The Formation of Public Morality. *Rhetoric Society Quarterly* 29 (1):5–23.

Haynes, Cynthia, and Jan Rune Holmevik, eds. [1998] 2002. *High Wired: On the Design, Use and Theory of Educational MOOs.* Ann Arbor: University of Michigan Press.

Hebdige, Dick. 1979. *Subculture: The Meaning of Style.* London: Methuen.

Heidegger, Martin. [1927] 1962. *Being and Time.* Trans. J. Macquarrie and E. Robinson. New York: Harper & Row.

Heidegger, Martin. [1952] 1971a. Building Dwelling Thinking. In *Poetry, Language, Thought.* Trans. A. Hofstadter, 145–161. New York: Harper & Row.

Heidegger, Martin. [1946] 1971b. What Are Poets For? In *Poetry, Language, Thought.* Trans. A. Hofstadter, 91–142. New York: Harper & Row.

Himanen, Pekka. 2001. *The Hacker Ethic.* New York: Random House.

History of the OSI. 2011. *Opensource.org.* Accessed February 20. http://www.open source.org/history.

History of the SCO Group. 2011. *SCO.com.* Accessed February 20. http://www.sco .com/company/history_1979-1999.html.

Holmevik, Jan Rune. 1994. *Educating the Machine. A Study in the History of Computing and the Simula Programming Languages.* Master's Thesis. Norwegian University of Science and Technology, Trondheim, Norway.

Holmevik, Jan Rune. 2004. *TraceBack: MOO, Open Source, and the Humanities.* Dr. Art. Dissertation. University of Bergen, Norway.

Holmevik, Jan Rune, and Cynthia Haynes. 2000. *MOOniversity: A Student's Guide to Online Learning Environments.* Needham Heights, Mass.: Allyn & Bacon.

Hopper, Grace. 1981. Keynote Address. In *History of Programming Languages.* Ed. Richard L. Wexelblatt, 7–20. New York: Academic Press.

How to Think about Narrativity and Interactivity. 2009. Colloquium. Georgia Technological University. October 16. http://www.bogost.com/blog/how_to_think _about_narrative_a_1.shtml. Archived live recording http://lcc.gatech.edu/graduate/ live.

Hubbard, Jordan. 2011. A Brief History of FreeBSD. FreeBSD Documentation Project. *FreeBSD Handbook.* Accessed February 20. http://www.freebsd.org/doc/en_ US.ISO8859-1/books/handbook/history.html.

Huizinga, Johan. [1938] 1955. *Homo Ludens: A Study of the Play Element in Culture.* Boston, Mass.: Beacon Press.

Jenkins, Henry. 2006. *Convergence Culture: Where Old and New Media Collide.* New York: New York University Press.

Jepson, Kevin. 2004. The Barn. *enCore Consortium.* http://www.encore-consortium.org/Barn/default.htm.

Jordan, Tim. 2008. *Hacking: Digital Media and Technological Determinism.* Cambridge, UK: Polity Press.

Joyce, Jim. 1984. Interview with Bill Joy. *Unix Review* 2 (5): 58–62. http://web.cecs.pdx.edu/~kirkenda/joy84.html.

Juul, Jesper. 2005. *Half-Real: Video Games between Real Rules and Fictional Worlds.* Cambridge, Mass.: MIT Press.

Juul, Jesper. 2009. *A Casual Revolution: Reinventing Video Games and Their Players.* Cambridge, Mass.: MIT Press.

Kant, Immanuel. [1790] 2000. *Critique of the Power of Judgment.* Ed.Paul Guyer. Trans. Paul Guyer and Eric Matthews. New York: Cambridge University Press.

Katz, Steven. (forthcoming). *Plato's Nightmare.* Anderson, S.C.: Parlor Press.

Kell, Jeff. 1987. Relay: Past, Present, and Future. Excerpt from presentation at NETCON, New Orleans. http://web.inter.nl.net/users/fred/relay/relhis.html.

Krueger, Myron. [1983] 1991. *Artificial Reality II.* New York: Addison-Wesley.

Kubrick, Stanley. 1968. *2001: A Space Odyssey.* Film. Metro-Goldwyn-Mayer.

Kuhn, Bradley, and Richard Stallman. 2001. Freedom or Power? *GNU.org.* http://www.gnu.org/philosophy/freedom-or-power.html.

Kuhn, Thomas. 1962. *The Structure of Scientific Revolutions.* Chicago, Ill.: University of Chicago Press.

LambdaMOO. 2011. Virtual World. Accessed February 20. Telnet://lambda.moo.mud.org:8888.

Lanham, Richard. 1993. *The Electronic Word: Democracy, Technology, and the Arts.* Chicago, Ill.: University of Chicago Press.

Latour, Bruno. 1987. *Science in Action. How to Follow Scientists and Engineers through Society.* Cambridge, Mass.: Harvard University Press.

Latour, Bruno. 1993. *We Have Never Been Modern.* Cambridge, Mass.: Harvard University Press.

Latour, Bruno, and Steve Woolgar. 1979. *Laboratory Life: The Social Construction of Scientific Facts.* Beverly Hills, Calif.: Sage Publications.

Laurel, Brenda. 1991. *Computers as Theatre*. Reading, Mass.: Addison-Wesley Publishing Company.

Lee, J. A. N. 1994a. Charles Babbage History. http://bandwidthco.com/history/babbage/Charles%20Babbage%20History.pdf.

Lee, J. A. N. 1994b. Konrad Zuse. http://ei.cs.vt.edu/~history/Zuse.html.

Leonard, Andrew. 1998a. Let My Software Go. *Salon.com*. http://www.salon.com/21st/feature/1998/04/cov_14feature.html.

Leonard, Andrew. 1998b. The Richard Stallman Saga, Redux. *Salon.com*. http://www.salon.com/21st/feature/1998/09/11feature.html.

Leonard, Andrew. 2000. BSD Unix: Power to the People from the Code. *Salon.com*. May 16. http://www.salon.com/technology/fsp/2000/05/16/chapter_2_part_one/print.html.

Lévi-Strauss, Claude. 1966. *The Savage Mind*. Chicago, Ill.: The University of Chicago Press.

Levy, Stephen. [1984] 1994. *Hackers: Heroes of the Computer Revolution*. London: Penguin Books.

LinguaMOO. [1995] 2011. http://electracy.net:7000.

Lyotard, Jean-François, and Jean-Loup Thébaud. 1985. *Just Gaming*. Trans. W. Godzich. Minneapolis: University of Minnesota Press.

Marx, Karl. [1867] 1906. *Capital: A Critique of Political Economy*. Ed. Frederick Engels. Trans. Samuel Moore and Edward Aveling. New York: The Modern Library.

McCarthy, John. 1959. Memorandum to P. M. Morse Proposing Time Sharing. http://www-formal.stanford.edu/jmc/history/timesharing-memo/timesharing-memo.html.

McCarthy, John. [1983] 1996. Reminiscences on the History of Time Sharing. http://www-formal.stanford.edu/jmc/history/timesharing/timesharing.html.

McKusick, Marshall Kirk. 1999. Twenty Years of Berkeley Unix: From AT&T-Owned to Freely Redistributable. In *Open Sources: Voices from the Open Source Revolution*. Eds. Chris DiBona, Sam Ockman, and Mark Stone, 31–46. Sebastopol, Calif.: O'Reilly Media.

McMillan, Robert. 2001. Our Man in Palo Alto: Talking with Bruce Perens. *Linux Magazine*. http://www.linux-mag.com/id/861.

Mercer, Charles. 1964. *Legion of Strangers: The Vivid History of a Unique Military Tradition—The French Foreign Legion*. New York: Holt, Rinehart, & Winston.

Miguel, Helft, and Ashley Vance. 2010. Apple Passes Microsoft as No. 1 in Tech. *New York Times*. May 26. http://www.nytimes.com/2010/05/27/technology/27apple.html?_r=1.

Montfort, Nick. 2003. *Twisty Little Passages: An Approach to Interactive Fiction*. Cambridge, Mass.: MIT Press.

Montfort, Nick, and Ian Bogost. 2009. *Racing the Beam: The Atari Video Computer System*. Cambridge, Mass.: MIT Press.

Montola, Markus. 2009. Games and Pervasive Games. In *Pervasive Games: Theory and Design*. Eds. Markus Montola, Jaakko Stenros, and Annika Waern, 7–24. Burlington, Mass.: Morgan Kaufmann.

Moulthrop, Stuart. 2005. After the Last Generation: Rethinking Scholarship in the Days of Serious Play. In *Proceedings of Digital Arts and Culture Conference*, 208–215. IT-University, Copenhagen. Copenhagen, Denmark.

Multics History. 2011. *Multicians.org*. Accessed February 20. http://www.multicians .org/history.html.

Murray, Janet H. 1997. *Hamlet on the Holodeck: The Future of Narrative in Cyberspace*. New York: The Free Press.

Nardi, Bonnie A. 2010. *My Life as a Night Elf Priest: An Anthropological Account of World of Warcraft*. Ann Arbor: University of Michigan Press.

Naur, P., and B. Randell. 1969. Software Engineering: Report on a Conference Sponsored by the NATO Science Committee. Garmish, Germany. 7–11 October 1968. http://homepages.cs.ncl.ac.uk/brian.randell/NATO.

NetBSD Formal Releases. 2011. *NetBSD.org*. Accessed February 20. http://www.netbsd .org/releases/formal.html.

Netscape Announces Plans to Make Next-Generation Communicator Source Code Available Free on the Net. 1998. *Netscape Communications Corporation*. January 22. http://www.prnewswire.com/news-releases/netscape-announces-plans-to-make -next-generation-communicator-source-code-available-free-on-the-net-76399462 .html.

Nietzsche, Friedrich. [1883] 1961. *Thus Spoke Zarathustra*. Trans. R. J. Hollingdale. Baltimore, Md.: Penguin Books.

Nietzsche, Friedrich. [1887] 1969. *On the Genealogy of Morals* and *Ecce Homo*. Trans. W. Kaufmann and R. J. Hollingdale. New York: Random House.

Nietzsche, Friedrich. [1886] 1973. *Beyond Good and Evil*. Trans. R. J. Hollingdale. New York: Penguin Books.

Nietzsche, Friedrich. [1873] 2006. Philosophy in the Tragic Age of the Greeks. In *The Nietzsche Reader*. Eds. Keith Ansell Pearson and Duncan Large, 101–113. Oxford, UK: Blackwell Publishing.

Nitsche, Michael. 2008. *Video Game Spaces: Image, Play, and Structure in 3D Worlds*. Cambridge, Mass.: MIT Press.

Oikarinen, Jarkko. 2011. IRC History. *IRCNet.org*. Accessed February 19. http://www .ircnet.org/History/jarkko.html.

Ong, Walter. 1982. *Orality and Literacy: The Technologizing of the Word*. New York: Routledge.

Open Source Definition (Annotated). 2011. *Opensource.org*. Version 1.9. Accessed February 20. http://www.opensource.org/osd.html.

Open Source Licenses by Category. 2011. *Opensource.org*. Accessed February 20. http://www.opensource.org/licenses/category.

Orwell, George. 1949. *1984*. London: Secker and Warburg.

OS Market Share News. 2011. Netmarketshare.com. Accessed February 20. http:// www.netmarketshare.com/os-market-share.aspx?qprid=9.

Pearce, Celia, and Artemesia. 2009. *Communities of Play: Emergent Cultures in Multiplayer Games and Virtual Worlds*. Cambridge, Mass.: MIT Press.

Perens, Bruce. 1999. It's Time to Talk about Free Software Again. Email to debian -devel@lists.debian.org. February 17. http://lists.debian.org/debian-devel/1999/02/ msg01641.html.

Portability and Supported Hardware Platforms. 2011. *NetBSD.org*. Accessed February 20. http://www.netbsd.org/about/portability.html.

Quartz, Steven R., and Terrence J. Sejnowski. 2002. *Liars, Lovers, and Heroes: What the New Brain Science Reveals About How We Become Who We Are*. New York: William Morrow.

Raessens, Joost, and Jeffrey Goldstein, eds. 2005. *Handbook of Computer Game Studies*. Cambridge, Mass.: MIT Press.

Raymond, Eric. [1993] 1996. *The New Hacker's Dictionary*. Cambridge, Mass.: MIT Press.

Raymond, Eric. 2001a. *The Cathedral and the Bazaar: Musings on Linux and Open Source by an Accidental Revolutionary*. Sebastopol, Calif.: O'Reilly Media.

Raymond, Eric. 2001b. Personal communication with the author. February 9.

Raymond, Eric. 2011. The Jargon File. Version 4.4.7. Accessed February 20. http:// www.catb.org/jargon/html/index.html.

Redmond, Kent C., and Thomas M. Smith. 1980. *Project Whirlwind: The History of a Pioneer Computer*. Bedford, Mass.: Digital Press.

Rheingold, Howard. [1985] 2000. *Tools for Thought: The History of Future of Mind-Expanding Technology*. Cambridge, Mass.: MIT Press.

Rheingold, Howard. [1993] 2000. *The Virtual Community: Homesteading on the Electronic Frontier*. Cambridge, Mass.: MIT Press.

Ritchie, Dennis. [1979] 1996. The Evolution of the Unix Time-sharing System. http://cm.bell-labs.com/cm/cs/who/dmr/hist.html.

Ritchie, Dennis. 2000. The Unix Time-sharing System—A Retrospective. http://cm.bell-labs.com/cm/cs/who/dmr/retro.html.

Rollings, Andrew, and Dave Morris. 2000. *Game Architecture and Design*. Scottsdale, Ariz:.: Coriolis.

Sagan, Carl, Ann Druyan, and Steven Soter. 1980. *Cosmos: A Personal Voyage*. Television series. Public Broadcasting Service.

Salen, Katie, and Eric Zimmerman, eds. 2005. *The Game Design Reader: A Rules of Play Anthology*. Cambridge, Mass.: MIT Press.

Sartre, Jean-Paul. 1965. *The Philosophy of Jean-Paul Sartre*. London: Random House.

Sicart, Miguel. 2009. *The Ethics of Computer Games*. Cambridge, Mass.: MIT Press.

Snow, C. P. [1959] 1993. *The Two Cultures*. Cambridge, UK: Cambridge University Press.

Stallman, Richard. 1983. Initial Announcement. *GNU.org*. http://www.gnu.org/gnu/initial-announcement.html.

Stallman, Richard. 1986. RMS Lecture at KTH. Royal Institute of Technology, Stockholm, Sweden. 30 October 1986. http://www.gnu.org/philosophy/stallman-kth.html.

Stallman, Richard. 1998. Why "Free Software" Is Better Than "Open Source." *GNU.org*. http://www.gnu.org/philosophy/free-software-for-freedom.html.

Stallman, Richard. 1999. The GNU Operating System and the Free Software Movement. In *Open Sources: Voices from the Open Source Revolution*. Eds. Chris DiBona, Sam Ockman, and Mark Stone, 53–70. Sebastopol, Calif.: O'Reilly Media.

Stallman, Richard. 2002. On hacking. http://stallman.org/articles/on-hacking.html.

Stallman, Richard. 2007. Why Open Source Misses the Point of Free Software. *GNU.org*. http://www.gnu.org/philosophy/open-source-misses-the-point.html.

Stiegler, Bernard. 1998. *Technics and Time, 1: The Fault of Epimetheus*. Stanford, CA: Stanford University Press.

Stiegler, Bernard. 2008. *Technics and Time, 2: Disorientation*. Stanford, CA: Stanford University Press.

Stiegler, Bernard. 2010. *Technics and Time, 3: Cinematic Time and the Question of Malaise*. Stanford, CA: Stanford University Press.

Stoll, Clifford. 1989. *The Cuckoo's Egg*. New York: Doubleday.

Sutton-Smith, Brian. 1997. *The Ambiguity of Play*. Cambridge, Mass.: Harvard University Press.

Taylor, T. L. 2006. *Play Between Worlds: Exploring Online Game Culture*. Cambridge, Mass.: MIT Press.

Ten O'clock News. 1988. *Channel 8 News Boston*. 3 minutes. http://www.youtube.com/watch?v=G2i_6j55bS0.

Toole, Betty A., ed. 1998. *Ada, the Enchantress of Numbers*. Mill Valley, Calif.: Strawberry Press.

Torvalds, Linus. 1991a. What Would You Like to See Most in Minix? *comp.os.minix*. http://groups.google.com/group/comp.os.minix/msg/b813d52cbc5a044b?pli=1.

Torvalds, Linus. 1991b. Free Minix-like Kernel Sources for 386-AT. *comp.os.minix*. http://groups.google.com/group/comp.os.minix/msg/2194d253268b0a1b.

Torvalds, Linus. 1999. The Linux Edge. In *Open Sources: Voices from the Open Source Revolution*. Eds. Chris DiBona, Sam Ockman, and Mark Stone, 101–112. Sebastopol, Calif.: O'Reilly Media.

Torvalds, Linus, and David Diamond. 2001. *Just for Fun: The Story of an Accidental Revolutionary*. New York: HarperCollins.

Turing, Alan M. 1937. On Computable Numbers: With an Application to the Entscheidungs Problem. *Proceedings of the London Mathematical Society* 2 (42):230–265.

Turkle, Sherry. 1995. *Life on the Screen: Identity in the Age of the Internet*. New York: Simon & Schuster.

Turkle, Sherry. [1998] 2002. All MOOs are Educational—The Experience of "Walking" through the Self. In *High Wired: On the Design, Use, and Theory of Educational MOOs*. Eds. Cynthia Haynes and Jan Rune Holmevik, ix–xix. Ann Arbor: University of Michigan Press.

Turkle, Sherry. [1984] 2005. *The Second Self: Computers and the Human Spirit*. New York: Simon & Schuster.

Ulmer, Gregory L. 1985. *Applied Grammatology: Post(e)-Pedagogy from Jacques Derrida to Joseph Beuys*. Baltimore, Md.: Johns Hopkins University Press.

Ulmer, Gregory L. 1989. *Teletheory: Grammatalogy in the Age of Video*. New York: Routledge.

Ulmer, Gregory L. 1994. *Heuretics: The Logic of Invention*. Baltimore, Md.: Johns Hopkins University Press.

Ulmer, Gregory L. 2003. *Internet Invention: From Literacy to Electracy*. New York: Longman.

Ulmer, Gregory L. 2005. *Electronic Monuments*. Minneapolis: University of Minnesota Press.

Ulmer, Gregory L. 2009. The Learning Screen Networked_Art. http://ulmer .networkedbook.org/the-learning-screen-introduction-electracy.

Ulmer, Gregory L. forthcoming. *Avatar Emergency*. Anderson, S.C.: Parlor Press.

Virilio, Paul. 1997. *Open Sky*. Trans. J. Rose. London: Verso.

Virilio, Paul. 2007. *The Original Accident. Trans. Julie Rose*. Cambridge, UK: Polity Press.

Virilio, Paul, and Sylvère Lotringer. 1983. *Pure War*. New York: Semiotext(e).

Vitanza, Victor. [1998] 2002. Of MOOs, Folds, and Non-reactionary Virtual Communities. In *High Wired: On the Design, Use, and Theory of Educational MOOs*. Eds. Cynthia Haynes and Jan Rune Holmevik, 286–310. Ann Arbor: University of Michigan Press.

Wardrip-Fruin, Noah. 2009. *Expressive Processing: Digital Fictions, Computer Games, and Software Studies*. Cambridge, Mass.: MIT Press.

Wardrip-Fruin, Noah, and Pat Harrigan, eds. 2004. *First Person: New Media as Story, Performance, and Game*. Cambridge, Mass.: MIT Press.

WarGames. 1983. Film. Director, John Badham. Metro-Goldwyn-Mayer.

Weishaus, Joel. 1998. IMAGING EmerAgency: A Conversation with Gregory Ulmer. *Postmodern Culture* 9 (1). http://pmc.iath.virginia.edu/text-only/issue.998/ 9.1weishaus.txt.

White, Stephen. 1991. Moospec.txt. Accessed February 20, 2010. http://www .linnaean.org/~lpb/muddex/moospec.txt.

Williams, Michael R. [1985] 1997. *A History of Computing Technology*. Los Alamitos, Calif.: IEEE Computer Society Press.

Index

Aarseth, Espen, 2–3
  CALLMOO and, 132
  Cybertext and, 14, 16, 21, 95
  ergodic literature and, 14, 16, 21, 95,
    153
  game studies and, 161
  ludology and, 14–16
  University of Bergen and, 20, 132
AberMUD, 98, 115
Aca-fandom, 161–163
Actor-network theory, 24
ADD, 33
Administrators, 27
  choral code and, 62, 68
  hackers and, 49
  MOOs and, 105, 113, 118, 121,
    124–130, 133
  as wizards, 105
Adventure (game), 97
Aesop, 12
Aesthetics, 7–8, 10, 12, 16, 20, 149–150
Afghanistan, 52–53
"After the Last Generation: Rethinking
  Scholarship in the Days of Serious
  Play" (Moulthrop), 91–92, 95, 115
Aldus PageMaker, 42
ALGOrithmic Language (ALGOL),
  35–36
Allen, Paul, 41
Allen, Tim (Gemba), 103, 107, 112
Alphabetic writing, 4
AlphaMOO, 101–104, 112

Altair computer, 40, 42
Ambiguity of Play, The (Sutton-Smith), 16
Amphibian identity, 1, 25, 162–163
Analytical Engine, 28–29
Anderson, Judy (Yduj), 104, 106–109,
  113–114
Anderson, Todd, 85
Angry Birds (game), 44
Anonymous, 53
Antifoundationalism, 2
API system, 103–104
Aporia, xii
Apostle, The (film), 8
Apparatus, 163
  Baudrillard and, xiv–xv
  behavior and, 9–10
  chora and, 56–57, 61, 64, 66, 69, 155
  conductive history and, 9, 61, 69
  digital, 6, 149
  hacker noir and, 28, 54
  institutions and, 8–9
  literacy and, 4, 8–9, 153–154, 157
  ludic ethics and, 143, 149, 151
  machine and, 4
  ontologies and, 11
  philosophy and, 10
  religion and, 8–11
  state of mind and, 9
  three registers of, xi
  Ulmer and, 6–7, 154
  venture and, 91
  widescope and, 4–12, 17, 20–21

Apple Computer, 40–44, 86, 89
Applets, 51, 126, 131–132
Application Program Interface (API),
    103–104
Applied Grammatology (Ulmer), 5–6
April Fool's Day hack of 1992, 109
Aristotle, xii, 147
ARPANET, 46–49, 65, 77, 97
Artaud, Antonin, 93
Artificial intelligence, 26, 35, 69–70, 97
Artificial Reality (Krueger), 93
Aspnes, James, 98–101, 166n4
Assange, Julian, 52–53
Assembler, 61, 70
AstroVR, 118
AT&T, 46, 62, 66–67, 79–80
Atanasoff, John Vincent, 32
Auger, Pierre, xvi
Augur, xvi
Augustin, Larry, 85
Avatar Emergency (Ulmer), 4, 8, 11, 143,
    146–147, 156
Avatars, ix
  body and, 21, 25
  chora and, 91
  as *eidos*, 149
  electracy and, 4 (*see also* Electracy)
  flash reason and, 17
  games and, 134, 141
  orality and, 146–147
  as prosthetic body, 11
  Ulmer and, 4, 8, 11, 25, 143, 146–147,
    149, 156
Axis of pleasure/pain, 3, 12–13, 21, 66,
    91, 143, 145, 151, 158

Babbage, Charles, 29, 147
Barber, John, 95
Barthes, Roland, 144
Bartle, Richard Allan, 96–99, 115
BASIC, 41, 76
Bataille, Georges, xiv
Batch processing, 38, 58–60, 63, 69

Baudelaire, Charles, x
Baudrillard, Jean, xiii–xv
Baudry, Jean-Louis, xi
Being and Becoming, x, 11, 21
Being and Time (Heidegger), 18
Bell Labs, 36, 60–62, 64, 79
Bellovin, Steve, 48
Benjamin, Walter, xiv
Bermel, Albert, xv
Berners-Lee, Tim, 66
Berry, Clifford, 32
Beyond Good and Evil (Nietzsche), 137
BioGate system, 126, 131–133
BioMOO, 117–121, 126
Birkerts, Sven, 157
BITNET, 49–50
Bizzell, Patricia, 2
Blanchard, Mark, 121
Blindspots, 155
Blizzard Entertainment, 166n6
Blogs, 16, 163
Bogost, Ian, x, 15, 41, 56, 95, 142–143,
    161–164
Brand, Stewart, 50–51
Bricoleurs, 92
  actor-network theory and, 24
  Altair and, 40, 42
  chora and, 66, 80–82, 88
  constructionism and, 24
  hackers and, 23–25, 28, 32, 37, 44,
    80–82
  heuretics and, 23–24, 28
  invention and, 23–24
  Lévi–Strauss and, 23–25
  meaning of term, 23
  morphisms and, 24–25
  protocol and, 66
  science, 32
  technology and, 24
British Legends (game), 97, 166n3
Broderick, Matthew, 26
Browser wars, 83
Bruckman, Amy, xxi, 114, 117–119, 129

BSD (Berkeley Software Distribution), 44, 46, 116
  breaks from Unix, 66–67
  choral code and, 57, 62–69, 74, 77–80, 85–86
  Computer Systems Research Group (CSRG) and, 65, 67
  consumer feedback and, 65
  copyright and, 67
  distinct flavor or, 65
  enCore and, 127
  FreeBSD and, 68
  layer model and, 66
  NetBSD and, 68
  new releases of, 64–65
  OpenBSD and, 68
  portable programming and, 67–68
  TCP/IP protocols and, 65
  386BSD and, 67–68
BSDi, 67
Buena Vista University, 119
Buffer overrun, 166n5
Bugs
  code and, 58, 66, 68–69, 72, 75, 128
  enCore and, 128, 133–134
  MOOs and, 100, 102, 111, 113, 121, 128–129, 133–134
"Building Dwelling Thinking" (Heidegger), 1
Bulletin board systems (BBSs), 49–50, 54
Bungle, Mr., 110–111
Burke, James, xi
Burning Chrome (Gibson), ix, 26, 157
Bush, Vannevar, 55
Byron, Lord, 29
Byte magazine, xix

C, 36, 48, 62, 70, 72–73, 76, 97–98
C++, 36, 72, 101
Caillois, Roger, xiii, xv
Caldera, 79
CALLMOO project, 132–133
Callon, Michel, 24

Career, 19
Carlson, Jay, 125
Carnegie Mellon University, 73
Carroll, Lewis, 162
Casual Revolution, A (Juul), 153
"Cathedral and the Bazaar, The" (Raymond), 81–83
Cha, Theresa Hak Kyung, xi
Chassell, Robert, 70–74, 127
Cherney, Lynn, 95
Chess, xviii, 7, 31
Chora, 54
  apparatus and, 56–57, 61, 64, 66, 69, 155
  assembler and, 61, 70
  avatars and, 91
  Being and Becoming and, x, 11, 21
  bricoleurs and, 66, 80–82, 88
  cloud computing and, 59, 88
  commercialization of software and, 70
  conflation of place/memory and, 56
  defined, x, 55–56
  Derrida on, 154
  dromospheric space and, 59, 156–157
  electracy and, 64, 66, 69
  ethics and, 58, 64, 87
  fantasy and, 56
  frontiers and, 55–56
  as genos, x
  hackers and, 56–58, 62–65, 69–70, 73–89, 154–155
  heuretics and, 56–58, 62–69, 89
  Lévi-Strauss and, 80, 82
  licenses and, 63, 71, 78, 85–87
  ludology and, 61
  MAC and, 60
  machines and, xiii, 58–63, 67, 76–77
  Multics and, 60–61
  mystory and, 73
  orality and, 64, 66
  personal computers and, 67–68, 75, 80, 88
  pioneers and, 55–56

Chora (cont.)
  Plato and, xi, 11
  play and, 56–57, 61, 64, 67–68, 72–74,
    77–79, 89, 155
  rhetoric and, 56, 86
  source code and, 63–66, 75, 83, 85
  TCP/IP protocols and, 65, 67
  technology and, 55–58, 61, 65, 77–81,
    84, 89
  time-sharing and, 57, 59–61, 69–70, 79
  Ulmer and, 55–57, 64, 66, 69, 72–73, 89
  Unix and, 58, 61–75, 77–80, 82, 88
Choral code
  BSD and, 57, 62–69, 74, 77–80, 85–86
  defined, 55–57
  Free Software movement and, 57–58,
    71–72, 74, 77–89
  GNU and, 57, 62, 69–75, 78–81,
    85–86, 88
  Linux and, 57, 62, 68–69, 75–88
  MIT and, 57–60, 69–70, 78–79
  operating systems and, 57–58, 62,
    75–79, 82, 84
  Project Whirlwind and, 58–59
  time-sharing and, 57, 59–61, 69–70, 79
Cinematographic Apparatus: Selected Writ-
    ings (Cha), xi
Clements, Brian, 121–122
Clemson University, x
Cleudo (game), xvii
Cloud computing, 59, 88
CNU C library, 73
Code jockeys, 36–40
CollegeTown MOO, 119–122, 126
Columbine High School, ix, xv–xvi
  Harris and, 140–144, 167n1
  Klebold and, 140–141, 144
  memorial for, 145
Commedia dell'Arte, xv
Commodore Business Machines, 40–41
Commodore 64 computer, xix
Common Business Oriented Language
    (COBOL), 35

ComMOOnity, 120
Community history, 19, 21
Compatible Timesharing System (CTSS),
    59–60
Compilers, 34, 39–40, 54, 60, 70, 72,
    78, 107
Computers, xviii, 5, 9, 14, 19, 21, 154,
    156
  access to, 37–39
  ALGOL and, 35–36
  Altair, 40, 42
  Analytical Engine, 28–29
  Apple 2, 41–43
  artificial intelligence and, 26, 35,
    69–70, 97
  Atanasoff and, 32
  batch processing and, 38, 58–60,
    63, 69
  Berry and, 32
  C and, 36
  C++ and, 36
  choral code and, 55–70, 74–77, 80,
    86, 88
  cloud computing and, 59, 88
  COBOL and, 35
  commercially available, 37, 39
  compilers and, 34, 39–40, 54, 60, 70,
    72, 78, 107
  as consuming interest, 37
  CPU power and, 38–39
  Dahl and, 36
  debugger and, 72 (see also Bugs)
  DEC VAX series, 67
  desktop publishing and, 42, 54
  Difference Engine, 28–29, 147
  Eckert and, 32–33
  ENIAC, 32–33
  FORTRAN and, 35
  GE-645, 60
  hackers and, 25–49 (see also Hackers)
  HAL 9000, 26
  Hopper and, 34
  IBM 709, 59–60

intervention and, 118, 123, 129, 132–133
Jacquard Loom and, 28–29
Java and, 36, 51, 72, 126, 131
Lovelace and, 29–30
ludic ethics and, 137, 139–140, 142–146, 151
Macintosh, 42–43
Mauchly and, 32–33
microprocessors and, 40–41, 54, 67
Nygaard and, 36
operating systems and, 43, 46, 54, 57–58, 62, 75–79, 82, 84
Pascal and, 36
PDP-11, 62
PDP-7, 61
personal, 40–45, 54, 67–68, 75, 80, 88
Project Whirlwind and, 58–59
Ritchie and, 36
Simula and, 36
Smalltalk and, 36
source code and, 63–66, 75, 83, 85 (see also Source code)
Sun workstations and, 67
time-sharing and, 38–39, 46–47, 57, 59–61, 69–70, 79
Turing and, 30
UNIVAC, 33–34
universal machine, 28–33
Unix and, 58, 61–75, 77–80, 82, 88 (see also Unix)
venture and, 94–95, 97–101, 104–105
Wirth and, 36
Z3, 30–31
Zuse and, 30–32
Computers and Writing (CW), 123
Computers as Theatre (Laurel), 9
Computer science, 34
Computer Systems Research Group (CSRG), 65, 67
Conductive history, 9, 61, 69
Conference On College Composition and Communication (CCCC), 123

Connections (Burke), xi
Constructionism, 24
Convergence Culture (Jenkins), 94
Copyleft, 71
Copyright, 67
Corbató, Fernando J., 60
Cosmos (TV show), 7
Counterstrike (game), 139
Count Zero (Gibson), 26
Cox, Alan (Anarchy), 98, 115
CPYNET, 47
Critical Art Ensemble, 51
Critique of Judgment (Kant), 150
Crowther, William, 97, 166n2
CRT-type monitors, 59
Cuckoo's Egg, The (Stoll), 27
Cult of the Dead Cow (cDc), 51–52
Cup-O MUD, 126, 131
Curtis, Pavel, 101–107, 109–114, 117
Cyberpunk: Outlaws and Hackers on the Computer Frontier (Markoff and Hafner), 27
Cybertext: Perspectives on Ergodic Literature (Aarseth), 14, 16, 95, 21
CyberText Yearbook (Eskelinen and Koskimaa), 16

DAC (Digital Arts and Culture), 16, 20
Dahl, Ole-Johan, 36
Darwin, 44
Dasein, 18–19
David and Goliath, 7
Debian Free Software Guidelines (Perens, et al.), 85
Debuggers, 72
DEC, 37, 67
Deconstruction, 5–6, 17, 21, 25, 55–56, 92, 148
Deleuze, Gilles, xiii, xvi, 165n1
Denial-of-service (DoS) attacks, 51
Derrida, Jacques, x
bricoleur and, 25, 32, 80
chora and, 56, 80, 154

Derrida, Jacques (cont.)
  ethics and, 138–139, 149
  free play and, 25, 138, 149
  jargon and, 163
  Nietzschean affirmation and, 138–139
  orality and, 151
  poststructuralism and, xi
  widescope and, 1–2, 4–6
Desktop publishing, 42, 54
Dewey, John, 149–150
Dibble, Julian, 110
Dick, Phillip K., 26
Diderot, D., xv
Difference Engine, 28–29, 147
Digital writing, 5
DiGRA, 16
Diversity University MOO, 126
Dominguez, Ricardo, 51
DOOM (game), ix, 140–144, 167n1
Dreistadt, 132
Dreyfus, Suelette, 52
Dromospheric space, 59, 156–157
Druyan, Ann, 7
Duke University, 48
Dungeons and Dragons (D&D), 96–97,
  166n2
Duvall, Robert, 8

Eastwood, Clint, 146
Eckert, J. Presper, 32–33
Eckert-Mauchly Computer Corporation,
  33–34
Eco, Umberto, 120
Ecstasy, xv
Eidos, 149
Electracy, 163
  aesthetics and, 7–8, 10, 12, 16, 20,
    149–150
  assemblage and, 92, 155
  avatars and, 11
  axis configuration of, 12–13
  Baudrillard and, xiv–xv
  choral code and, 64, 66, 69

concept of, 3–14
entertainment and, 7–9, 19–21
figure and, 12, 21, 44, 80
hackers and, 23 (see also Hackers)
heuretics and, 3, 6, 9–10, 17
intervention and, 134
invention of, 2–3, 9, 17–21, 89, 134
  (see also Heuretics)
literacy and, 4 (see also Literacy)
ludic ethics and, 138–139, 143–144,
  149, 154–155
meaning of term, x
modes and, 12
as new approach to learning, 3–4
ontologies and, 11
operant and, xi–xii
orality and, 4
pedagogical experiments and, ix
play and, 2 (see also Play)
politics and, 8
practice of, 7
procedure of, 8
religion and, 8, 10–11
style and, 8
Ulmer and, 3–14, 15, 17–21, 44, 155
venture and, 91
Electronic Civil Disobedience and Other
  Unpopular Ideas (Critical Art Ensemble), 51
Electronic Disturbance Theater, 51
Electronic Literature Organization
  (ELO), 123
Electronic Monuments (Ulmer), 8,
  143–144, 153, 156
Electronic Numerical Integrator and
  Computer (ENIAC), 32–33
Electronic Word, The (Lanham), 100
Eliot, T. S., 162
Ellis, Jim, 48
Emacs (Editor MACroS), 70–73, 79, 82
Email, 109, 118
  choral code and, 81–83, 88
  hackers and, 46–49, 54

intervention and, 128, 134
EmerAgency, ix, 6, 72–73, 135,
    156–157, 163
encore
  beta version of, 128–129
  BioGate system and, 126, 131–133
  BSD and, 127
  development of, 125–128
  Documentation Project and, 134
  GNU GPL and, 127
  intervention and, 114, 116–117,
    124–135
  LambdaCore distribution and,
    125–127
  licensing and, 126–127
  Open Source project and, 114, 116,
    133
  reflections on, 133–135
  technical support and, 128
  Xpress and, 130–133
enCore Consortium, 134
enCore exChange, 129
enCore Xpress, xxi
Enlightenment, 4, 12, 56
Entelechy, xii
Entertainment, 154
  electracy and, 7–9, 19–21
  hackers and, 28, 44, 53
  ludology and, 145
  mystory and, 19
  violence and, 145
Equinox community, ix–x, 157–158
Ergodic literature, 3, 15–16, 21, 153
Eskelinen, Markku, 2, 14–16
ESR. See Raymond, Eric Steven
Essex MUD, 96–98, 166n3
Ethics, 3
  chora and, 58, 64, 87
  defined, 138–139
  Derrida and, 138–139, 149
  electracy and, 138–139, 143–144, 149,
    154–155
  epideictic rhetoric and, 145–149

as experience of lived virtue, 148
hermeneutic circle and, 139
intervention and, 135
justice and, 137, 146, 150–151
ludic, 21, 137–151 (see also Ludology)
Lyotard and, 150–151
machines and, 140, 147
morality and, 137–138, 142–143, 151
negative, 138
Nietzsche and, 137–139, 143, 148–
    149, 151
phenomenology and, 139
play and, 15, 137–139, 143, 148–149,
    151
religion and, 12
Sicart and, 137–139, 142–143, 146,
    151
technology and, 146, 148
unnatural experience and, 149–151
venture and, 143, 149, 151
violence and, 137, 139–146, 148, 150
Ethics of Computer Games (Sicart), 137,
    139, 151
Experience engines, 3, 147, 149–150

Fabry, Robert, 62, 65
Facebook, 45
Family, 19
Fantasy
  chora and, 56
  games and, 20, 96–97, 107, 115, 151,
    166n3
  role-playing and, 97, 107, 117–118,
    141, 157, 166n2
  Ulmer and, 9, 56
  violence and, 137, 139–146, 148, 150,
    163
Far Cry 2 (game), 139
Farmville (game), 154
Fatal Strategies (Baudrillard), xiv
Figure, 12, 21, 44, 80
Flash reason, 12, 17, 57, 148, 156–157
FLOW-MATIC, 35

Ford, John, 146
Foresight Institute, 85
FORmula TRANslation (FORTRAN), 35, 72, 97
Forrester, Jay, 58–59
Foss, Adam, 140
Foundationalism, 1–2
Fox, Ken, 125
Frand, 101, 104, 109
Frasca, Gonzalo, 14–15
Free play, 2, 25, 51, 135
Free Software movement, x
  choral code and, 57–58, 71–72, 74, 77–89
  Free Software Foundation (FSF), 71–74, 77, 80–81, 86, 88, 102, 127
  venture and, 102, 123–124, 127, 133
Freud, Sigmund, xiv
Frogger (game), xix
"Frog Prince, The" (fairy tale), 163–164
FTP, 47, 68, 71
FurryMUCK, 115

Gademerian hermeneutics, 139
Galloway, Alexander, 65–66
Games. *See also* Specific game
  aca-fandom and, 161–163
  avatars and, 134, 141
  Bogost on, 161–164
  drama and, xviii
  effort needed for, 153
  as electrate expressions, 153–154 (*see also* Electracy)
  epideictic rhetoric and, 145–149
  as experience engines, 3, 147, 149–150
  fantasy and, 20, 96–97, 107, 115, 151, 166n3
  hand-eye coordination and, xviii
  high scores and, xviii–xix
  monumentality and, 3, 145
  motivations for, 154
  MUDs, xxi, 95–96, 99–107, 116–119

personal computers and, 41
pervasive, 166n1
role-playing, 97, 107, 117–118, 141, 157, 166n2
serious, 15, 20
social atmosphere of, xvii
text-based, xx–xxi, 100, 119, 126, 129, 132
venture and, 91–101, 107
violence and, 137, 139–146, 148, 150, 155
Games and Culture journal, 16
Games Studies magazine, 14
Game studies, x, 1–2, 10, 14–17, 94, 138–139, 161, 165n2
Gamestudies.org, 14, 16
Game Theory, xv
Gates, Bill, 41–43, 45
GDC, 16
Gee, James Paul, 92
General Economy, xiv
General Electric (GE), 60
General Public License (GPL), 71, 78, 85–86, 88, 127
Genos, x
Gibson, William, ix, 26–27, 55, 157–158
Gillogly, Jim, 97
Glusman, Gustavo, 117, 121, 126
GNU, 37, 46, 102, 116
  C and, 70
  choral code and, 57, 62, 69–75, 78–81, 85–86, 88
  contributors to, 72–73
  copyleft and, 71
  Emacs and, 70–73, 79, 82
  first version of, 71
  Free Software Foundation (FSF) and, 71–74, 77, 80, 81, 86, 88, 102, 127
  General Public License (GPL) and, 71, 78, 85–86, 88, 127
  HURD and, 74–75
  Linux and, 78

Mach and, 73–74
Stallman and, 69–73, 78, 80, 86–88
GNU C Compiler (GCC), 72–73, 75, 78
Goody, Jack, xi
Google, 89
Goux, Jean-Joseph, xi
Grammatology, x–xi, 4–5, 18
Grand Theft Auto IV (game), 145–146
Grigar, Dene, 95, 122
Guattari, Félix, xiii, xvi, 155
Gutenberg Elegies, The (Birkerts), 157

Hackers, ix–x
  ALGOL and, 35–36
  Altair and, 40, 42
  Analytical Engine and, 28–29
  apparatus and, 28, 54
  arrogance and, 65–66
  Assange and, 52
  Atanasoff and, 32
  Bellovin and, 48
  Berry and, 32
  bricoleurs and, 23–25, 28, 32, 37, 44,
    80–82
  brilliance and, 65–66
  C and, 36
  C++ and, 36
  chora and, 154–155
  choral code and, 56–58, 62–65, 69–70,
    73–89
  COBOL and, 35
  as code jockeys, 36–40
  collaborative software model and, 39
  common perception of, 25
  compilers and, 34, 39–40, 54, 60, 70,
    72, 78, 107
  Curtis and, 101–107, 109–114, 117
  Dahl and, 36
  debugger and, 72
  denial-of-service (DoS) attacks and, 51
  Difference Engine and, 28–29, 147
  Eckert and, 32–33
  Ellis and, 48

email and, 46–47
ENIAC and, 32–33
entertainment and, 28, 44, 53
FORTRAN and, 35
free play and, 51
fringe of society and, 52
Gibson and, 26–27
Hess and, 27
heuretics and, 3
high reputation of, 80
Hopper and, 34
Jacquard Loom and, 28–29
Jargon File and, 37, 81
Java and, 36, 51, 72, 126, 131
Kell and, 49
leet speak and, 140, 143
Lévi-Strauss and, 23–25, 40
Lovelace and, 29–30
machines and, 26–35, 38–44, 48, 50,
  53–54
Mauchly and, 32–33
microprocessors and, 40–41, 54, 67
Mitnick and, 27–28, 52
Morris and, 27
MUDs/MOOs and, 95–111, 114
Nygaard and, 36
Oikarinen and, 49–50
Pascal and, 36
play and, 24–28, 31, 37–38, 44–45, 49,
  51, 53, 56–57, 61, 64, 67–68, 72–74,
  77–79, 89
public perception of, xx, 28
Raymond and, 80–87
rhetoric and, 51
Ritchie and, 36
Simula and, 36
Smalltalk and, 36
social media and, 44–50
source code and, 39–40
Stallman and, 37–38, 57, 69–73,
  77–78, 80, 84, 86–88
Stoll and, 27
style and, 76, 79, 82, 85–88, 134

Hackers (cont.)
  technology and, 24–26, 36–37, 40,
    44, 54
  time-sharing and, 38–39
  Tomlinson and, 46–47
  Truscott and, 48
  Turing and, 30
  Ulmer and, 25, 44
  UNIVAC and, 33–34
  universal machine and, 28–33
  Unix and, 27, 36, 44, 46, 48–50, 54
  as unsung heroes, 28
  White and, 100–103, 106, 111
  Wirth and, 36
  worms and, 27, 166n5
  Zuse and, 30–32
Hackers (Levy), 28, 37, 51
Hacker's Conference, 51
Hacktivism, 50–54
Hactivismo, 51–52
Hafner, Katie, 27
Haley, Chuck, 64
Half-Life (game), 92
Hall, John, 85
Hamlet on the Holodeck (Murray), 9
HAL 9000, 26
Harpold, Terry, 2
Harrell, Fox, 15
Harris, Eric David, 140–144, 167n1
Hauser, Gerard, 147
Havelock, Eric, x–xi
Hawisher, Gail, 94–95
Haynes, Cynthia
  educational MOOs and, 20, 92, 94–95,
    124, 130, 134
  LinguaMOO and, 116, 119–121,
    124
  play/writing connections and, 16
  University of Bergen and, 20
Hebdige, Dick, 8
Heidegger, Martin, xii–xiii, 1, 18, 91,
    148, 151
Heraclitus, 137

Hermeneutics, 18, 57, 66, 139
Hess, Marcus, 27
Heuretics
  behavior and, 9–10
  bricoleurs and, 23–24, 28
  chora and, 56–58, 62–69, 89
  electracy and, 3, 6, 9–10, 17
  hackers and, 3
  intervention and, 120, 134
  mystory and, 18, 20–21
  pleasure/pain axis, 3, 12, 21, 66, 91,
    143, 145, 151, 158
  style and, 8, 19–20, 41, 79, 82, 85–88,
    134, 143, 163
  venture and, 91
Heuretics: The Logic of Invention (Ulmer),
    55–57
High Wired enCore, 116, 124–125
High Wired: On the Design, Use, and The-
    ory of Educational MOOs (Holmevik
    and Haynes), 20, 92, 94, 124, 130
Hilbert, David, 30
HIRD, 74
Holmevik, Jan, ix, 36
  Bogost on, 162–163
  educational MOOs and, 20, 92, 94–95,
    124, 130
  play/writing connections and, 16
Homer, 162
Homo Ludens (Huizinga), xii, 9–10
Homophones, 6
Hopper, Grace M., 34
Howard, Tharon, 95
HTML, 66, 126, 131
Hubbard, Jordan, 68
Huizinga, Johan, 9–10
HURD, 74–75

IBM, 35, 37, 42–43, 59–60, 67, 89
Identity
  amphibian, 1, 25, 162–163
  apparatus and, xi (see also Apparatus)
  entertainment and, 53

flash reason and, 12, 17, 57, 148,
156–157
group awareness and, ix, 8
interpellation and, 19, 21, 145
literacy and, x (*see also* Literacy)
ludology and, 146–147
morphisms and, 24–26, 154–155
mystory and, 18–19 (*see also* Mystory)
new dimension of, 11
punctum and, ix–x, 144–145, 155,
157–158, 160
venture and, 94
IGN.com, 145
Ilynx, xv
Industrial Revolution, xi, 53
Institutions
apparatus and, 7–9
career and, 19
choral code and, 63–64, 71, 79
community and, 19
electracy and, 3–4, 44
entertainment and, 19
family and, 19
hackers and, 44, 53
Internet and, 8–9, 20
intervention and, 123–124, 129, 135
ludic ethics and, 149
play and, 6
rewriting of, 64
technology and, 18 (*see also*
Technology)
venture and, 102
Instrumentalism, 6, 73
Intellectual property
copyleft and, 71
copyright and, 67
licenses and, 63, 71, 78, 85–87,
126–127
Internet Explorer, 83
*Internet Invention: From Literacy to Elec-
tracy* (Ulmer), 3–4, 8–9, 19, 156
Internet Relay Chat (IRC), 46, 49–50,
54, 81, 99

Interpellation, 19, 21, 145
Intervention
electracy and, 134
enCore and, 114, 116–117, 124–135
ethics and, 135
heuretics and, 120, 134
LinguaMOO and, 116, 119–124
machines and, 132
MUDs and, 115–119, 125–126, 131
play and, 115, 117–118, 120–123,
134–135
rhetoric and, 117, 155
technology and, 3, 115–125, 130, 132,
135
Ulmer and, 135
Unix and, 119, 123
venture and, 91–96, 114
Xpress and, 117, 124, 130–133
Invention. *See also* Heuretics
bricoleurs and, 23–24, 28
hackers and, 45 (*see also* Hackers)
retrospection and, 23–24
universal machine and, 28–33
iOS App Store, 44
Iran, 45
Iraq, 52–53
Irvin, Lennie, 134
iTunes, 44

Jacquard, Joseph-Marie, 28
Jacquard Loom, 28–29
Jargon File, 37, 81
Java, 36, 51, 72, 126, 131
Jay's House MOO, 125
Jenkins, Henry, 15, 161–162
Jepson, Kevin, 134
JHCore, 125
Jobs, Steve, 44
Johnson-Eiolola, Johndan, 95
Jolitz, Bill, 67–68
Jolitz, Lynne, 67–68
Jopp, Carsten, 132
Joy, Bill, 63–65

Jung, Daniel, 134
Jupiter project, 113
Juul, Jesper, 14, 153

Kant, Immanuel, xiv–xv, 150
Karper, Erin, 134
Katz, Steven, 1
Kell, Jeff, 49
Klebold, Dylan Bennet, 140–141, 144
Kolko, Beth, 95
Koskimaa, Raine, 16
Kretschmer, Tim, 139, 141
Kreuger, Myron, 93
Kubric, Stanley, 26
Kuhn, Thomas, 5

Lakoff, George, 142
LambdaCore distribution, 113–114,
   116, 124–127
LambdaMOO
   code sharing and, 103
   Curtis and, 102–114, 117
   development of, 96, 102–120
   mailing list of, 113–114
LambdaMOO Takes Another Direction
   (LTAND), 110
Lanham, Richard, 100
Lanier, Jaron, 93
Latour, Bruno, 24–25, 57
Laurel, Brenda, 9
Law, John, 24
Leet speak, 140, 143
Leone, Sergio, 146
Leroi–Gourhan, André, xi
Lévi–Strauss, Claude
   Altair and, 40
   bricoleurs and, 23–25
   chora and, 80, 82
   hacker noir and, 23–25, 40
   ludic ethics and, 23–25
Levy, Steven, 28, 37, 64
Liars, Lovers, and Heroes: What the New
   Brain Science Reveals about How We

Become Who We Are (Quartz and
   Sejnowski), 141–142
Licenses, 63
   copyleft, 71
   copyright, 67
   enCore Open Source Project and,
      126–127
   General Public License (GPL), 71, 78,
      85–86, 88, 127
Life on the Screen (Turkle), 16, 94
Lingo.uib, 132
LinguaMOO, xxi, 114, 116, 167n1
   academic conferences and, 123–124
   Classroom and, 122, 125
   Clements and, 121–122
   ComMOOnity and, 120
   The Courtyard and, 120
   development of, 119–124
   intervention and, 119–124
   Moderated Room and, 122
   Recording and Intercom System of,
      122
   space redesign of, 121
   technology potential of, 122–123
   University of Texas at Dallas UTD)
      and, 119–121, 123
Linux, 98
   choral code and, 57, 62, 68–69, 75–88
   criticism of, 75–77
   GNU and, 78
   hackers and, 46, 49, 54
   intervention and, 116, 133
   MacDonald and, 78–79
   monolithic design of, 75–77
   popularity of, 76–78
   release of, 76
   Tanenbaum and, 75–77, 88
   Torvalds and, 74–82, 85–88
Linux International, 85
Linux Magazine, 87
Literacy
   alphabetic writing and, 4
   apparatus and, 4, 8–9, 153–154, 157

deconstruction and, 5–6, 17, 21, 25,
    55–56, 92, 148
institutions and, 8–9
machine and, 4, 10
orality and, 4–10, 12, 64, 66, 151
Western metaphysics and, x
writing and, 4–6, 16
Lord of the Rings, The (Tolkien), 97
Lovelace, Ada, 29–30
LPC, 99
LPmud, 99, 115
Ludic electrate transversal, 3, 25, 155
Ludo (game), xvii
Ludology, 3
    chora and, 61
    concept of, 14–17
    conducting, 14–17, 61
    dromospheric time warp and, 156–157
    egency and, 156–157
    entertainment and, 145
    ethics and, 137–151 (*see also* Ethics)
    hackers and, 23 (*see also* Hackers)
    identity and, 146–147
    morality and, 137–138, 142–143, 151
    play and, 137–151, 156
    rhetoric and, 14–16, 138–150
    Ulmer and, 17–21, 143–151, 155,
        156–157
    widescope and, 14–17
LulzSec, 53
Lunar Lander (game), xix
Lyotard, Jean-François, 150–151

MAC (Multiple Access Computers/Man
    and Computer), 60
MacDonald, Peter, 78–79
Mach, 73–74
Machines, 166n3
    abstract, 155
    apparatus and, 4
    chora and, xiii, 58–63, 67, 76–77
    desiring, xiii
    faith and, 15

flattery and, xv
hacker noir and, 26–35, 38–44, 48, 50,
    53–54
Industrial Revolution and, xi, 53
intervention and, 132
literacy and, 4, 10
ludic ethics and, 140, 147
science and, 15
smart, 26
social, xi, 12
universal, 28–33
venture and, 91, 101–104
MacMOOSE, 129
Man, Play, and Games (Caillois), xiii
Mandrake, 79
Manning, Bradley, 52–53
Man the Player, 10
Markoff, John, 27–28
Marx, Karl, xv
Massachusetts Institute of Technology
    (MIT), 37–38
    Artificial Intelligence Lab and, 69–70
    Bruckman and, 114
    choral code and, 57–60, 69–70, 78–79
    code-sharing environment of, 70
    Compatible Timesharing System
        (CTSS) and, 59–60
    Computation Center and, 59–60
    Incompatible Time-sharing system
        (ITS) and, 70
    Lincoln Lab and, 59
    MAC and, 60
    McCarthy and, 59
    Media Lab and, 117
    Project Whirlwind and, 58–59
Mastermind (game), xvii
Mauchly, John W., 32–33
McCarthy, John, 59
McGrath, Roland, 73
McIlroy, Doug, 61
McKusick, Marshall, 62–66, 68–69
McLuhan, Marshall, x–xi
McManus, Barbara, 134

MediaMOO, xxi, 114, 117–120
Media studies, xi, 117, 161
Meier, Sid, 146
Memex, 55
MEmorial, 144–145
Mendax, 52
Mercer, Charles, 55
Mercer, Eric, 126
Microsoft
  choral code and, 77, 83, 86, 88
  hackers and, 41–46
  IBM and, 42–43
  Internet Explorer and, 83
  as monopoly, 77
  MS-DOS and, 43, 67, 75
  Windows and, 43–44, 46, 123
  XENIX and, 67
Minix, 49, 54, 74–78
Mitnick, Kevin, 27–28, 52
MIT Press, 17
Modernism, 24, 146
Modernity, 12
Modern Language Association (MLA),
  123
Moment, 148–149
Mona Lisa Overdrive (Gibson), 26
Monopoly (game), xvii
Monster (game), 98
Montfort, Nick, 41
Monumentality, 3, 145
MOO Cows, 113
Mooniversity: A Student's Guide to Online
  Learning Environments (Holmevik and
  Haynes), 20, 95, 130
Moore School of electrical Engineering,
  32–33
MOOs (Multiuser Dungeons,
  Object-Oriented)
academic, 118
administrators and, 105, 113, 118,
  121, 124–130, 133
AlphaMOO, 101–104, 112
API system and, 103–104

ASCII maps and, 121
AstroVR, 118
The Barn and, 134
BioMOO, 117–121, 126
code community and, 109–111
code sharing and, 111–114
CollegeTown MOO, 119–122, 126
Diversity University, 126
educational use of, 116–119
enCore and, 114, 116–117, 124–135
intervention and, 115–135
Jay's House MOO, 125
LambdaCore distribution and,
  113–114, 116, 124–127
LambdaMOO, 96, 102–120
LinguaMOO, xxi, 114, 116, 119–124,
  167n1
MediaMOO, 114, 117–120
online meetings and, 117–118
professional communities and,
  117–119
real-time collaboration and, 120
source code and, 102, 111, 115, 119,
  128, 131, 134–135
venture and, 92, 94–96, 100–114,
  111
verbs for, 107–108, 113, 129
VRoma MOO, 134
White and, 100–103, 106, 111
Xerox PARC and, 101–102, 111
Morality
  ludic ethics and, 137–138, 142–143,
    151
  religion and, 12
Moral Politics (Bogost), 142
Morphisms, 24–26, 154–155
Morris, Robert Tappan, 27, 166n5
Moses, 7
Moulthrop, Stuart, 2–3, 69, 91–92, 95,
  115
MS-DOS, 43, 67, 75
MUDS (Multi–User Dungeons), xxi
AberMUD, 98, 115

Aspnes and, 98–101, 166n4
Bartle and, 96–99, 115
code sharing and, 111–114
commands for, 99
Cup-O MUD applet and, 126, 131
Curtis and, 101–107, 109–114, 117
DikuMUD, 115
Essex, 96–98, 166n3
golden age of, 98
hackers and, 96
intervention and, 115–119, 125–126, 131
LPC and, 99
LPmud, 99, 115
MUD1, 97, 99, 166n3
MUD2, 97–98
source code and, 98, 100, 102, 111, 115, 131
TinyMUD, 98–102, 105, 115, 166n4
Trubshaw and, 96–98, 115
venture and, 95–96, 99–107
MUL, 33
Multics (Multiplexed Information and Computing Service), 60–61
Murray, Janet, 2, 9, 15
MUSE, 98, 115
Museum of the Accident, xiv
MUSH, 115
My Life as a Night Elf Priest (Nardi), 149–150
Mystory, ix, xvii–xxi, 3, 163
  career and, 19
  chora and, 73
  community history and, 19, 21
  dasein and, 18–19
  digital games and, 154
  elusion of, 154
  entertainment and, 19
  family and, 19
  heuretics and, 18, 20–21
  ludic egency and, 156
  principles of, 18–19
  Ulmer and, 18–21

Myth (game), 20
Mythology, 8

Name of the Rose, The (Eco), 120
Nardi, Bonnie, 149–150
NASA, 7
National Security Agency (NSA), 27
Naur, P., 35
Nausea (Sartre), xv–xvi
Nemesis, xiv
NetNews. *See* Usenet
Netoric Project, 117
Netscape Communications Corporation, 83–85
Neuromancer (Gibson), 26
New Hackers Dictionary (Raymond), 37
News of the World, 53
Nichomachean Ethics (Aristotle), 147
Nietzsche, Friedrich, xvii, 12–13, 137–139, 143, 148–149, 151, 165n1
1984, (Orwell), 26
Nokia, 86
Norwegian Computing Center, 36
Nygaard, Kristen, 36

Objective C, 72
Ockman, Sam, 85
Of Grammatology (Derrida), 4
Oikarinen, Jarkko, 49–50
Old Testament, 7
"On Computable Numbers" (Turing), 30
Ong, Walter, x–xi, 4–5
Open Source Definition (OSD), 85–86
Open Source Initiative (OSI), 85–88
Open Source movement, x, 8
  bazaar model and, 81–83, 85, 88, 134
  enCore and, 114, 116–117, 124–135
  GNU and, 37, 46, 57, 62, 69–75, 78–81, 85–86, 88, 102, 116, 127
  ideologies and, 83–89
  LambdaCore distribution and, 113–114, 116, 124–127

Open Source movement (cont.)
Linux and, 46, 49, 54, 57, 62, 68–69,
75–88, 98, 116, 133
Netscape and, 83–85
Stallman and, 57, 69–73, 77–78, 80,
84, 86–88
Torvalds and, 49, 74–82, 85–88
Operant, xi–xii
Operating systems. *See also* specific
system
choral code and, 57–58, 62, 75–79,
82, 84
Stallman and, 57, 69–73, 77–78, 80,
84, 86–88
Torvalds and, 74–82, 85–88
Orality
avatars and, 146–147
chora and, 64, 66
literacy and, 4–10, 12, 64, 66, 151
politics and, 5
religion and, 5, 12
*Orality and Literacy: The Technologizing of
the Word* (Ong), 4–5
Orwell, George, 26
OS X, 44
Othello (game), xvii

Pac-Man (game), xviii
Pascal, 36, 63–64
PDP-11, 62
PDP-7, 61
Pedagogy, 3, 8, 112, 123, 125, 147
Pensjø, Lars, 99, 116
Perens, Bruce, 85
Peripheral monuments, 145
Persian Gulf War, 50
Personal computers
Apple 2, 41–43
choral code and, 67–68, 75, 80, 88
hackers and, 40–45, 54
IBM and, 42–43
Macintosh, 42–43
Minix and, 49, 74–78

open standards and, 43–44
popularization of, 67–68
Windows and, 43–44, 46, 123
XENIX and, 67
Persuasive Games (Bogost), 95, 142
Pervasive games, 166n1
Pervasive life, xiv, 89, 92–95, 100, 135
Peterson, Chris, 85
Philosophy in the Tragic Age of the Greeks
(Nietzsche), 137–138
PL/1, 60
Plankalkül, 31–32
Plato, x–xi, 1, 5, 11, 56
Play, xii, 160–161, 163
as aesthetic experience, 149–150
Agon and, xiii
Alea and, xiii
amphibian identity and, 25
avatars and, 11 (*see also* Avatars)
axis of pleasure/pain and, 3, 12, 21, 66,
91, 143, 145, 151, 158
behavior and, 9–10, 20–21
bricoleurs and, 25 (*see also* Bricoleurs)
choosing not to, 153–154
chora and, 56–57, 61, 64, 67–68,
72–74, 77–79, 89, 155
embodied, 1
end of, 138
epideictic rhetoric and, 145–149
ethics and, 15, 137–139, 143, 148–
149, 151
fantasy and, 96–97, 107, 115, 151,
166n3
free, 2, 25, 51, 135
hackers and, 24–28, 31, 37–38, 44–45,
49, 51, 53, 56–57, 61, 64, 67–68,
72–74, 77–79, 89
Huizinga and, 10
Ilynx and, xiii
intervention and, 115, 117–118,
120–123, 134–135
ludology and, 14–17, 137–151, 156
Mimicry and, xiii

modality and, 1
motivations for, 154
Nietzschean affirmation and, 138–139,
   143
praxis and, 15, 17, 56, 139
punctum and, 157–158
reflection and, 3
rhetoric and, 14
simulation and, xiii
sure, 6
Ulmer and, 9
unnatural experience and, 149–151
venture and, 91–100, 103, 105–110,
   114
vertigo and, xiii
violence and, 139–145
widescope and, 19–21
work and, 6
writing and, 6
PMC magazine, 8
Politics
   electracy and, 8
   hacktivism and, 50–54
   morals and, 142
   orality and, 5
   violence and, 139
Popcycle, 19, 21
Porter, James, 95
Poststructuralism, xi, 19
Praxis, 15, 17, 56, 139
Print culture, 157
Programming
   ADD, 33
   ALGOL, 35–36
   Analytical Engine and, 28–29
   applets and, 51, 126, 131–132
   applied mathematics and, 34–35
   artificial intelligence and, 26, 35,
      69–70, 97
   assembler, 61, 70
   Atanasoff and, 32
   BASIC, 41, 76
   beginnings of, 33–36

Berry and, 32
bugs and, 58, 66, 68–69, 72, 75,
   100, 102, 111, 113, 121, 128–129,
   133–134
C, 36, 48, 62, 70, 72–73, 76, 97–98
C++, 36, 72, 101
Chess and, 31
chora and, 61 (*see also* Chora)
COBOL, 35
code jockeys and, 36–40
compiler and, 34, 39–40, 54, 60, 70,
   72, 78, 107
Dahl and, 36
debugger and, 72
Difference Engine and, 28–29, 147
Eckert and, 32–33
ENIAC and, 32–33
FORTRAN, 35, 72, 97
Hopper and, 34
Jacquard Loom and, 28–29
Java, 36, 51, 72, 126, 131
language rules of, 34–35
Lovelace and, 29–30
LPC, 99
making a living from, 39
Mauchly and, 32–33
microprocessors and, 40–41, 54, 67
MS-DOS and, 43, 67, 75
MUL, 33
Nygaard and, 36
Objective C, 72
Pascal, 36, 63–64
PDP-7 assembly, 61
PL/1, 60
Plankalkül and, 31–32
portable, 67–68
Ritchie and, 36
Short Code, 33–34
Simula, 36
Smalltalk, 36
source code and, 63–66, 75, 83, 85 (*see
   also* Source code)
Turing and, 30

Programming (cont.)
UNIVAC and, 33–34
Wirth and, 36
XENIX, 67
Zuse and, 30–32
Project Whirlwind, 58–59
Protocol: How Control Exists after Decentralization (Galloway), 65–66
Prufrock, J. Alfred, 162
Punctum, ix–x
assemblage and, 92, 155
ludic ethics and, 144–145
play and, 157–158
World of Warcraft and, 157–160
Puns, 6
Purdue University, 134
Pure Forms, 1, 137

Quake (game), 50
Quarterlife (game), 92
Quartz, Steven, 141–142, 144

Racing the Beam: the Atari Video Computer System (Montfort and Bogost), 41
Radio Shack, 40
Rameau's Nephew (Diderot), xv
Rand Corporation, 97
Randell, B., 35
"Rape in Cyberspace" (Dibble), 110
Raymond, Eris Steven, 37, 80–87
RCID program, x
Red Dead Redemption (game), 146
Red Hat, 79
Relay, 49
Religion, xx, 5
apparatus and, 8–11
electracy and, 8, 10–11
ethics and, 12
miracles and, xiii
morality and, 12
Old Testament and, 7
orality and, 12
televangelists and, 8

Rheingold, Howard, 94
Rhetoric, 1, 3, 8, 10, 156, 163
chora and, 56, 86
disavowal and, 145
epideictic, 145–149
ethics and, 145–149
flash reason and, 12
hackers and, 51
intervention and, 117, 155
ludology and, 14–16, 138–150
Man the Player and, 10
the Moment and, 148–149
pervasive life and, 93
play and, 14
procedural, 56, 142
venture and, 93–95, 100
Ring of Remembrance, 145
Ritchie, Dennis M., 36, 60–62
Rockstar Games, 145–146
Roger, 107–109
Role-playing games, 97, 107, 117–118, 141, 157, 166n2
Rousseau, Jean-Jacques, 4

Sagan, Carl, 7
San Antonio College, 134
Santa Cruz Operation (SCO), 67
Sartre, Jean-Paul, xv–xvi
Savage Mind, The (Lévi–Strauss), 23
Schneider, Jeff, 134
Schweller, Ken, 119, 122, 125, 131–132
Science and technology studies (STS), 24
Scotland Yard (game), xvii
Second Life (game), 92–94
Second Self, The (Turkle), 94
Seinfeld (TV show), xix
Sejnowski, Terrence, 141–142, 144
Selfe, Cynthia, 94–95
Severn, Gary, 103, 107
Shakespeare, 162
Short Code, 33–34
Sicart, Miguel, 137–139, 142–143, 146, 151

SIGGRAPH, 16
Silicon Valley Linux User's Group, 85
Simondon, Gilbert, xi
Simula, 36
Simulation, xiii, 35–36, 61, 142
Smalltalk, 36
SNDMSG, 47
Snow, C. P., 24
Social machines, xi, 12
Social media, 20, 44–50
Socrates, 5
Softlanding Linux Software (SLS), 78–79
Software Arts, Inc., 41
Sørensen, Sindre, 132
Soter, Steven, 7
Source code
  chora and, 63–66, 75, 83, 85
  distribution of, 98
  hackers and, 39–40
  licenses and, 63, 71, 78, 85–87,
    126–127
  MOOs and, 102, 111, 115, 119, 128,
    131, 134–135
  MUDs and, 98, 100, 102, 111, 115, 131
Space Invaders (game), xviii
Space Travel (game), 61
Sperry Rand Univac, 37
Sprawl trilogy (Gibson), 26–27, 157
Stallman, Richard
  commercialization of software and, 70
  distribution business of, 71
  GNU and, 69–73, 78, 80, 86–88
  hacker noir and, 37–38
  open source movement and, 57,
    69–73, 77–78, 80, 84, 86–88
  papers of, 87
Stiegler, Bernard, xi–xiv
Stoll, Clifford, 27
"Structure, Sign, and Play in the
  Discourse of the Human Sciences"
  (Derrida), 1–2
Structure of Scientific Revolutions, The
  (Kuhn), 5

Style
  hackers and, 76, 79, 82, 85–88, 134
  heuretics and, 8, 19–20, 41, 79, 82,
    85–88, 134, 143, 163
Sun Microsystems, 66, 67, 89
Sun OS, 46
Surf and Turf client, 131–132
S.u.S.E., 79
Sutton-Smith, Brian, 16
Swiss Federal Institute of Technology, 36

Tanenbaum, Andrew, 75–77, 88
TCP/IP protocols, 46, 65, 67
Teaching Online in Higher Education
  (TOHE), 123
Technics and Time (Stiegler), xi
Technology
  Analytical Engine and, 28–29
  apparatus and, xi (*see also* Apparatus)
  Atanasoff and, 32
  batch processing and, 38, 58–60, 63, 69
  Berry and, 32
  bricoleurs and, 24
  C and, 36
  C++ and, 36
  chora and, 55–58, 61, 65, 77–81,
    84, 89
  cloud computing and, 59, 88
  compiler and, 34, 39–40, 54, 60, 70,
    72, 78, 107
  computers and, xviii, 5, 9, 14, 19, 21
    (*see also* Computers)
  constructionism and, 24
  Dahl and, 36
  debugger and, 72
  Difference Engine and, 28–29, 147
  Eckert and, 32–33
  ENIAC and, 32–33
  hacker noir and, 24–26, 36–37, 40,
    44, 54
  Hopper and, 34
  human-technics rhizome and, xi–xii
  Industrial Revolution and, xi, 53

Technology (cont.)
intervention and, 3, 115–125, 130,
   132, 135
Jacquard Loom and, 28–29
Java and, 36, 51, 72, 126, 131
licenses and, 63, 71, 78, 85–87,
   126–127
Lovelace and, 29–30
ludic ethics and, 146, 148
machines and, xi, 166n3 (see also
   Machines)
Mauchly and, 32–33
microprocessors and, 40–41, 54, 67
Nygaard and, 36
regulation and, 166n6
Ritchie and, 36
Smalltalk and, 36
Turing and, 30
UNIVAC and, 33–34
venture and, 96, 102, 106, 111, 114
Virilio and, 156
widescope and, 2, 5, 7, 11, 15, 18–19
Wirth and, 36
Zuse and, 30–32
Techno-Rhetoricians, 117
Teletheory: Grammatology in the Age of
   Video (Ulmer), 18
Televangelists, 8
Thompson, Ken, 60–63, 88
Timaeus (Plato), x, 56
Time-sharing
choral code and, 57, 59–61, 69–70, 79
computers and, 38–39, 46–47, 57,
   59–61, 69–70, 79
TinyMUCK, 100–101, 115
TinyMUD, 98–102, 105, 115, 166n4
Tolkien, J. R. R., 97
Tomlinson, Ray, 46–47
Torvalds, Linus
autobiography of, 78
Linux and, 74–82, 85–88
Minix and, 49, 74–78

open source movement and, 74–82,
   85–88
Toth, Viktor, 166n3
Travels in Cybertextuality: The Challenge
   of Ergodic Literature and Ludology to
   Literary Theory (Eskelinen), 15
Trubshaw, Roy, 96–98, 115
Truscott, Tom, 48
Tuesday Café, 117
Turing, Alan, 30
Turkle, Sherry, 16, 94
"Twenty Years of Berkeley Unix"
   (McKusick), 69
Twitter, 45
2001: A Space Odyssey (Kubric), 26

U.A.C. Labs (game), 143–144
Ulmer, Gregory, ix–xvi, 2, 153, 160
apparatus theory and, 6–7, 154
avatars and, 25
axis configuration of, 12–13
chora and, 55–57, 64, 66, 69, 72–73,
   89
dimension pollution and, 17
electracy and, 3–21, 44, 155
EmerAgency and, 6, 72–73, 135,
   156–157, 163
fantasy and, 9, 56
flash reason and, 12, 17, 57, 148,
   156–157
hackers and, 25, 44
heuretics and, 91 (see also Heuretics)
intervention and, 135
ludology and, 17–21, 143–151, 155,
   156–157
mystory and, 18–21
transversals and, 12–14
venture and, 91
writing and, 5–6
Underground (Dreyfus), 52
Unit Operations (Bogost), 95
Univac, 35

Universal Automatic Computer
(UNIVAC), 33–34
University College of Wales, 98
University of Bergen, Norway (UiB), 20,
132–134
University of California at Berkeley, 49,
62–64, 66, 69, 79, 101–104
University of Michigan, 124
University of Oulu, 49
University of Pennsylvania, 32
University of Tennessee, 49
University of Texas at Dallas (UTD),
119–121, 123
Unix, 97
BSD and, 44, 46, 57, 62–69, 74, 77–80,
85–86, 116, 127
chora and, 58, 61–75, 77–80, 82, 88
commercialization of, 66–67
hackers and, 27, 36, 44, 46, 48–50, 54
intervention and, 119, 123
Minix and, 49, 54, 74–78
venture and, 97–98, 107
Usenet, 46, 48–50, 54, 69–71, 75, 81,
99, 101
U.S. Navy, 59

Venture, 21
apparatus and, 91
code community and, 109–111
code sharing and, 111–114
electracy and, 91
games and, 91–101, 107
Heidegger on, 91
heuretics and, 91
identity and, 94
intervention and, 91–96, 114
machines and, 91, 101–104
MOOs and, 92, 94–96, 100–114
MUDs and, 95–96, 99–107
pervasive life and, 92–95, 100
play and, 91–100, 103, 105–110, 114
rhetoric and, 93–95, 100

technology and, 96, 102, 106, 111, 114
Ulmer and, 91
Unix and, 97–98, 107
virtual reality and, 93, 100–101, 119
Vertigo, xiii, xv
Village Voice journal, 110
Violence, 11, 51, 155
Brothers Grimm and, 163
DOOM and, 140–144, 167n1
ethics and, 137, 139–146, 148, 150
games and, 137, 139–146, 148, 150,
167n1
Harris and, 140–144, 167n1
Klebold and, 140–141, 144
Kretschmer and, 139, 141
motivations for, 139–144, 167n1
politics and, 139
punctum and, 144
Virilio, Paul, xiv, 57, 156–157
Virtual Community, The (Rheingold), 94
Virtual reality, 93, 100–101, 119
VisiCalc, 41–42
Vitanza, Victor, x
VMS, 75
Von Neumann, John, xv, 154
VRoma MOO, 134

WADs, 143–144, 167n1
Wall of Healing, 145
WarGames (film), 26–27
WaterCooler Games, 16
Wayne, John, 146
We Have Never Been Modern (Latour), 24
Weishaus, Joel, 8
WELL (Whole Earth 'Lectronic Link),
50–51
"What Are Poets For?" (Heidegger), 91
White, Stephen, 100–103, 106, 111
Whole Earth Catalong (Brand), 50–51
Widescope, ix
apparatus and, 4–12, 17, 20–21
bridge construction and, 1–3, 7, 16

Widescope (cont.)
  Derrida and, 1–2, 4–6
  electracy and, 3–14
  foundationalism and, 1–2
  grammatology and, 4–5, 18
  ludology and, 14–17
  mystory and, 3, 18–19, 21
  reference point and, 1–2
  technology and, 2, 5, 7, 11, 15, 18–19
Wikileaks, 52–53
Wire, The (TV show), 163
Wired magazine, 83–84
Wirth, Niklaus, 36
Wittgenstein, L., 73
Wizards
  choral code and, 69, 82
  MUDs/MOOs and, 97, 99, 104–114,
    118, 121
Woods, Don, 97
Woolgar, Steve, 24
Wordplay, 6
World of Warcraft (game)
  Equinox community and, ix–x,
    157–158
  game studies and, 161–162
  ludic ethics and, 141, 149–151
  punctum and, 157–160
  raids and, 17, 154, 157–158, 163
World Trader (game), xvii–xviii
World Wide Web, 45–46, 54, 121, 126
Worms, 27, 166n5
Writing, 4–6, 16
Wysocki, Anne, 95

XENIX, 67
Xerox PARC, 101–102, 111
Xpress Graphical User Interface, 117,
  124, 130–133

Zanni, xv
Zapata, Emiliano, 51
Zapatista FloodNet, 51
Zapitista Army of National Liberation, 51

Zarathustra (Nietzsche), 148
Zedillo, Ernesto, 51
Z4 computer, 31
Z3 computer, 30–31
Zuse, Konrad, 30–32

P 90 .H655 2012

Holmevik, Jan Rune.

Inter/vention